M000158134

"Drew resists the faddish en[...] they are, instead inviting eac[...] exploring every obstacle to [...] ing our unlived lives, and discovering our hidden vocation. This immensely practical gift holds the possibility of transformation, for yourself and for a hungry and hurting world. Savor it!"

Dr. Chuck DeGroat, author, *When Narcissism Comes to Church*; Professor of Pastoral Care and Christian Spirituality at Western Theological Seminary; therapist, spiritual director

"Drew writes on the enneagram with both clarity and conviction, not as a mere spectator gleaning from the sidelines, but a journeyman who has traveled the road thoroughly and brought back wisdom to share. I highly recommend this book to the enneagram student."

AJ Sherrill, lead pastor, Mars Hill Bible Church, author, *The Enneagram for Spiritual Formation*

"In this work, Drew has curated a wonderful tour for how the enneagram can helpfully guide us all to deeper exploration of vocation, calling, and life passion. Drew's writing style—like his teaching style—is both accessible and deep. New and long-time students of the enneagram will find gifts of wisdom in Drew's pages."

Hunter Mobley, enneagram teacher with Suzanne and Joe Stabile's Micah Center in Dallas, Texas; Nashville-based pastor and attorney; author, *Forty Days on Being a Two*

"This is a brilliant book! If you want to know and experience the life you desire to live, *The Enneagram of Discernment* delivers a map to get from here to there. You can read this book all at once but take your time. Dr. Drew's work with college students, along with his keen intellect, palpable empathy, and instinctual wisdom, serves as a GPS for young and old alike. Savor the landscape. Search your inner terrain, the heights, depths, and breadth of your soul with Drew as a faithful guide to help you discover more of the magnificent life you are meant to live."

Rev. Clare Loughrige, co-author, *Spiritual Rhythms of the Enneagram*; pastor at Crossroads Church (Marshall, MI); spiritual director

"Drew does a remarkable job of establishing separation between type and person while also writing about each type in such a way that we are all sure to be deeply seen. I appreciated the way he spoke of my dominant type (Seven) from a deep and nuanced perspective. In addition, he was able to offer tangible mindset shifts for working with the enneagram that take the information from understanding into application. I'm excited for you to start or continue your enneagram journey with *The Enneagram of Discernment* in your tool belt."

Sarajane Case, founder, @enneagramandcoffee; author, *The Honest Enneagram*

"*The Enneagram of Discernment* is an essential resource in the journey of self-discovery. Dr. Moser has accomplished what few others have in his ability to detail the extensive landscape of our human experience in a beautifully complex yet practically uncomplicated manner. His deft capacity to effectively guide each of us as we navigate past the shallowness of personality typing into the depths of true personal exploration can not be understated. This resource is a life-giving map for all of us seeking wisdom via practical applications in our efforts to discover our unique purpose."

Dr. Jerome D. Lubbe, author, *The Brain-Based Enneagram: You are Not a Number*

"Drew invites us to step past the shallow earth of simple self-awareness into the wider world of wholeness. This book is more than a map to flourishing. It's an excavation of the soul. Let Drew's kind, practical wisdom guide you to the gift of coming home to who you really are."

KJ Ramsey, licensed professional counselor; author, *This Too Shall Last: Finding Grace When Suffering Lingers*

"On the surface, 'discernment' is about answering the occasional pressing question: 'What should I do?' However, with profound depth, clarity, and insight, *The Enneagram of Discernment* shows us how cultivating discernment is more essentially about braving with tenderness and vulnerability the sacred space of our authentic selfhood—and doing this as a devoted practice each and every day of our 'wild and precious' lives. If you are feeling lost, uncertain, or confused, Dr. Moser will help direct you to the trailhead of your own identity and gently offer you a map home."

Rev. Nhiên Vương, founder, Evolving Enneagram; International Enneagram Association accredited professional; ordained inter-spiritual minister

"*The Enneagram of Discernment* has quickly become one of the top resources we recommend for people wanting to use the ancient wisdom of the enneagram for its intended purpose of liberation. Drew's unique take on cultivating discernment through the enneagram provides a much-needed accessibility to an intimidating subject. This book not only provides a map but also the wisdom and guidance from the heart of a teacher who kindly and thoughtfully leads you each step of the way on the journey of finding your identity, purpose, and direction. We are thankful for Drew's gift to the conversation and believe you will be as well."

Rebekah TenHaken, co-founder and Director of Content and Collaboration for *Enneagram Magazine*

"With the acumen of a scholar, the heart of a servant-leader, and the wisdom of a sage, Drew Moser has created a landmark book. *The Enneagram of Discernment* is deeply rooted in tradi-tion while simultaneously weaving fresh, illuminating insights on identity, vocation, wisdom, and practice. Whether you're a seasoned student of the enneagram or just being introduced to this ancient tool for holistic transformation, there is no better companion for deepening your journey into the true self. This book is sure to stand the test of time and belongs on the shelf alongside the great contemporary enneagram teacher."

Ryan Kuja, writer, spiritual director, & author, *From the Inside Out: Reimagining Mission, Recreating the World*

"When it comes to exploring our vocation—or helping others do the same—many leaders feel ill-equipped. We're desperate for resources that go beyond navel-gazing, pop-psychologizing, or slapping a spiritual shellac on standard decision-making advice. *The Enneagram of Discernment* does none of this. Instead, it invites us to look inward in a new way—to take a trip to the center of ourselves, not only to better our understanding, but ultimately to see the *Imago Dei*. For those who want to apply the ancient enneagram tool to our output in today's world, Drew Moser is a humble, encouraging, and incredibly insightful guide. This book has the power to transform anyone who is willing to embark on the discernment journey!"

Erica Young Reitz, author, *After College*; founder and Principal, After College Transition

"If you are new to the enneagram or an enneagram expert, this book will speak to you. Drew Moser has written an inspired book! Drew's lifelong passion for helping young people discern their pathway in life has been transformed into a guide for us all. Drew clearly and skillfully uses the fundamental tenets of the enneagram to help us see and uncover our authentic selves. This allows us to listen and respond to the wisdom of a deeper calling. Challenging and meaningful questions and exercises at the end of chapters help us find a felt sense of what we are discovering and takes this wonderful information from head knowing to a full body, heart and head understanding. Like Drew, I have a literal room full of books on the enneagram. I have multiple copies of my favorite books and those I find most helpful, to lend to clients, students and friends. Rest assured there will be multiple copies of *The Enneagram of Discernment* in my library!"

Nan Henson, International Enneagram Association Accredited Professional, Riso-Hudson Certified Teacher & Authorized Workshop Leader; founding board member of IEA Georgia; owner, Enneagram Atlanta

"Drew Moser's *The Enneagram of Discernment* is beautifully written, powerfully engaging, and rich in its depth! At a time when 'thrown together' enneagram books are flooding the marketplace, Drew Moser has come forth with a solid and authentic piece of work—a genuine contribution to the enneagram field. *The Enneagram of Discernment* offers a framework for working with the enneagram that keeps the true purpose of the ennea-gram alive throughout the book by staying true to a focus on us-ing the enneagram for 'doing the Work' as opposed to a focus on the enneagram itself. The Type Chapters present a fresh view of each enneagram type from an 'inside out' perspective —describ-ing more the experience of each Type than the typical 'outside in' descriptions of characteristics and behaviors. The exercises and practices offered throughout the book are purposeful and practical invitations for inquiry, one of the most effective tools for real and lasting personal and spiritual growth. I highly rec-ommend this book to those new to the enneagram as well as to seasoned enneagram journeyers. Thank you, Drew, for this enneagram gem!"

Lynda Roberts, Riso-Hudson certified enneagram teacher, past president, International Enneagram Association, Accredited Professional, www. enneagramhorizons.com

"I have long considered my work with students at Christian col-leges as 'standing at the crossroads' with them as they discern their futures, settle important questions about who they are and determine the purpose for their lives. In this volume, Drew Mos-er has developed an elegant and useful articulation of insights from the enneagram that will help me guide students in these crucible moments of their growth. For the reader who is new to the enneagram, Drew points out basic insights. For the sea-soned pilgrim, he extracts and weaves together the concepts of vocation, wisdom and practice, thus helping any reader of any enneagram type to develop discernment. This is a book to which I will return often, for myself and as a recommended resource for students, colleagues, and leaders."

Dr. Edee M. Schulze, Vice President for Student Life at West-mont College (CA)

"As the enneagram has grown in popularity, it has unfortunately often been treated as a static personality profile, leaving unac-cessed its greatest gifts for our evolution. But Drew's book is one of the rare ones that grasps and shares the dynamic power of this tool for our transformation as we confront the most challenging questions of vocation and discernment. With Drew's expert guidance, we can use the enneagram to pursue our best work and our truest lives."

Jason Adam Miller, founder and Lead Pastor, South Bend City Church (IN)

"This book beautifully unpacks how better understanding ourselves through the enneagram can lead us on a path of discernment. The nine questions serve as practical tools that nurture wisdom in making good life decisions."

Dr. Kris Hansen-Kieffer, Vice Provost for Student Success and Engagement at Messiah College (PA)

"This is not just another enneagram book, like many of them out there, regurgitating what was written in the first books. Drew's approach is unique in its depth and practicality, giving readers a fresh approach to understanding the 'why' of type and the 'how' of practicing loosening our addictive patterning to reclaim our innate capacity for wisdom needed to flourish where we are."

Seth Abram, enneagram writer/teacher, @integratedenneagram; Nashville-based singer/songwriter, co-host, Fathoms | An Enneagram Podcast

"Dr. Drew Moser is a national leader in defining the struggles that the 20-something generation is going through and moreover, how to overcome those struggles. His new book on the enneagram is his best work helping people understand their type and how to best use knowledge of that type to live abundantly. As someone in his 50s, I learned a lot from Moser's brilliant work on the enneagram. Thus, I trust that people of all ages will learn and grow from reading this fantastic title. Moser notes that in a world of beauty, we often listen to our earbuds and social media. He astutely asks, 'What are we tuning out?' I encourage you to tune in to Moser's book and learn about how to live a more authentic life through discernment and hearing the voice of God."

Dr. John D. Foubert, dean and professor, College of Education, Union University (TN)

"Knowing and being able to integrate the enneagram's wisdom with my journey of discernment over the past two years was a gift just as Drew Moser describes it to be: to decide and live from the wholeness of the claim 'This is who I am.' That others can experience that integration because of Drew's work here is a similar gift! The enneagram is meant for so much more than trendy Facebook posts and Instagram pics. With *The Enneagram of Discernment*, we are taken into the 'so much more' in a rich, comprehensive, yet exceedingly clear and helpful way. Would you expect anything less from a college professor who's spent his years walking alongside young adults in the pursuit of their vocation? No doubt I will recommend this work again and again to those I serve of all ages."

Dr. David A. Bell, Executive Director of Circle City Fellows (Indianapolis, IN); founder of Enneagram Insight

"Understanding the way forward involves a willingness to experience self-awareness and a desire for transformation. *The Enneagram of Discernment* offers an invitation for both of these to take place through wisdom and practice. The integration of theory and reflection are intertwined in a thorough way through this insightful resource. Drew emulates a life of discernment through his own evolution of transformation."

Dr. Julia Hurlow, author, *Transcendence at the Table*; Director of Discipleship, Taylor University (IN)

"Discernment is one of those things that we all think we have finally obtained at one point in our lives. When in reality, we soon realize that this difficult & precarious balancing act, only dares us to continue confronting the ways in which we see, perceive and believe. Drew has skillfully and efficiently conveyed the deep wisdom of the enneagram in which, every fathom you descend you feel more and more at home in your body, soul, & mind. Drew has managed to gracefully hold in tension, the complexities of you, while still giving you access to the practicality of this ancient system."

Seth Creekmore, experiential enneagram teacher/musician; co-host, Fathoms | An Enneagram Podcast

"Each of us makes seemingly unimportant decisions every day and then every so often a monumental life decision must be made. This book harnesses the power of authentic self-discovery through the enneagram and provides an invitation into wisdom to discern life's decisions. Dr. Drew Moser is a gifted educator whose words will adeptly guide readers into a deeper understanding and application of the enneagram."

Dr. Amy VanDerWerf Carroll, Senior Consultant for Student Success at Credo

"The Enneagram of Discernment is an invitation to tend to your soul. While there's no shortage of resources on the enneagram, none marry story-telling, education, and reflective questions the way this book does so beautifully. Drew created a rare gift that we'll get to open over and over again."

Manda Carpenter, Jesus-follower, foster care advocate, & author, *Space: An Invitation to Create Sustainable Rhythms of Work, Play, and Rest*

THE ENNEAGRAM OF DISCERNMENT

The Enneagram of Discernment:

The Way of Vocation, Wisdom, and Practice

Drew Moser, Ph.D.

Foreword by Dr. Chuck DeGroat

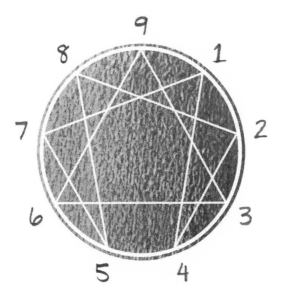

Falls City Press

THE ENNEAGRAM OF DISCERNMENT
The Way of Vocation, Wisdom, and Practice

© 2020 Falls City Press by Drew Moser

2108 Seventh Avenue
Beaver Falls, PA 15010
www.fallscitypress.com

Cover Design by Rafetto Creative
www.rafettocreative.com

Interior Illustrations by Rachel Aupperle

Library of Congress Cataloging-in-Publication Data

Moser, Drew, 1979—

    p. cm.
  Includes bibliographical references.

Identifiers:
  ISBN: (paper) 978-0-9864051-6-7
  ISBN: (ebook) 978-0-9864051-7-4
  LCCN: 2020937836

Subjects: LCHS: Enneagram | Personality—Religious Aspects—Christianity | Typology (Psychology)—Religious Aspects I. Title.

  BV4597.57.M79 2020 (print)

Printed in the USA

Dedication

To all the brave souls in search of a deeper and better way...

To those in search of greater clarity, awareness, and wisdom...

To those with a holy discontent living in a world increasingly frenetic, tiring, isolating, and polarizing...

...this book is for you.

I wish I could share a cup of coffee and talk about these things with each of you. Alas, this will have to suffice. I hope it helps.

One step at a time, together.

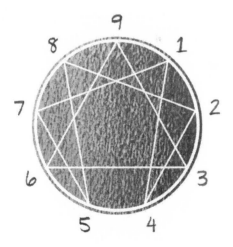

Contents

FOREWORD

At 50, I look back at my life and see distraction, fragmentation, confusion, and reactivity. Even as one committed to spiritual disciplines and interior silence, I've too-often bounced upon the waves, without a mooring. As a result, I've found myself exhausted, grumpy, and sometimes desperate. Can you relate?

In the late 1990s, a wise guide provided a helpful map for me in the Enneagram, a tool with ancient roots, yet one crafted for contemporary challenges. This tool, with great precision, named certain adaptive patterns in my life, coping mechanisms that locked me into self-sabotaging habits. Given its relative obscurity in my Christian community, I pieced together an Enneagram-education of my own, using the tool in my pastoral work and in my clinical counseling practice. I taught a class for a seminary on vocation featuring the Enneagram as the central wisdom-tool for discernment and practice. In every realm, it proved helpful. In my own life, it proved transformational.

And then, as I often say, the Enneagram got sexy. With an evangelical and pop-psychology makeover, this tool, which once lurked in the shadows, became mainstream, through a flurry of books, in podcasts, through social media Ennea-influencers, and more. Suddenly, this wisdom tool became another quick-fix strategy. I was receiving phone calls to help evangelical church staffs fix their relationship problems through half-day Enneagram seminars. But with growing attention came growing suspicion. Those suspicious of this new tool outlawed its use in some circles. Discouraged, I stopped teaching it and talking about it for a while.

And yet, I'm beginning to see new, wise-and-seasoned engagements with the Enneagram. Engagements like the book you're holding right now. Drew resists the faddish Enneagram-talk that tells people who they are. Instead, he invites each of us on a journey of discernment, exploring every obstacle to becoming our true selves, uncovering our unlived lives, and discovering our hidden vocations. He takes up the ancient task once again, offering the Enneagram not as the easy-fix or instant-remedy, but as wisdom for the journey—a time-honored tool for discernment.

Drew writes, "Discernment is the gift and practice of living our lives from a deep sense of vocation, with wisdom, in the fullness of time." And are we not all eager for discernment in a world that seems more chaotic and lives that feel more fragmented by the day?

Years ago, the sage Evelyn Underhill wrote, "Vocation is a gradual revelation—of me, to myself, by God—it is who we are, trying to happen." This is also true of the broader gift and practice of discernment. Drew invites you into this gradual revelation, providing a map with trails to follow, questions to ponder, and practices to engage. He trusts that God, who dwells at the center of your being, whispers this wisdom and leads the way. He believes that you are God's image-bearer, born to flourish, designed for significance and meaning and impact in your world.

This immensely practical gift holds the possibility of transformation, for yourself and for a hungry and hurting world. Drew has written it in a spiritually hospitable way: Readers from any faith tradition (or no faith tradition) will find it helpful. But it doesn't promise an easy path. Drew asks you, the reader, to commit to engaging it with your whole selves—not just heads, but hearts and bodies. If you're ready, this wise companion for your journey will take you into the profound depths of your own heart and into the deep needs of our hurting world. Savor it.

Dr. Chuck DeGroat
Author, *When Narcissism Comes to Church: Healing Your Community from Emotional and Spiritual Abuse*; Professor of Pastoral Care and Christian Spirituality at Western Theological Seminary; therapist, spiritual director

AUTHOR'S NOTE

The enneagram is ancient and open source, which often puts it at odds with our modern world of intellectual property. Many teachers have left their mark through trainings, books, articles, and the like. They are right to be mindful of how their content is being used by others. I've had good friends warn me about entering my own writing into the fray. Writing something new about the enneagram can be stepping into a mine field. Since Claudio Naranjo began teaching the enneagram in Berkeley, California, there have been hundreds of books, countless schools, institutes, trainings, conferences, podcasts, and the list goes on.

I've noticed a tension between two approaches to enneagram writing. The first approach fails to properly recognize (in citations and references) source material. A lack of citations implies that everything in a resource is of the author's own creation. We all learn from others, so this seems silly. The second approach is to cite whenever and wherever possible, which to some in the enneagram community implies a lack of originality. As a trained scholar and academic, my inclination is to build upon the good work of others. I can't bring myself to the first approach, and I disagree with those who look down upon the second. In my guild, citations and references convey honor and respect, meant to communicate that others' work is important enough to remain in the conversation. I hope those I cite feel honored that their work is influential to others. I've been tediously careful in trying to note where I sourced material and tried to let the reader know when I chart my own path with the content.

In general, my own enneagram training comes in a few forms. I've sat at the feet of some of the best enneagram teachers in intensive workshop environments. This book stands on their shoulders. As a scholar, another important mode of training comes from research. My own ever-expanding enneagram library bolsters my learning, and you'll see references to it throughout these chapters. I'm also active in the International Enneagram Association, and have learned much from my peers in workshops, conversations, and digital communication. In today's age, social media is ubiquitous, and beyond the memes and gifs can be found some truly profound content from enneagram friends around the world. All to say, I turned over as many rocks as possible in the enneagram world and did my best to let you know what I found. Thanks in advance for your grace and understanding.

Part I

Introducing the Way
of Discernment

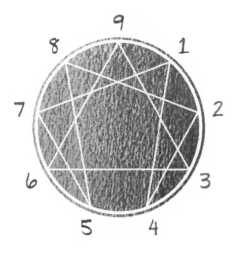

INTRODUCTION

This is Who I Am

*"Do I contradict myself? Very well, then I contradict myself.
I am large, I contain multitudes."*
—Walt Whitman

This is not who I am. The words were in response to the firestorm surrounding Philadelphia Eagles running back LeSean McCoy in a tragic 2013 twitter spat with an ex-girlfriend.[1] After first claiming his Twitter account was hacked, McCoy finally owned up to his actions, and issued an apology statement.

This is not who I am. The now infamous University of New Mexico women's college soccer player Elizabeth Lambert expressed deep regret when a 2009 video went viral showing her dragging an opponent to the ground by her ponytail. "I look at it and I'm like, 'That is not me,'" said Lambert.[2]

This is not who I am. A freshman Chi Omega sorority member at American University thump-tapped the sentence in an Instagram post apologizing for using the "n-word" in a video filmed by another sorority sister.[3]

This is not who I am. The legendary professional wrestler/ entertainer Hulk Hogan invoked the phrase when an audio transcript surfaced in 2015 in which Hogan used racial slurs in a conversation with his daughter.[4]

This is not who I am. The sentence was invoked yet again in 2019 by then Virginia Governor Ralph Northam after old racist yearbook photos came to light.[5]

This is not who I am. When a leader or celebrity gets sideways with the public, lawyers and public relations firms swoop in to manage the crisis. Apparently these six words are standard boiler plate apology language used to deescalate the situation. In each instance, they are meant to convey an incongruence of past decisions made and the true character of a person.

And every time a statement is released or a remorseful person utters them in a press conference, the collective reaction is almost always the same: *that's not a real apology. We teach our children to give better apologies than that.*

It's a fair critique, because it truly is a terrible apology. It's an attempt to prove that while I own up to my mistakes, this one time was an aberration. It's an effort in diminishing the disaster to minimize the damage. Each time such bad apologies are offered, the temptation is to roll our eyes and mutter: *You're not sorry.*

Here's the thing: each time a person shuffles to a microphone at a press conference and implores to the masses that *this is not who I am*, I now think about the situation differently. I still see it for the contrived charade that it often is. I still hear the formulaic, crafted message. I still sense the inadequacy of the "apology." But along with it, I now have a different response. When someone claims that *this is not who I am*, I think:

You're exactly right.

Our decisions have the powerful role in forming and representing who we are. These apologies at least acknowledge the interconnectedness of our identity (being) and our decisions (doing). Such public failures remind me that on the other side of my sanctimony is a recognition that I too struggle with the idea of who I am, and make decisions that feel incongruent. I also find myself in situations in which, with hindsight, I feel regret or remorse about the encounter. At the risk of projection, I'd say we all do. The human experience is full of dissonance, where our behaviors seem mismatched with who we want to be.

And it's a uniquely human issue. The poet-philosopher David Whyte reminds us that: "We are the only creation that refuses to be ourselves."[6] We seem to be plagued by a collective identity crisis. Psychologist David Benner agrees: "In all of creation, identity is a challenge only for humans. A tulip knows exactly what it is. It is never tempted by false ways of being. Nor does it face complicated decisions in the process of becoming."[7]

I'm not claiming that celebrity apologies convey the full weight of our identity issues. But I think they point to it, even if unbeknown to the celebrity. It's a glimpse of the internal tug of war we all wage: the battle between a *persona* and an authentic self. Our inability to grapple with identity leads us to make poor decisions. They may not be for the world to see, but they are poor decisions nonetheless. Our struggles with identity also significantly inhibit our ability to make decisions altogether. Left unchecked, we can come to a place of poverty (of wisdom) and paralysis (of action). When faced with life's decisions, we need both wisdom and right action.

We need to know who we truly are… and how to make good and wise decisions accordingly. Why is this so difficult? Why do we suffer from such confusion about who we are? There are probably a multitude of reasons, but three loom the largest:

1. We lie to ourselves, often for very understandable reasons.
2. We are overwhelmed, which inhibits our ability to live with congruence.
3. We've neglected our capacity to listen well, choosing to listen to the wrong voices.

Let's take each in turn.

We lie to ourselves. The Dutch Catholic priest Henri Nouwen wisely acknowledges our tendency for self-deceit, outlining the three lies of identity:[8] *I am what I do, I am what I have,* and *I am what others say about me.*

When we believe these lies, we live in some unhealthy ways. We devote ourselves to activities that aren't true to who we are. We collect material possessions in hopes that they bring a sense of fulfillment. We cling to the approval of others. Our minds, hearts, and bodies search and scan for an elusive form of validation and approval. When we feel we've failed at this, we turn to contriving schemes and tweaking formulas to craft a better persona, one that is perhaps more effective at these things.

We are overwhelmed. In addition, we are an overwhelmed bunch. We are overworked and overstressed. In our digital age, we are bombarded with information, we are consumed by work and stress, and we fail to slow down enough to listen to the wisdom within. Despite the promise of technology to make our lives easier, it often has the opposite effect. Rather than reducing our workload, it has increased it. Tending to emails outside of normal business hours is now the norm, not the exception. A study conducted by a Virginia Tech professor indicates that the mere expectation (regardless of the time we spend) to check work emails after business hours harms the health of employees and their families.[9]

We also tend to not use the paid time off we earn. A 2019 poll revealed that only 28% of Americans planned to max their vacation time.[10] The average American worker used, on average, only 54% of their time off. This is despite the many studies that prove the health benefits of taking time away from work.

A nice ending to this story would be to believe that, *The reasons we overwork are because we love it so much.* But other studies reveal that we aren't enjoying life as much as we hope. A global poll conducted by Gallup finds that Americans are among the most stressed people in the world.[11] And stress is increasing with each generation. Generation Z, those born after 1997, are the most "stressed out Generation in American history."[12]

And despite our perpetual digital connectivity, adults in America are lonely. Since 1985, the number of Americans who report having no close friends has tripled.[13] Living in a perpetual state of burnout, stress, and loneliness results in a lack of authentic identity void of any purpose and direction.

We aren't listening well. Most people I know who have committed to the difficult path of living a more authentic life often look back and can clearly see the signs, the voices, and the opportunities ignored or dismissed. And most, if honest, admit "I wasn't listening." Parker Palmer, in his profound book *Let Your Life Speak*, writes, "We listen for guidance everywhere except from within."[14] I work on a college campus, which affords me the opportunity to observe young adults and how they live. Ours is a sprawling, beautiful campus, full of trees and creeks and walking paths. And yet, such beauty and space can't compete with earbuds and social media. I often wonder, what are we listening to? Perhaps a better question: What are we tuning out?

Palmer implores us to listen to our lives, for they have something to say. This requires us to tune our listening differently, inwardly, tending to our soul.

He writes:

> The soul is like a wild animal—tough, resilient, savvy, self-sufficient, and yet exceedingly shy. If we want to see a wild animal, the last thing we should do is to go crashing through the woods, shouting for the creature to come out. But if we are willing to walk quietly into the woods and sit silently for an hour or two at the base of a tree, the creature we are waiting for may well emerge, and out of the corner of an eye we will catch a glimpse of the precious wildness we seek.[15]

In our current state, we don't have much time and space for soul work. Such inner work requires a different sort of listening. It requires a different pace of life. It requires an honesty with ourselves that can seem scary.

But to avoid who we truly are and continue living otherwise is actually scarier. If we lie to ourselves long enough, we start to forget what's true. We overwhelm ourselves and wonder if we can sustain the pace. We doubt our ability to listen, and wonder if we'll never be able to hear the right voices. Our persona gradually shifts from that which helps us feel a sense of comfort in our world to that which feels suffocating. To continue in our default patterns and settings will result in further confusion about our identity, further division within the various parts of our lives, and a diminishment of our purpose and direction.

We are desperate for discernment, searching for wisdom to make good decisions. This requires a sacred journey to authentic identity, demanding a different pace than our calendar apps typically allow. Workaholism, stress, and loneliness aren't very helpful places from which to make decisions. What would it look like to live free of them? What if we reconsidered the question, *What should I do with my life?*

May Sarton captures the journey well:

Now I become myself.
It's taken time, many years and places.
I have been dissolved and shaken,
Worn other people's faces...[16]

To know who we are and then live accordingly is not easy. The path to an authentic identity that makes wise decisions takes time, and we must acknowledge our prior efforts to wear "other people's faces." I used the word *persona* previously to discuss how we tend to live out of false places of identity. The Latin root for *persona* is "theatrical mask." The personas we present to the world are masks. In fact, it seems easier to live from persona and consider it identity. But we only put on the mask because we want to shape how others see us. It's a response to perception rather than reality. To live from an authentic sense of identity is a response to how I see myself.[17]

If you've ever worn a mask, you know that it often impedes your vision. Most costume masks have holes for your eyes, but even when you line your eyes up with the holes your vision is restricted. To live well requires that we name the masks that we wear, take them off, and then see our lives with more clarity, range, and depth. The initial glance can be tough, because it leads to the acknowledgement that "the life I am living is not the same as the life that wants to live in me."[18]

When we do this, we're beginning to scratch the surface of the essence of life. Mary Oliver, in her poem "The Summer Day," asks "Tell me, what is it you plan to do with your one wild and precious life?"[19]

It's a rich question, full of simplicity and complexity. Those that read it fall into two camps. The first camp is inspired. Oliver assumes that our lives are wild and precious. Our plans for life should honor the wildness and preciousness. Such "wild" living beckons us to adventure and anticipation. The second camp is anxious. *I don't know! That's what I'm trying to figure out!* A lack of plans cause many to worry that their lives will be a waste. Confusion, frustration, and even depression can creep in.

If we are willing to name the masks we wear, take them off, and explore what's underneath, we can carry the weight of inspiration and discovery Oliver gives, and make decisions accordingly. That is the essence of this book. We each desperately need to find the path back to our true selves, and then live from that place of identity to make wise decisions. By exploring the ancient wisdom of the enneagram, coupled with the gift and practice of discernment, we will. By becoming ourselves, we learn to discern our path with wisdom.

Discerning Identity, Discerning Life

To arrive at a point of authentic identity is rare. Most continue to live with the mask on. But for those who are willing to put in the work, a sacred space emerges. It's a place of raw vulnerability. It's a tender place, full of sensitivity, goodness, fear, and courage. Entering it can conjure two responses. The first is defensive, where we shame ourselves for our inadequacies and shortcomings, heaping criticism. This is engaging the space with *judgment*. We become our own worst enemy: an inner critic.

The second is hospitable, where we see ourselves as we truly are, and welcome with love. And to see is to love.[20] This is engaging the space with *discernment*.

The result of a shift from persona to identity is this ability to discern a wild and precious life. In your hands is no ordinary self-help book. The realm of discernment is too challenging for simplistic formulas. Nor is this your ordinary enneagram book, some of which tend to introduce the reader to recycled types and tips.

Instead, I hope to explore the ways in which the enneagram can illuminate the path to authentic identity, and in so doing, cultivate the wisdom to discern life's decisions, big and small. In short, I call it the **Enneagram of Discernment**; a framework of becoming ourselves so we can discern with wisdom. The tragic irony of our "information age" is that our unfettered access to information has failed to make us wiser. It fails to help those who confess: *This is not who I am.*

Imagine the shift from the brokenness of *This is not who I am* to the wholeness of living in such a way that you can claim *This is who I am*. To do so would allow us to get out of some unhelpful patterns of behavior. This is what discernment provides. To do so requires an integrity and authenticity saturated with wisdom, the holistic intelligence that guides us to effectively engage the many decisions of life. The enneagram invites us into how we can bring our full and authentic selves into the world with this sort of wisdom.

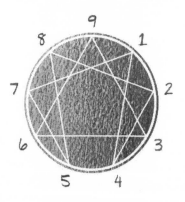

When the enneagram comes up at parties or other social settings, it's often discussed as a way to describe who people *ARE*. This is understandable, but unfortunate. The enneagram is truly about understanding who you are *NOT*. Through the awareness that comes with discovering your dominant type, one can begin to see our habitual patterns, behaviors, reactions, defenses, barriers and capacities.

If you're new to the enneagram framework and don't know your dominant type, no worries. Chapter One will be a helpful introduction. You can read this book in its entirety and make sense of it. You may even discover your dominant enneagram type once you finish. If you'd like help discovering your type before you read on, check out the appendices, which provide tips for typing and exercises to help you discover your type.

Discovering your dominant enneagram type is just the beginning. In this present surge in popularity of the enneagram, there are untold amounts of information out there, much of it being peddled by people eager to sell you their knowledge. Such fervor isn't all bad, but it risks creating a culture of superficiality. There's a lot of repackaged content about personality types out there. Discovering your personality type is merely the trailhead to a deep, complex, and important journey to self-discovery. It's the place we start, not the place we end. When working with the enneagram we must remember that:

INFORMATION < KNOWLEDGE < WISDOM

Any enneagram fan can master the enneagram of personality with enough information and knowledge. The Enneagram of Discernment invites us into wisdom and cultivates it. In order to discern who we are and what we should do, we have to plunge deeper. Information leads to simple formulas and knowledge simply gives us tools. The Enneagram of Discernment provides something much more profound. It provides a way that allows us to explore a crucial question:

How do we hold the map of our lives and make sense of it?

Introducing the Enneagram of Discernment

By drawing from the wisdom of the enneagram to cultivate the gift and practice of discernment, we can live from a grounded, working definition of discernment:

*Discernment is the gift and practice of living our lives
from a deep sense of vocation, with wisdom, in the
fullness of time.*

Simply, discernment is applied identity. Wisdom comes from a place of authenticity, where we can approach challenging situations not just by looking at it, but beneath it and through it.[21] When we see through, we see what's truly at stake.

Hannah Anderson writes, "Discernment does not change the challenges we face; it changes our ability to face them."[22] This is where the wisdom of the enneagram engages the challenges of our lives.

What we need is a map. Like many 90s American teens, my Thursday nights revolved around the TV show *Friends*. In a memorable episode, the main characters took a trip to London, England. Joey, in an effort to find his way in this foreign land, opened up a paper map of London, placed it on the sidewalk, and literally stepped onto the map in an attempt to orient himself. Joey's friend Chandler was characteristically exasperated. The scene, while funny, conveys a profound truth: A map is only as good as your ability to hold it and make sense of it.[23]

The enneagram can provide a map of our lives, but we must learn to hold it and make sense of it. This is the enneagram work that is beneath simply understanding the nine personality types. This book is an invitation to discover your authentic self so that you can discern your life with wisdom.

The Enneagram of Discernment is a triadic map of applied identity:

- Triad 1—Vocation: the Divine Call of identity, purpose, and direction.

- Triad 2—Wisdom: the holistic intelligence that guides us to engage our lives with integrity and authenticity.

- Triad 3—Practice: our intentional work in the fullness of time.

Together the triads of discernment provide nine key questions of discernment:

Vocation

- Who am I?
- Why am I here?
- Where am I going?

Wisdom

- What am I thinking?
- What am I feeling?
- What am I doing?

Practice

- What am I remembering?
- What am I experiencing?
- What am I anticipating?

Each type has its own journey of discernment through these triads and questions. I must warn you that this journey isn't easy. This book will illuminate ways of transformation, but the process can be painful. In the words of David Benner, "No one should work with the enneagram if what they seek is flattery."[24] Surrendering our ego-centered[25] perspective on life can hurt. But it's also liberating.

In Chapter One, we'll explore the enneagram a bit more deeply and consider the three primary emotional barriers to discernment. For newcomers to the enneagram, this will provide enough context to make sense of the book. For those well-versed in the enneagram, we'll explore some new content on the triads and discernment.

In Chapter Two, we'll explore the first triad of the Enneagram of Discernment: Vocation. I'll unpack this ancient theological concept and remind us of our Divine Call to flourish in our identity, purpose, and direction. We'll walk through the shadows of the false self in pursuit of the true. From this place, we'll consider a more grounded purpose and direction.

In Chapter Three, we'll consider the Enneagram of Discernment's second triad: Wisdom. The cultivation of wisdom draws from the full range of intelligence available: head, heart, and body. We'll explore the enneagram's ancient wisdom of three centers of intelligence, which are now being corroborated with neuroscience.

In Chapter Four, we'll expand our understanding of time through the Enneagram of Discernment's third triad: Practice. By deepening our understanding of enneagram type, we can see how our egoic personality hinders our ability to live in the fullness of time: past, present, and future. We'll explore yet another helpful grouping of the enneagram: the stances.

Chapters Five through Thirteen each reconsider the nine Types of the enneagram and provide a deeper exploration in how each type helps, and hinders, the process of discernment. These chapters will give additional type-specific content that shed light on how each type digresses from a place of personality and will explore the way of discernment through the triadic map of applied identity.

I conclude the book with some encouragement and perspective to aid your lifelong cultivation of discernment. I also provide a number of helpful resources in the appendices for further study and exploration.

Each chapter concludes with exercises to aid you in your journey to discern life from authentic identity. Readers of enneagram books are notorious for reading the introduction and then skipping to the content that is specific to their dominate type. Here I want to highlight the idea of the "dominant" type. If something is dominant, it tends to have more weight or authority than others. Your dominant type likewise carries more authority than the other types. For this reason, I encourage you to consider that you have all nine types within you and therefore will benefit from the entirety of this book. You will see aspects of yourself in all of the chapters. Reading through all the type-specific content will not only be relevant to you; it will also help you better understand others.

In our present digital age, our brains have become accustomed to scanning and skimming as quickly as possible. Deep transformative work requires observation, time, and reflection. Savor this text. Take your time.

Finally, heed the words of Parker Palmer: "Inner work, though it is a deeply personal matter, is not necessarily a private matter: inner work can be helped along in community."[26] This journey requires intentional time alone and with others. Be sure to develop healthy rhythms of solitude and community that allow you to incorporate these ideas.

This is not who I am. It's a subpar apology. But with the wisdom of the Enneagram of Discernment, it's a powerful statement acknowledging our confused and distorted identity.

No longer. *This is who I am*. Time to hold the map of your life and make sense of it.

Notes

[1]Adam Wells, "LeSean McCoy's Twitter Account Deleted After Public Blowup with Ex-Girlfriend," *Bleacher Report*, last modified, January 28, 2018, accessed October 1, 2019, https://bleacherreport.com/articles/1503592-lesean-mccoys-twitter-account-deleted-after-public-blowup-with-ex-girlfriend.

[2]Jere Longman, "Those Soccer Plays, in Context," *The New York Times*, last modified November 17, 2009, accessed October 1, 2019, https://www.nytimes.com/2009/11/18/sports/soccer/18soccer.html.

[3]The Eagle News Staff, "Video circulates on social media of Chi Omega member saying racial slur," *The Eagle*, accessed Feb 29, 2020, https://www.theeagleonline.com/article/2020/02/video-circulates-on-social-media-of-chi-omega-member-saying-racial-slur.

[4]Colen Gorentein, "Hulk Hogan apologizes for 'n-word' audio: 'This is not who I am,'" *Salon*, last modified July 24, 2015, accessed October 1, 2019, https://www.salon.com/2015/07/24/hulk_hogan_apologizes_for_n_word_audio_this_is_not_who_i_am/.

[5]Ari Shapiro and Gene Demby, "Why Calls for Racial Dialogue So Rarely Lead to It," *NPR*, last modified February 3, 2019, accessed October 1, 2019, https://www.npr.org/2019/02/04/691427223/why-calls-for-racial-dialogue-so-rarely-lead-to-it.

[6]David Whyte interview with Krista Tippett, "The Conversational Nature of Reality," *On Being*, last modified, December 27, 2018, accessed Oct 1, 2019, https://onbeing.org/programs/david-whyte-the-conversational-nature-of-reality-dec2018/.

[7]David G. Benner, *The Gift of Being Yourself: The Sacred Call to Self-Discovery* (Downers Grove, IL: IVP Books, 2015), p. 16.

[8]Nouwen explores these three lies in a video series on YouTube, delivered in 1992. I think they are so profound that they are worth another look here. See Henri Nouwen, "Being the Beloved," https://www.youtube.com/watch?v=SFWfYpd0F18&app=desktop.

[9]Nouwen, "Being the Beloved," https://www.youtube.com/watch?v=SFWfYpd0F18&app=desktop.

[10]Megan Leonhardt, "Only 28% of Americans Plan to Max out Their Vacation Days This Year," *CNBC Make It*, last modified April 27, 2019, accessed Oct 1, 2019. https://www.cnbc.com/2019/04/26/only-28percent-of-americans-plan-to-max-out-their-vacation-days-this-year.html.

[11]Niraj Chokshi, "Americans are Among the Most Stressed People in the World, Poll Finds," *The New York Times*, last modified April 25, 2019, accessed Oct 1, 2019, https://www.nytimes.com/2019/04/25/us/americans-stressful.html#targetText=Americans%20are%20among%20the%20most%20stressed%20people%20in%20the,according%20to%20a%20new%20survey.&targetText=The%20data%20on-%20Americans%20is,with%20just%2035%20percent%20globally.

[12]American Psychological Association, *Stress in America: Generation Z*, October 2018: https://www.apa.org/news/press/releases/stress/2018/stress-gen-z.pdf.

[13]General Social Survey data, https://gss.norc.org/.

[14]Parker J. Palmer, *Let Your Life Speak: Listening for the Voice of Vocation* (San Francisco: Jossey-Bass, 1999), p. 5.

[15]Ibid, p. 8-9.

[16]May Sarton, "Now I Shall Become Myself," in *Collected Poems, 1930-1993* (New York: W.W. Norton & Company, 1993).

[17]David Benner's work deeply informed this perspective.

[18]Palmer, *Let Your Life Speak*, p. 2.

[19]Mary Oliver, "The Summer Day," in *Devotions: The Selected Poems of Mary Oliver* (New York: Penguin Press, 2017).

[20]Frederich Beuchner wrote about this beautifully. See Frederich Buechner, *The Remarkable Ordinary: How to Stop, Look, and Listen to Life* (Grand Rapids: Zondervan, 2017), p. 33.

[21]Henri Nouwen, *Discernment: Reading the Signs of Daily Life* (San Francisco: HarperOne, 2015), p. 6.

[22]Hannah Anderson, *All That's Good: Recovering the Lost Art of Discernment* (Chicago: Moody Publishers, 2018), p. 25.

[23]My brilliant friend and enneagram teacher Annie Dimond introduced me to this language of "learning to hold the map." Check out her work on Instagram: @enneagramforwholeness.

[24]Benner, *The Gift of Being Yourself*, p. 63.

[25]By ego I mean a psychological concept that is one of the three parts of psychoanalytic theory (along with the id and the superego). This is how you have learned to identity yourself. This, when combined with our dominant enneagram type, forms the adapted self.

[26]Palmer, *Let Your Life Speak*, p. 92.

CHAPTER ONE

The Enneagram and Barriers to Discernment

"If you can find a path with no obstacles,
it probably doesn't lead anywhere."
—Frank A. Clark

The enneagram is a framework of nine pilgrimages of personhood. In its essence, it's that simple. But it's a simplicity of understanding who we are that comes while working though the complexity of life. Each person's enneagram journey contains profound questions of vocation, wisdom, and practice that comprise the Way of Discernment.

My take on the enneagram is different than much of what is out there in print and on podcasts. It's worth explaining what the enneagram is (and isn't). The reality is that there are a lot of "enneagrams" out there and I want to be clear about the one I'm using.

The name "enneagram" derives from two Latin and Greek words: figure (*gram*) and nine (*ennea*). Figures of nine things have

been found throughout antiquity. The enneagram's is a complicated and sorted history, without a definitive narrative.[1]

The modern enneagram framework typically contains a circle with nine interconnected points, like this:

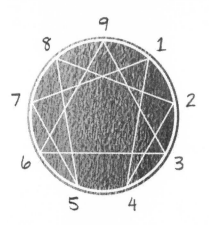

Recently, the ennea-
gram has exploded in pop-
ularity, producing countless
books, workshops, coaches,
podcasts, and the like. Current use of the enneagram
tends to fall into two camps.
The first is primarily *psychological*, employing the
enneagram as a personality
typing tool; a handy way to
understand people. In this
way, the enneagram is com-
pared to other typologies, such as the Myers-Briggs Type Indicator
(MBTI), the Dominance influence Steadiness Conscientiousness
Profile (DiSC), StrengthsFinder, etc. This use has been extended
to social media (referred to by many as the "memefication" of the
enneagram). In these instances, enneagram content takes on a
digital pop-psychology tone. It risks becoming an object we con-
sume, yet another opportunity to commodify one another.

The second realm of enneagram work is primarily spiritual,
employing the enneagram as an esoteric tool—a means to enlight-
enment and spiritual transformation. This is why you'll find the
enneagram used within mystical streams of every major religious
tradition, as well as non-religious spiritualities. Used this way, the
enneagram becomes an integral resource on the spiritual journey.
This approach risks elevating the spiritual over our physicality.

With any resource, different understandings have their
critics. Some find the psychological approach reductive and a
departure from the enneagram's ancient roots. The enneagram
only found its footing within the field of psychology in recent
decades, and critics of "psychologizing" the enneagram point to

its predation of modern psychology and the wisdom found be-neath the "types." There's legitimate concerns about the shifts in enneagram content from an oral tradition to a written tradition and now to social media "content." Is it really appropriate to go to Instagram to find a series of posts on the best type of health smoothie for each type? For the purposes of discernment, which require time, reflection, and contemplation, digital spaces prove challenging, as they train our brains to merely skim and scan.[2]

Others find many offerings from the spiritual approach to esoteric and impractical, ignoring the important contribution modern psychology provides. Such critics scoff at "elitist" or "in-sider" tendencies within some spiritual camps in the Enneagram community. There are legitimate concerns in these spaces about privilege and practicality. Not everyone can afford to attend a seven-day spiritual retreat in luxury accommodations. And for those who can, connecting the experience to the everyday grind of life can be confusing.

The Enneagram of Discernment is an attempt to avoid the potential traps of both, offering invitations into the spirituality, psychology, and practicality that the enneagram provides. This maintains a sense of integrity when encountering the enneagram and the gift and practice of discernment.

With this approach in mind, a basic introduction is war-ranted. For the newcomers, consider this a crash course. For the ennea-savvy, consider this a return to the fundamentals.

A Way-Too-Brief-but-Still-Helpful Introduction to the Enneagram

- As mentioned above, the enneagram is a framework of nine pilgrimages of personhood.
- There are nine points (types) on the enneagram frame-work, with each point representing a particular persona. Each person has a dominant enneagram type that they lead with for the balance of their lives. Each person also contains aspects of all eight other types, but lead with

their one dominant type. All nine types have strengths and weaknesses. There is no hierarchy to the types.

- These types are labeled by numbers (1-9) and often by nicknames (more on these later). Your dominant type represents the set of habits and patterns you've developed over the course of your life to cope (in good and bad ways) in this world. It is your egoic personality; the character structure you've developed over time. Your egoic personality isn't necessarily a bad thing, but believing that this is identity leads to some unhealthy places. Many teachers refer to this as the "false self," or "adapted self." This is the *persona* that we put on to relate to others, express ourselves, defend ourselves, and survive.

- Your dominant "type" also helps you understand the ways in which you've lost sight of your authentic identity. Many teachers refer to authentic identity as the "true self" or "authentic self."

- The enneagram isn't really about behaviors. The enneagram is about core motivations and fears that drive certain behaviors. This distinguishes it from other typologies.

- The enneagram is perpetually triadic. Beyond a surface-level understanding of type lies a wealth of wisdom by grouping the ennea-types into various groups of three. These triads contain powerful wisdom for the pilgrimage. (Note: This book will explore a few of those triadic groupings.)

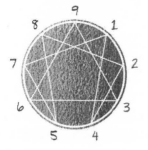

- The enneagram is a dynamic resource. While each person leads with a dominant type, the presence of the other eight types provides considerable movement throughout the framework. This is represented through the interconnected lines that traverse the circle. These inner dynamics represent how each type experiences stress and security. Each point on the circle has lines connecting it to two other types. One of those lines is the direction of stress (a coping mechanism) and the other is the direction of security (a place of safety, ease, and/or comfort)

- The enneagram is wonderfully simple, yet endlessly complex. It's tempting to read a short description of the nine types and believe you've figured everyone out. The reality is that to explore the enneagram with depth requires an acknowledgement that there is always more to learn and more to discover. This is because it is a dynamic framework, with opportunities for integration, disintegration, growth, maturity, and so much more. Thus, while each of us has a dominant type, we are so much more than our number.

The Nine Types of the Enneagram

There are many ways to introduce the nine types. For the Enneagram of Discernment, it's helpful to describe the types by what they truly want, not only what they too often settle for. These "wants" are core desires for each type. It's important to note that each of the type's "wants" are common to all, but explored in different ways. In other words, we all want these things, but the ways in which we go about them (and why) differ by type. It's here that each type's response to anxiety emerges. By anxiety, I mean the human response to stress in life. This is different than a clinically diagnosed anxiety disorder. Experiencing anxiety is a universal human phenomenon. Our responses to that anxiety vary by type. Each type's response results in a "settling," a settling for less than what we truly "want."

Granted, there are healthy ways to settle. But when our enneagram type settles, it tends to find a seemingly fixed default setting; one that is short of who we truly are. In the Enneagram of Discernment, it's helpful to be aware of a primary "want" that drives us, and the ways in which we typically "settle." (Remember: There is no hierarchy to the types, and each has its strengths and weaknesses.)

Type Eight ("The Challenger")–Type Eights want protection but settle for control.

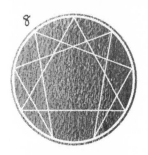

Type Eights are often labeled as "challengers." While this describes some common expressions of Eights, it doesn't capture what Eights are truly after. Eights, at their core, want protection. They want to be protected, and they want the world to be marked by protection. But when confronted with a world that isn't always protecting, the vulnerability feels threatening. They can see need for protection everywhere, and they see it most prominently within themselves. This leads Type Eights to feel anxious about life, and that stress manifests as a particular type of anger toward vulnerability: controlling their environment on their own terms. In order to keep the need for protection in check, Type Eights settle for the control they can manifest in their world. This pursuit of control can cause Eights to overlook the goodness of vulnerability in safe places.

Type Nine ("The Peacemaker")–Type Nines want peace but settle for calm.

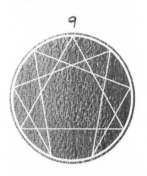

Type Nines are often labeled as "peacemakers." While this describes some common expressions of Nines, it doesn't capture all that Nines experience. Nines, at their core, want peace. They want peace within, and they want the world to be marked by peace. But when confronted with a world that isn't always peaceful, the vulnerability feels threatening. They can see need for peace everywhere, and they see it most prominently within themselves. This leads Type Nines to feel anxious about life, and that stress manifests as a particular type of anger toward disruption: passive aggression. In order to keep the need for peace in check, and to not disrupt with passive aggression, Type Nines settle for the calm they can maintain in their world. This pursuit of calm can cause Nines to forget themselves.

Type One ("The Reformer")–Type Ones want goodness but settle for order.

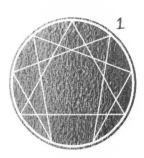

Type Ones are often labeled as "perfectionists." While this describes some Ones, it doesn't capture what Ones are truly after. Ones, at their core, want goodness. They want to be good, and they want the world to be good. But when confronted with a world that isn't always good, it feels like a consuming wrongness. They can see wrongness everywhere, and they see it most prominently within themselves. This leads Type Ones to feel anxious about life, and that stress manifests as anger. But because of their sensitivity to being good, they hold that anger down whenever possible. Anger then takes on a more subtle and acceptable version: resentment. In order to keep the resentment in check, Type Ones settle for order in their world: self-improvement, rules, a sense of fairness, a sense of being right, ordering their environment, etc. Little releases of resentment help to keep things in check. Small attempts at improvement aim to satisfy the pursuit of goodness.

Type Two ("The Helper")–Type Twos want unconditional love but settle for niceness.

Type Twos are often labeled as "helpers." While this describes some Twos, it doesn't capture what Twos are truly after. Twos, at their core, want love. They want to embody love, and they want the world to be marked by love. But when confronted with a world that isn't always loving, it feels like insufficiency.

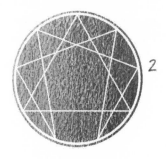

They can see need for love everywhere, and they see it most prominently within themselves. This leads Type Twos to feel anxious about life, and that stress manifests as shame. But because of their sensitivity to being loved, they hold that shame down whenever possible, and resolve it through focusing on others' needs. This helps Twos experience a more subtle and acceptable version: pride in their sacrificial love. It is subtle and acceptable because Type Twos settle for being nice in their world: service, helping, other-focused acts, giving of themselves, etc. This results in Twos receiving flattery for being so sacrificial, kind, and thoughtful. These small doses of flattery can confuse the altruism of twos, and feed their subtle pride. Twos' acts of helping are small attempts at giving love to try to satisfy the pursuit of unconditional love.

Type Three ("The Achiever")–Type Threes want worth but settle for image.

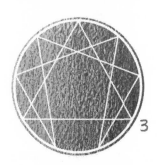

Type Threes are often labeled as "achievers." While this describes common behaviors of Threes, it doesn't capture what Threes are truly after. Threes, at their core, want worth and value. They want to be worthy, and they want the world to be marked by the inherent value of all. But when confronted with a world that doesn't always value the good, the right, and the beautiful, it feels threatening. They can see need for value everywhere, and they see it most prominently within themselves. This leads Type Threes to feel anxious about life, and that stress manifests as shame. But because of their sensitivity to being valued, they hold that shame down whenever possible. Shame then takes on a more subtle and acceptable version: image-crafting to impress and prove their worth. In order to keep the need for worth in check, Type Threes settle for the image(s) they create in their world: accomplished, polished, goal-oriented, and determined. This results in Threes receiving accolades and compliments for being so driven, focused, and successful. These small doses of recognition can confuse the inherent value and worth of Threes, and feed their sense of vanity. The Three's ability to get-things-done are small attempts at seeking the validation we all need.

Type Four ("The Individualist")–Type Fours want belonging but settle for longing.

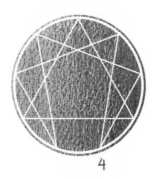

4

Type Fours are often labeled as "individualists." While this describes some expressions of Fours, it doesn't capture what Fours are truly after. Fours, at their core, want belonging and connection. They want to belong, and they want the world to be marked by connection. But when confronted with a world that doesn't always make space for all as they are, it feels threatening. They can see need for belonging and connection everywhere, and they see it most prominently within themselves. This leads Type Fours to feel anxious about life, and that stress manifests as a particular type of shame: deficiency. Because of their sensitivity to being truly known and accepted, deficiency takes on a more subtle and acceptable version: deep and extraordinary longing for connection. In order to keep the longing in check, Type Fours settle for secondary longings they conjure in their world: the extraordinary, the creative, and the unique. This results in Fours shunning the ordinary and mundane in search of re-establishing depth and connection.

These small doses of uniqueness can confuse the inherent belonging of Fours, and feed their sense of deficiency or inadequacy. Fours' attunement toward being misunderstood drives this pursuit of the unique.

Type Five ("The Investigator")–Type Fives want competency but settle for knowledge.

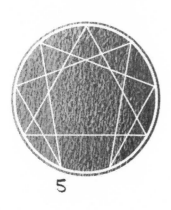

5

Type Fives are often labeled as "investigators." While this describes some common expressions of Fives, it doesn't capture what Fives are truly after. Fives, at their core, want competency and sufficiency. They want to be capable, and they want the world to be marked by sufficiency of understanding. But when confronted with a world that doesn't always makes sense, or in which they don't feel prepared, it feels threatening. They can see need for competency everywhere, and they see it most prominently within themselves. This leads Type Fives to feel anxious about life, and that stress manifests as a particular type of fear: being useless and empty. Because of their sensitivity to competency, this fear of scarcity takes on a more subtle and acceptable version: depth of knowledge and insatiable curiosity about complex things. In order to keep the need for competency in check, Type Fives settle for the knowledge they acquire in their world: deep dives on complex topics, ideas, or hobbies. This results in Fives' allergies to superficiality, small-talk, and high-energy social engagement. This pursuit of knowledge can cause Fives to withdraw to their safe places to study or tinker, which can further isolate and feed their fear of being useless or incompetent.

Type Six ("The Loyalist")–Type Sixes want loyalty but settle for safety.

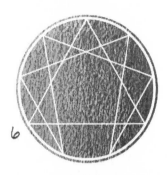

Type Sixes are often labeled as "loyalists." Unlike many other types, this nickname accurately captures what Sixes are truly after. Sixes, at their core, want loyalty. They want to be loyal and supported, and they want the world to be marked by fidelity to one another. But when confronted with a world that isn't always loyal, it feels threatening. They can see need for security everywhere, and they see it most prominently within themselves. This leads Type Sixes to doubt their intuition and feel anxious about life, and that stress manifests as a particular type of fear: being in an unfaithful environment. Because of their need to cope, this fear of infidelity takes on a more subtle and acceptable version: ensuring one's surroundings are safe and secure. In order to keep the need for loyalty in check, Type Sixes settle for the safety they can acquire in their world. This pursuit of safety can cause Sixes to threat-forecast wherever they go, which can further isolate themselves from others and feed their fear of disloyalty.

Type Seven ("The Enthusiast")–Type Sevens want contentment but settle for excitement.

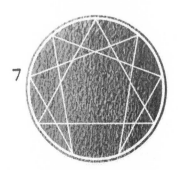

Type Sevens are often labeled as "enthusiasts." While this describes some common expressions of Sevens, it doesn't capture what Sevens are truly after. Sevens, at their core, want contentment. They want to be content, and they want the world to be marked by contentment.

But when confronted with a world that isn't always satisfactory, it feels threatening. They can see need for satisfaction and contentment everywhere, and they see it most prominently within themselves. This leads Type Sevens to feel anxious about life, and that stress manifests as a particular type of fear: being in a painful or deprived environment. Because of their need to cope, this fear of pain or deprivation takes on a more subtle and acceptable version: planning[3] for the next adventure or immersing themselves in another story. In order to keep the need for contentment in check, Type Sevens settle for the excitement they can manifest in their world. This pursuit of excitement can cause Sevens to hyper-plan wherever they go, which can cause Sevens to overlook the goodness of the ordinary and mundane.

Barriers to Discernment

Discernment is the gift and practice of living our lives from a deep sense of vocation, with wisdom, in the fullness of time.

In the Introduction, I argued that our ability to discern our lives well is diminished by lying to ourselves, being overwhelmed, and neglecting to listen. But underneath is another layer of resistance, a marshland of the soul that further impedes. To discern well, we must enter these murky and shadowy places and identify these impediments. More difficult to recognize, these impediments' ability to remain in the shadows makes them more powerful.

Notice how I began the type descriptions above with Type Eight and ended with Type Seven. This is not by mistake (I promise I know how to count). This ordering is a traditional and common approach to exploring the enneagram, because it groups the nine types into the three triads known as the three "centers" of intelligence available to us. We'll explore the centers in depth in Chapter Three, but for now it's helpful to know that types Eight, Nine, and One form the Gut Center Triad, types Two, Three, and Four form the Heart Center Triad, and Types Five, Six, and Seven form the Head Center Triad. Each type tends to lead from their center.

With this in mind, take another look at the descriptions I provide above of the nine types. Look specifically for a word common to the three types in each center.

With this second read, you'll notice three words tend to lift from the pages: anger, shame, and fear. These are the triads' responses to anxiety. We've all been angry. We've all felt shame. We've all been afraid. Any time we experience these emotions, our chances of making poor decisions increase. Our anger blinds. Our shame smothers. Our fear freezes us in our tracks.

Granted, there are healthy expressions of each of these emotions. Righteous anger is a healthy response to injustice or oppression. Shame can give way to remorse and play a healthy role in response to our own wrong and foolish behavior. Many fears are rational and legitimate as a response to real danger.

And it's important to highlight that emotions are vital to our lives. In this book we'll explore how emotions are a form of intelligence. They are a critical component to our wisdom formation. The temptation when we notice how certain emotions impede our discernment is to dismiss them, flee from them, or repress them. Any form of rejecting emotion will lead to poor discernment.

In our adapted states, anger, shame, and fear can result in negative, unhealthy consequences. The enneagram helps us see how each center of intelligence suffers from one of these impeding emotions in a more pronounced way.

- **The Gut Center Triad** types all suffer from anger—a state of displeasure, annoyance or hostility.
- **The Heart Center Triad** types all suffer from shame—a state of painful negative thoughts about oneself, humiliation or distress caused by the experience of being wrong or foolish.
- **The Head Center Triad** types all suffer from fear—an unpleasant state caused by the belief that someone or something is dangerous, likely to cause pain, or a threat.

When we are disconnected from an authentic sense of self, each type slams into a powerful impeding emotion, one they share in common with the other two types in their center. Riso and Hudson refer to this as each center's *dominant* emotion. The enneagram invites us into further exploration of our dominant impeding emotion and its excessive qualities as evidenced in our dominant type. This is the emotion that tends to surface most often to the point that we are nearly fixated on it. And that fixation can bring discernment to a screeching halt.

In the settling statements and descriptions you can see how each type tries to control this dominant emotion in some unhealthy ways. The "settling" for less than what they really want is a sort of compromise. Each type makes an internal deal: "If I settle for _____, it'll keep the dominant emotion (anger, shame, or fear) in check."

This process of controlling the dominant emotion thwarts our discernment in tragic ways.

How Anger Impedes Discernment

When angry, our thoughts become hyper focused on that which caused the anger. Our ability to consider just about anything else wanes, as the brain shunts blood away from itself to our muscles, preparing us for a fight. Our brain's cognitive efficiency (the ability to think clearly and quickly) decreases, and our anxiety increases. The overall effect is that our thinking gets simplified, impeding our ability to slow down, reflect, and engage the complexity of discernment.

In addition, when our bodies are angry we're prone to headaches, migraines, chest pains, or other physical ailments. When our bodies ache, it's difficult to think about anything else. It's a challenge to engage in complex thinking or sustained contemplation when your head is pounding.

Our anger often leads to projecting a false confidence that attempts to minimize risk and increase control. Think of the way many animals strut to appear larger and more menacing. The result is often impulsive behavior causing us to make more mistakes. The humility required of discernment is tossed aside. Our anger can damage relationships, cutting ourselves off from those who could potentially be most helpful in our discernment.

In the Gut Center Triad, Types Eight, Nine, and One are prone to anger in unique ways that impede their ability to discern.

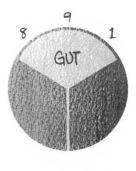

- Type Eights suffer from anger when they sense a lack of protection. They tend to express their anger outwardly, when they anticipate vulnerability or weakness in their world. This type of anger is easy to see as it is often unfiltered. For Eights, it's an efficient way to plow through difficulty or confusion.

- Type Nines suffer from anger at disruption. They tend to resort to a sort of self-forgetting to deny their anger, especially when their environment causes them to remember other disruptive contexts. This denial of anger often seeps out as passive aggression and stubbornness.

- Type Ones suffer from anger at a lack of goodness or rightness. They tend to internalize their anger, shifting its focus to themselves in the form of self-criticism, especially when they experience their world in ways that lack goodness or rightness. This exposes their own limits and shortcomings and anger can only stay suppressed for so long until it leaks out as resentment.

How Shame Impedes Discernment

Anger smolders until it erupts. Shame comes at us differently. When shame creeps in, it can feel suffocating. When we feel shame, our brains will act to avert any sort of risk, because the possibility of failure reinforces the shame. Our discernment becomes truncated to that which feels safest. Shame has a way of convincing us that we don't deserve any rewards that may come when we risk, so why bother risking at all. Along the way, our self-esteem plummets.

When the body experiences shame, it powers down. Shame has a way of dragging us down like we're sinking in our own quicksand. Momentum wanes, as does the motivation to act out of a sense of discernment. Shame also has a fog-like quality, impeding our vision to see anything but our own shortcomings.

The result is isolation, where we avoid others out of worry about being exposed. In isolation, we're prone to relapse into the same cycles of unhealthy behaviors, which reinforces the shame we loathe. It's a tragic cycle that drains generative discerning energy redirecting it at our own self-loathing.

In the Heart Center Triad, Types Two, Three, and Four are prone to shame in unique ways that impede their ability to discern.

- Type Twos suffer from the shame of being unlovable. They tend to turn their shame into serving and helping others to compensate for the perception of being unloved. This focus on the experience of being loved (or unloved) brings an other-focus. Their shame 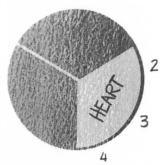 convinces them that their needs are not worth fulfilling, but others' needs are.

- Type Threes suffer from the shame of being without worth or value. They tend to accomplish and achieve to ward off their anticipation of shame. Their shame tells them that without their abilities to get things done, and look good doing it, they have no worth in their world. This causes Threes to craft personas that they feel are compelling to those around them in order to manufacture a sense of worth.

- Type Fours suffer from the shame of not belonging to something greater than themselves. They tend to channel their shame into longing for what is real and significant. This is often a response to painful memories of not belonging, encouraging Fours to withdraw as a defense. Their shame prods them to search for depth and significance in longing without belonging internally, and re-emerge into their world as one unique: an image that is simultaneously different and yet compelling.

How Fear Impedes Discernment

When we experience fear, our brain short-circuits pathways of rational thinking, reacting more from the amygdala in a survival mode. This process plays tricks with our memory, breeding uncertainty. The uncertainty can be overwhelming, causing us to freeze in our tracks.

When the body is in a state of fear, breathing quickens, the heart races, and muscles tighten in a panic state. The body is not built for sustained fear states, inevitably leading to fatigue and exhaustion, both of which work against the discernment process.

Succumbing to fear over time results in patterns of irrational behavior and/or learned helplessness. When we believe we're in a survival state, we do whatever it takes to survive in the present moment. If fear cripples us, we freeze in a state in which we can't help ourselves. In either situation, the wisdom to discern seems distant.

In the Head Center Triad, Types Five, Six, and Seven are prone to fear in unique ways that impede their ability to discern.

- Type Fives suffer from the fear of being incompetent and insufficient. They can clearly remember times of being without what they deem critical knowledge or information, and they don't want to relive them. This fear drives them to withdraw to study and compile a competency that they feel will protect them when they reemerge in their world.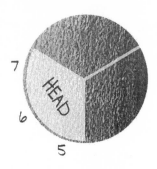

- Type Sixes suffer from a fear of being without loyalty or support. They tend to experience a lack of security in their environment, which causes them to doubt the support and safety around them. Sixes often want to resolve their perceived threats before they can relax and move ahead. They struggle to trust their own intuition, often looking for assurance from others.

- Type Sevens suffer from a fear of being deprived. They have a sensitivity toward depletion: when excitement, resources, and intrigue will run out. Their fear of being in a state of lack compels them to anticipate how to escape it and move on. This causes them to have one eye on their current environment and one eye on where to go next to maintain a level of contentment.

Anger. Shame. Fear. Their ability to thwart the gift and practice of discernment is pervasive and persistent. But this isn't the end of the story. The more familiar we become with our obstacles, the less ominously they loom over us. When we can name that which is in our way, it doesn't loom over us so ominously. When we can raise our awareness of the unique ways in which our dominant emotion impedes our discernment, its power can diminish. The temptation is to find a way around our anger, around our fear, and around our shame. But avoidance rarely works. We must journey through. When we do, our experiences with anger, shame, and fear can transform from impediments to invitations. These invitations beckon us to the landscape of the Holy.[4] They provide opportunities to listen and decide if the voices of anger, shame, and fear should be the loudest. When we sort through our dominant emotion's voice, we clear the way to hear another Voice. This is God, the Divine Voice of Love, which calls us to authentic identity, purpose, and direction.

Notes

[1]For a brief history of the enneagram, check out a piece written by Mike Morrell and John Luckovich in my friend Dr. Jerome D. Lubbe's beautiful and innovative work, *Whole Identity: A Brain-Based Enneagram Model for (W)holistic Human Thriving, Volume 1,* (Atlanta: Thrive Neuro Theology, 2019), p. 15-17. For a more thorough take, check out Fatima Fernandez Christlieb's *Where (On Earth) Did the Enneagram Come From?* (Fatima Editores, 2016).

[2]See the work of Nicholas Carr, *The Shallows: What the Internet is Doing to Our Brains* (New York: W.W. Norton & Co, 2011).

[3]A word on the "planning" of the Type Seven is needed, as it is often misunderstood by other types. Everyone plans, but the difference with Sevens is that they often plan in the middle of something that they've already planned. Think of planning the next vacation while presently on vacation.

[4]K.J. Ramsey gave me this landscape imagery. It's explored more deeply in her book. See K.J. Ramsey, *This Too Shall Last: Finding Grace When Suffering Lingers* (Grand Rapids: Zondervan, 2020).

CHAPTER TWO

The Vocation Triad: Identity, Purpose, and Direction

"We must make the choices that enable us to fulfill the deepest capacities of our real selves."
—Thomas Merton

Every step we take is a journey into the unknown. And in between the present moment and the one to come is a space. It's a space of transition, from the now to the next.

At times it's a space pregnant with possibility, where imagination, hope, expectation, all dwell. Not knowing what's next can be exciting. The anticipation can be palpable, fueled by the energy of creativity.

At times it's a space of great confusion, pain, and suffering. Not knowing what's next is often excruciating. The anxiety can be crippling, fueled by the energy of fear. Dare we dream and hope for good things?

Where we are right now is familiar ground. The next step is uncharted territory.

This is liminal space. The word "liminal" comes from the Latin word "limen," which means *threshold*—the sill of a door that marks the transition from one space to another. Many cultures hold special significance for thresholds and pass down customs to bring good luck or ward off bad luck.

Our lives contain many liminal spaces, thresholds from what is quickly becoming old to what is quickly becoming new. The liminal space from the lived to the unlived is sacred ground. Father Richard Rohr refers to liminal space as "God's waiting room."[1]

In God's waiting room, where we don't know what's next, we wait expectantly. In this liminal space, we find the expanse of vocation.

Modern expressions of vocation are unfortunately truncated to one's "job." That's not what I mean. The ancient theological concept of vocation existed long before the age of modern work. It derives from the Latin root *vocare*, which means "to call." Its scope is much broader and deeper. When we talk about calling, we are talking about vocation.[2]

It's a simple, yet profound idea. In the liminal spaces of our lives, where we wonder what's next, a call comes to us from the Divine.[3]

Nearly every religious tradition includes stories of a divinity calling to humanity. Most sacred texts provide dramatic tales of supernatural calls: a bush that burns without being consumed, angelic appearances, donkeys who talk, pillars of fire, golden plates unearthed, etc.

I have to be honest: None of those things have ever happened to me. I've had experiences I can't explain, but nothing so dramatic. Spiritual inspiration in my life has been far more in the realm of faint whispers of guidance, of subtle glints and glimmers. Some drama would make things easier. A bolt of lightning would get my attention.

This is the challenge of vocation: *attention*. Distracted by the enormity of it all, it's tough to pay attention to the Divine, others, and self in the present. Our confusion, anxiety, and worry about what's ahead can max our cognitive load.

But when we pay attention, the whispers of inspiration compel us to widen our eyes, perk our ears, set our jaw, and cross the threshold. It's easier said than done.

For if God calls, what's the Divine saying? And, how are we to respond? Those are hefty questions, loaded with all sorts of baggage.

Such hefty questions emerge in all sorts of important thresholds. We're often faced with decisions that have no simple answer:

- How should I continue my education?
- What should I study?
- Where should I live?
- Whom should I marry?
- Or, should I marry at all?
- What's my ideal career path?
- Do I want to become a parent?

When faced with such important questions, a common response for the religious and non-religious alike is to look to a higher authority (God), to help us make sense of the options before us, or perhaps, provide some validation for what we choose. It's been said that there are no atheists in foxholes.[4] When we feel stuck in indecision, we find ourselves in an existential foxhole.

This isn't all bad. To explore a calling is a noble thing. It's a means of placing one's life in a larger picture. Also, a calling assumes a Caller. That's also a good thing. To bring calling into our discernment means acknowledging our search for wisdom's source in making decisions.

To hear and respond to a sense of calling beckons us to cross the threshold into our unlived lives. How does this work? To be honest, much of what occurs in liminal space is spiritual and mystical, difficult to describe in words. It's more alchemic than formulaic. Our lives are marked by both clarity and confusion when it comes to our thresholds. Each of us can remember times in which the way forward was crystal clear. In my own life, the decisions to marry my wife was one such "crystal clear" threshold. We can also recall moments in which we had no idea what to do next. I've faced numerous career-related decisions that felt like a coin-flip was my only help. The temptation is to try to find a shortcut—a way to get from here to there (whatever there we hope and dream) as quickly as possible. We want to jump from our current place to a destination.

A definition is helpful to begin to wrap our minds, hearts, and bodies around vocation. I consider vocation to be *receiving the Divine Call of identity, purpose, and direction*.

A few aspects of this definition are worth highlighting. First, vocation is a gift more than it is a goal. Western culture has exalted the driven life, which often compels us to set goals ahead and then work toward them. This isn't necessarily wrong. Goal setting can be healthy. But importing it into the realm of vocation can distort the beautiful gift of the Divine Call. Palmer perhaps says it best when he describes vocation "not as a goal to be achieved but as a gift to be received. Discovering vocation does not mean scrambling toward some prize just beyond my reach but accepting the treasure of true self I already possess."[5] Receiving the gift is a lifelong process. There very well may be important destinations along the way, but they are cairns in the expanse of vocation.

Second, this definition surveys the expanse of vocation, which includes three sacred territories: identity, purpose, and direction. To discern our lives well, we can't bypass identity, purpose, and direction. Calling isn't something we simply descend upon. We make this road by walking it. The journey to a wild and precious life emerges from the Divine Call to traverse these territories.

In the expanse of Vocation Triad, we encounter the first three key questions of discernment:

- Who am I?—This is the question of identity.
- Why am I here?—This is the question of purpose.
- Where am I going?—This is the question of direction.

And in this space, these beautiful and brave questions emerge. Trace your confusion, frustration, and pain…you'll eventually get to one of these questions.

Navigating the big questions is not easy. These three territories don't always provide specific answers when crossing life's thresholds. But they provide us with something better: the confidence to cross any threshold with authenticity and integrity.

Let's explore each of these territories in turn, and how the Enneagram of Discernment provides insight.

The First Territory: Identity

Our Caricatures

Not too long ago I was on vacation with my family and there was a street artist offering to draw caricature portraits. I'm sure you've seen them: cartoonish likenesses of a person with exaggerated features. I think there's a reason they play well on streets and boardwalks the world over: in such drawings we see a comical version of ourselves. They're fun and funny, an impulsive artifact from the day.

Caricature artists can produce a portrait for you in mere minutes, which is astonishing. Their ability to produce a mimicked version of a person fascinates the passerby. There's also a deeper truth to it. The word, which derives from the Italian language, originally meant "loaded portrait." Caricatures are simultaneously loaded with simplifications and exaggerations.

It's an art with a hustle, which I can respect. But it's also something we've all been doing to ourselves for the entirety of our lives. Psychologists, theologians, and spiritual directors have long talked about the idea of the "false self" (in contrast with the "true self"). Different teachers have different ways of talking about the false and true selves, but all agree that, as children, we all develop a sense of self that helps us survive and navigate our worlds. Let me be clear that this is not a bad thing. Survival and coping are essential. But we, like the caricaturists, find ways to simplify and exaggerate who we are. Over time, we become a version of ourselves that we can recognize, but isn't truly who we are.

Gradually, we begin to rely too heavily on an ego that we've developed. Again, recall Nouwen's three lies of identity:

- I am what I have.
- I am what I do.
- I am what others say about me.

Living the lies over time develops a dependence on a false self that seeks to live our lives out of our own strength, disconnected from God. Consider how each lie falls into this trap:

- I am defined by the wealth I possess. Therefore, I must continue to accumulate more money and possessions in order to understand who I am.
- I am defined by the work that I do. Therefore, I must continue to work harder and move up the "ladder" in order to understand who I am.
- I am defined by how other's perceive me. Therefore, I must find ways to please and impress those around me in order to understand who I am.

Read over the above again. Notice the perpetual striving required. Notice how identity is defined by external forces. This is the false self. Albert Haase, in his book, *Coming Home to Your True Self*, expands this idea, providing ten "Empty P's of the False Self:" pleasure, praise, power, prestige, position, popularity, people, productivity, possessions, perfection.[6]

Our ability to develop our identity in unhealthy places abounds. Enneagram author and teacher Marylin Vancil describes this development in a helpful way. She refers to this as the "adapted self," the self we believe we must be in order to survive and have our needs met.[7]

This false/adapted self is the result of an over-identification with our ego. Granted, part of being human is having an ego. In fact, the ego is responsible for some important functions of our overall self. Beware the teachers who claim to help you eradicate your ego, allowing you to simply live from "essence." The goal is not to have our ego disappear. To have an ego is not a problem. To have an ego is to be human.

The problem is over-identifying with our ego, letting it run our lives. This is *egocentricity*. David Benner describes it this way: "it (the ego) cannot fulfill the role it is uniquely equipped to fill while it functions as chief executive officer."[8] In other words, our ego must be put in its proper place, letting our authentic self lead the way.

Authentic Self

You can probably see where I'm going. A helpful way to understand the adapted self is the enneagram types. My friend Seth Abram has a helpful take. He considers this false/adapted self a part of us that "lacks trust in being created in the image of the Divine."[9] The absence of trust in one's own authentic identity is a powerful motivator to place trust in other things, hoping they will help us understand who we are. Coupled with a lifetime of results in which our adapted self has worked fairly well for us, discovering a different way of being is no small task.

And the current go-to methods of self-improvement aren't all that helpful. They're full of willfulness (more on this later) and striving. The path to a more authentic self isn't a hot topic in the self-help space. Peeling back the adapted self to a more authentic way of living takes great time and care. We relax into it more than we go get it. We receive it as a gift more than we create it.[10] And that authentic self, for every person, regardless of enneagram type, is this:

You are a beloved self-in-God, made in the image of the Divine.

The word *beloved* has been reduced to mere sentimentality, but let's look at the original meaning. The prefix "be" conveys ideas such as "completely covered," and "encompassing." Your authentic self is one who is completely covered and encompassed in love. In this way, your authentic self has nothing to do with your behavior. It has everything to do with love.

This love is also generative. We are created in the *Imago Dei*, as an imprint of the Divine. Consider David Benner's explanation:

> ...our being is grounded in God's love. The generative love of God was our origin. The embracing love of God sustains...Love is our identity...Created from love, of love and for love, our existence makes no sense apart from Divine love.[11]

This is the beautiful irony of identity. We are prone to craft our own imprints to survive and thrive in our world. But our authentic identity is an imprint of a different sort, one that authenticates instead of imitates.

By excavating our way through the layers of adapted self that we've confused with identity, we reach the core of who we are: love in the *Imago Dei*.[12] Love doesn't simplify to reduce. Love doesn't exaggerate to compensate. Love doesn't divide. Love doesn't diminish. Love has a way of re-joining, re-conciling, re-deeming, and re-membering. In word, love is the way of wholeness.

And here we find the starkness of contrast between the adapted self and the authentic self. One is a caricature self with clever features. The other is a core self defined by wholeness.

Thomas Kelly, the Quaker mystic, calls this authentic self the "Divine Center," a holy place within us with a speaking Voice.[13] Many traditions call this Spirit. In the Christian tradition, St. John refers to the Spirit using the Greek word "*paraclete*," which translates as "helper," "advocate," or "counselor." What is more essential to discernment than a loving advocate/helper/counselor?

Now we've rounded an important circle: We too often look for a voice "out there" to guide us, when very often the voice we need to listen to is within. External voices and influences can certainly help, but we should never rely upon them at the expense of the Divine within. From this place of Divine Love we can hear guidance without pretense, insight without agenda, and encouragement without disclaimers. In our authentic self, union with God is available. This Divine Love helps us distinguish from the other inner voices (inner critics) that seek to sabotage us: chiefly anger, shame, and fear.

From Adapted Self → Authentic Self

To authentically live from this place is not easy. It requires much of us in areas we've learned to ignore. This work of excavation requires seven steps.

First, we must be more *aware* of our adapted self. It starts with an awareness of the ways in which we have learned to survive and cope, even when it has produced some great results.

Second, we must *acknowledge* the Divine Voice who calls us "beloved." This union with God that is available to us is a beautiful relationship defined by love that frames all relationships. The question *Who am I?* leads us to another question: *Whose am I?*. Our selfhood resides in the realm of relationships. To receive this call as a gift requires us to acknowledge a Giver, and be grateful for the gift. Benner writes, "Nothing is more important, for if we find our true self we find God, and if we find God, we find our most authentic self."[14]

Third, we must *relinquish* our adapted self. Over many years we've developed strong attachments to our adapted self. It's a place of some comfort and familiarity. To let it go can be scary. I've often heard that spirituality is really the art of letting go. When it comes to identity, we must begin to loosen our grip on our caricatured notions of self in order to receive the gift of identity.

Fourth, we must approach the path with *humility*. The journey to the authentic self is rarely triumphant. It's more of a humble quest in which we confront ways in which we've simplified and exaggerated ourselves in unhealthy ways. Think of a time in which you were humbled. Such instances have a way of bringing us back down to earth. It can hurt, but it can also ground us. The firmness of the ground provides a measure of safety and firmness upon which to walk.[15]

Fifth, we must *befriend* ourselves. Palmer reminds us that "true self is true friend."[16] If we are made in the image and likeness of God, and our identity is that of beloved, we must claim this as our identity and befriend it.

Sixth, we must live from a place of *agency*. The energetic nature of Love cannot be contained. From our identity as beloved we draw loving energy from the Divine Source. This is fertile ground from which to live, and here our sense of being and our sense of doing find congruence. Our activity in the world flows from this place of identity.

Seventh, we must continually do all of the above. I wish I could tell you that this chapter is a one-time ride. With honesty I can tell you that this journey of awareness, acknowledgement, befriending, humility, and surrender is lifelong and comprised of many iterations. But please don't mistake this journey for any other journey that calls you to strive or manufacture. The path from adapted to authentic is a descent. A journey inward and downward through our shadows. In many ways, this is the more difficult path. When Jesus told his disciples that to save their lives they must lose it (Mark 8:34-36), this is what he was talking about. There is a death we must suffer: a death to our over-identification with the ego. We must slay our overreliance of the unhealthy adapted self. Out of this death is resurrection.

Thomas Merton once wrote, "For me to be a saint means to be myself." This is what it means to live from authentic self. While this journey from adaptation to authenticity is available to us all, the places from which we start may differ. This is where enneagram wisdom helps us identify our dominant place of the adapted self (dominant type).

Enneagram Type → Authentic Self

The personality we've developed helps us survive, but it creates problems as it solves others. While it keeps us safe, it also conspires in our own diminishment and division.[17] This is where the enneagram provides a deep well of understanding. When we look at the specific ways in which each enneagram type seeks to present an adapted self to survive in the world, we can begin to find our way back to a more authentic self. We'll explore each types' path to authentic self in Part II of the book, but for now let's consider how each type adapts:[18]

- Type 1: Those dominant in Type One believe they must be right and live up to high ideals to be safe.

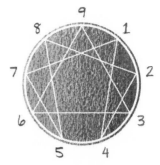

- Type 2: Those dominant in Type Two believe they must be "loving" and connected to others to be safe.

- Type 3: Those dominant in Type Three believe they must be successful and impressive to be safe.

- Type 4: Those dominant in Type Four believe they must be unique and significant to be safe.

- Type 5: Those dominant in Type Five believe they must be competent and at a safe distance from others to be safe.

- Type 6: Those dominant in Type Six believe they must be responsible and secure in their surroundings to be safe.

- Type 7: Those dominant in Type Seven believe they must be free and occupied to be safe.

- Type 8: Those dominant in Type Eight believe they must be powerful and in control to be safe.

- Type 9: Those dominant in Type Nine believe they must be peaceful and easygoing to be safe.

From our dominant type, we begin to see how we each deploy the human instincts of survival to develop an adapted self. In this adaptation, like the caricature, we simplify certain aspects of ourselves and exaggerate others. Our simplifications diminish a full and authentic sense of who we truly are. And our exaggerations further divide ourselves from a sense of wholeness.

This is why, when we take the time to honestly look at the life we're living, we so often see misplaced priorities, disordered and distorted loves, and fragmentation.

But the good news is that this isn't the end of the story. Wholeness and authenticity are within. While the enneagram teaches us that we will lead with our dominant type for the rest of our lives, its dominance in this adapted state can experience its own diminishment. We can put the ego in its proper place. When we reclaim a sense of authentic self, the simplicities and exaggerations of the adapted self soften their grip. This is the path to authenticity, to a sense of self defined not by external forces but from a deeper Source.

The path to authenticity requires a great *unknowing*, where we unlearn some messages that bolster the adapted self, so that we can begin to know what it means to live from the authentic self.

Look again at the list above, where I provide a statement for how each enneagram type adapts. If you know your dominant type, consider this: What if you lived as if your adaptation statement wasn't true?

It would require some "unknowing." For my dominant Type Three, I would have to unknow my patterns and habits that reinforce the idea that my safety and survival hinges upon my ability to be successful and impress others. For many types, that's not a big deal. For a Type Three, it's the tallest mountain to climb.

This process of unknowing begins with the acknowledgment of what needs to be challenged.

Riso and Hudson provide two lists of childhood messages that highlight what I believe to be the unknowing work for each type. First let's consider the "Unconscious Childhood Messages" for each type. These are the messages we believed to be true as children, which catalyze the development of the dominant enneagram types:

Unconscious Childhood Messages:[19]

Type 1 - "It's not okay to make mistakes."

Type 2 - "It's not okay to have your own needs."

Type 3 - "It's not okay to have your own feelings and identity."

Type 4 - "It's not okay to be too functional or too happy."

Type 5 - "It's not okay to be comfortable in the world."

Type 6 - "It's not okay to trust yourself."

Type 7 - "It's not okay to depend on anyone for anything."

Type 8 - "It's not okay to be vulnerable or to trust anyone."

Type 9 - "It's not okay to assert yourself."

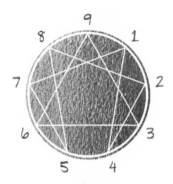

Next compare this with Riso and Hudson's other list of childhood messages, the "Lost Childhood Messages." Here we see that somewhere along the way we lost sight of these truths and instead starting living from a place of being "not okay":

Lost Childhood Messages:[20]

Type 1 - "You are good."

Type 2 - "You are wanted."

Type 3 - "You are loved for yourself."

Type 4 - "You are seen for who you are."

Type 5 - "Your needs are not a problem."

Type 6 - "You are safe."

Type 7 - "You will be taken care of."

Type 8 - "You will not be betrayed."

Type 9 - "Your presence matters."

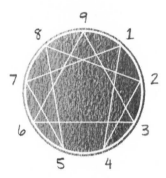

Let's combine the two lists to begin to explore the way of unknowing for each type. We must unknow the first message to embrace what was once lost.

Unconscious Childhood Messages → Lost Childhood Messages

Type 1 - "It's not okay to make mistakes." → "You are good."

Type 2 - "It's not okay to have your own needs." → "You are wanted."

Type 3 - "It's not okay to have your own feelings and identity." → "You are loved for yourself."

Type 4 - "It's not okay to be too functional or too happy." → "You are seen for who you are."

Type 5 - "It's not okay to be comfortable in the world." → "Your needs are not a problem."

Type 6 - "It's not okay to trust yourself." → "You are safe."

Type 7 - "It's not okay to depend on anyone for anything." → "You will be taken care of."

Type 8 - "It's not okay to be vulnerable or to trust anyone." → "You will not be betrayed."

Type 9 - "It's not okay to assert yourself." → "Your presence matters."

For many, the chasm between your unconscious childhood message and lost childhood message seems enormous. But with awareness and intention, each dominant type can navigate the territory of identity. Our dominant type is the trailhead to a sacred journey to the authentic self as beloved. Meister Eckhart once said, "God is at home. It is we who have gone out for a walk."[21] To live our lives with discernment, we must first go home. From there we receive the gift of our authentic purpose.

The Second Territory: Purpose

Olympic athletes are well known for their one pure and clear purpose: to get the gold medal. Every summer and winter Olympic games of my childhood were marked with televised biographical stories of athletes who sacrificed many things in the pursuit of Olympic glory. I was an aspiring athlete myself as a child, so I got it. But one athlete's story complicated things for me: Eric Liddell. Liddell was a Scottish Olympic Gold medalist whose story is recounted in the movie *Chariots of Fire*. Perhaps the most famous quote from the film subverted my simplistic idea of purpose. "I believe that God made me for a purpose. . . and when I run, I feel his pleasure. . .to win is to honor him."[22] Liddell's story raised more questions within me than answers: *Why did I want to win? Why did I want to be first?* Purpose, I eventually learned, is a complex thing. Even among the world's elite athletes, purposes can differ. The "why" behind something has many layers.

Remember that when we embark on the journey from the adapted to authentic self, we eventually discover a new energy of agency. This agency activates our journey through vocation's second territory: purpose.

It is in this territory we engage the second question of the Vocation Triad: *Why am I here?*

This territory is also fraught with dangers. In our striving and our ambition, we are tempted to cast purpose as a motivating force that drives us toward a goal. It's good to have goals. But pursuing a goal must come from a deeper place. If we only tend to the shallower purposes in life, we live from a place of willfulness. It's a forced set of "yeses" and "nos" that come from an external place. It's conjured and mustered. Parker Palmer goes so far to consider willfulness as an act of violence toward the self.[23] Our response to the Divine Call isn't one of willfulness but willingness. Willfulness is oppositional. Willingness is consensual.[24] To live in agreement with the Divine Call sets a purpose that is deeper than our goals and ambitions and flows directly from our identity as the beloved self-in-God.

An identity doesn't exist in a vacuum. It's a lived experience in homes, schools, neighborhoods, families, congregations and relationships. This is where purpose resides, in the **intention** of our identity. Once we discover our authentic self, how do we live from it?

This is the central *why* of vocation, the intent of our identity. It's here that I believe another ancient theological concept is truly helpful.

Shalom is an ancient Hebrew concept found throughout the Jewish *Tanakh* (to the Christians, the Old Testament). It's commonly translated as "peace" in English, which is a travesty. A more proper translation of *shalom* is "flourishing." In the ancient Hebrew wisdom tradition, *shalom* means flourishing in the expanse of life. It's a call to live a life in pursuit of flourishing in one's relationships with God, self, others, and creation. So, when we talk about purpose in our vocation, we're talking about a process of living in healthy trajectories of shalom in the many dimensions of our lives.

It's a beautiful notion: to live as the beloved self-in-God is to be about the belovedness of others. The Divine Love is self-giving rather than self-serving. It flows from God to our self-in-God and to other selves-in-God through our relationships. When we live from a place of authentic identity in the *Imago Dei*, our self also gives from this same Source. This allows us to consent to right relationships with God, self, others, and creation.

Shalom thus provides an even greater vision of wholeness. The journey of discovering the *Imago Dei*, moving from adapted self to authentic self heals us from our egocentricity, unifying our self with God. This is an internal wholeness. Shalom helps us seek flourishing wholeness around us. It aligns our self-in-God with others in generative, reciprocating ways.

When our identity and purpose are aligned, we can name how our dominant enneagram type settles for a life that is less than flourishing. We can also see more clearly the gifts we offer the world, one that acknowledges our *Imago Dei* and seeks to flourish from this identity. Consider this a way of willingness for each type.

Purpose: From Settling → Flourishing

Type 1 – Ones want goodness but settle for order. → Goodness is within. → Pursue flourishing from this inner goodness.

Type 2 – Twos want unconditional love but settle for niceness. → Love is within → Pursue flourishing from this inner love.

Type 3 – Threes want worth but settle for image → Worth is within. → Pursue flourishing from this inner worth.

Type 4 – Fours want belonging but settle for longing → Belonging is within. → Pursue flourishing from this inner belonging.

Type 5 – Fives want competency but settle for knowledge → Competency is within → Pursue flourishing from this inner competency.

Type 6 – Sixes want loyalty but settle for safety → Loyalty is within. → Pursue flourishing from this inner loyalty.

Type 7 – Sevens want contentment but settle for excitement. → Contentment is within. → Pursue flourishing from this inner contentment.

Type 8 – Eights want protection but settle for control. → Protection is within. → Pursue flourishing from this inner protection.

Type 9 – Nines want peace but settle for calm. → Peace is within. → Pursue flourishing from this inner peace.

There's much more to say about willingness of purpose for each type. Part II of the book will explore this more deeply. For all types, a helpful starting place for flourishing relationships is approaching others with the following mantra: *The image of God in me sees the image of God in you.* By stating this in our encounters with others (even if internally), we name and acknowledge the identity of others. This is the beginning of the pursuit of flourishing.

The Third Territory: Direction

We've crossed the first two territories of the Vocation Triad, and now we encounter the third: direction. This territory explores the third question of discernment: *Where am I going?* It's a question about the future, an expressed hope to see where things end. We're all prone to look ahead, squinting our eyes to notice what's in the distance.

This third territory is uniquely challenging. We can't fast forward our lives. Our predictions of the future are often incorrect.

The unforeseen nature of life can cause anxiety. We run into all sorts of things for which we did not prepare.

When we align this third question, *Where am I going?* with the questions of identity and purpose, our direction shifts. Rather than anxiously looking ahead, we discern with depth our present trajectory. And here we encounter another ancient concept: the *fathom.*

The term "fathom" originally meant "outstretched arms." Well before sophisticated marine technology, sailors and mariners would use a sounding line to measure the depths of the water beneath their boats. This ancient nautical tool was brilliantly simple: a thick rope with a weight on the one end. A member of the crew would take a length of rope equivalent to their outstretched arms and then drop it into the water.

This was one fathom. Again: two fathoms. Again: three.

Repeat the process until the weight reaches bottom, and you could comprehend the depths of where you are by the number of fathoms.

Fathom by fathom, sailors could measure the depth of where they were. Over time, "fathom" came to mean the way in which we understand a difficult problem or situation. We take the time to penetrate the surface, and, bit-by-bit, come to a place of comprehension.

This is the Divine Call to discern direction. We comprehend where we are going by considering what we can reach with our arms. Then we do it again. And again. In this is a great mercy. If we attempt to comprehend all that awaits us, we'll be overwhelmed. But fathom by fathom, we make our way.

The direction of vocation is one of depth before distance. With arms outstretched, we discern by seeing beneath the surface of where we are and seeing through with wisdom: we notice complexities and intricacies. We take the necessary time to understand this fathom, and then we measure the next.

Then, from an authentic identity as self-in-God, in the pursuit of flourishing, we take the next right step. Then the next.

Each enneagram type is called to fathom in ways that are congruent with our identity and purpose and uncomfortable to our adapted self. We'll consider them in Part II.

Conclusion

In the many thresholds of our lives, God is calling. The Divine rarely (if ever) provides a formula. This is not the realm of 10 year strategic plans. What God gives in this liminal space are deeper truths: identity, purpose, and direction. These territories of vocation transcend all our plans. This is true vocation: an understanding of who you are, why you are here, and where you are going.

- *Who are you?* A beloved self-in-God.
- *Why are you here?* To pursue flourishing; wholeness in your relationships with God, self, others, and creation.
- *Where are you going?* Fathom, by fathom, you will comprehend the depths of your journey.

Our egocentricism blinds us to these truths, relying on our own willfulness to make our way in the world. But freedom from this "false self" loosens the chains of our anger, shame, and fear, and allows us to take a posture of willingness, where we say "Yes!" to God's call.

Notes

[1]https://cac.org/liminal-space-2016-07-07/.

[2]Since vocation's etymological roots are so similar to that of "calling," I use the two terms synonymously. Therefore, I won't use the common phrase, "vocation and calling" because I think it's redundant.

[3]Admittedly, words fail when describing the transcendent. They are limiting the limitless; attempting to define the indescribable. God, the Divine, Ultimate Reality, Essence, the Universe all carry certain meaning and connotation, attempting to grasp at that which is transcendent and universal. For consistency, I'll be using God and the Divine. I approach my experience in this world from a Christian perspective but am hoping to present this material from a more inclusive "faith positive" perspective.

[4]The origin of this quote is unknown and disputed.

[5]Palmer, *Let Your Life Speak*, p. 10.

[6] Albert Haase, *Coming Home to Your True Self: Leaving the Emptiness of False Attractions* (Downers Grove, IL: InterVarsity Press, 2008).

[7]Marilyn Vancil, *Self to Lose, Self to Find: A Biblical Approach to the 9 Enneagram Types* (Enumclaw, WA: Redemption Press, 2016).

[8]David G. Benner, *Soulful Spirituality: Becoming Fully Alive and Deeply Human* (Grand Rapids: Brazos Press, 2011), p. 64.

[9]Follow Seth's brilliant work on Instagram at @intedgratedenneagram.

[10]Benner's *The Gift of Being Yourself* helped me with this language.

[11]Benner, *The Gift of Being Yourself*, p. 47.

[12]Throughout this book, especially in Part II, I call each enneagram type to return to, discover, or reclaim that which it truly "wants." I often use language such as "inherent worth, peace, value, protection," etc. When I do, I'm referring to this *Imago Dei* within us, the Divine imprint which reflects these characteristic of God.

[13]I found this in Chuck DeGroat's fabulous book *Wholeheartedness: Busyness, Exhaustion, and Healing the Divided Self* (Grand Rapids: Eerdmans Publishing, 2016), p 130-131.

[14]Benner, *The Gift of Being Yourself*, p. 17.

[15]Palmer's *Let Your Life Speak* talks similarly about the benefits of "humiliation."

[16]Palmer, *Let Your Life Speak*, p. 69.

[17]Again, I'm channeling Parker Palmer's work here in *Let Your Life Speak*.

[18]The language here is mine, but informed by some underlying motivations work provided by Don Richard Riso and Russ Hudson.

[19]Don Richard Riso and Russ Hudson, *The Wisdom of the Enneagram: The Complete Guide to Psychological and Spiritual Growth for the Nine Personality Types* (New York: Bantam Press, 1999).

[20]This list is from Riso and Hudson's *The Wisdom of the Enneagram*.

[21]This quote is widely attributed to the German mystic Meister Eckhart. Mentz, George, See Meister Eckhart, *The Complete Mystical Works of Meister Eckhart* (New York: Crossroad Publishing, 2009).

[22]Anderson, Lindsay, Cheryl Campbell, Ian Charleson, Dennis Christopher, Ben Cross, Nigel Davenport, Brad Davis, et al. 2011. *Chariots of Fire*: Warner Home Video.

[23]Palmer, *Let Your Life Speak*, p. 4.

[24]In David Benner's *Desiring God's Will: Aligning Our Hearts with the Heart of God* (Downers Grove, IL: InterVarsity Press, 2015), this is a central concept.

CHAPTER THREE

The Wisdom Triad: Doing, Feeling, Thinking

"Blessed are those who find wisdom,
those who gain understanding."
—Proverbs 3:13

"Love is the highest form of intelligence."
—Serge Benhayon[1]

When we consider the many decisions of life, how do we *know* that the decisions we make are the 'right' ones? Questions of identity, purpose, and direction are weighty ones. They often lack the general consensus that accompanies "harder" science such as gravity. I know that if I jump off a cliff I will fall instead of fly. But when it comes to discerning with wisdom, we must honestly confront the question: How do we know what we need to know in order to live a flourishing life?

For philosophers, it's a question of epistemology. For psychologists, it's a question of consciousness. For neuroscientists, it's a question of biology. For sociologists, it's a question of context. For theologians, it's a question of divine inspiration.

To consider how we know what we know can take our thoughts to some strange and confusing places. First, we must consider the process (or pathways) by which we gain insight to take good and healthy steps of progress in our lives. In other words, our experience of knowing matters greatly.

And when it comes to matters of discernment, not all content is created equal. It's tragically ironic in our information-saturated culture; when we can access anything with our smart phones, we are no wiser when it comes to life's most important questions. Information must be perceived, analyzed, filtered, considered, and critiqued. We have more than enough *information* to make decisions. What we often lack is proper understanding, application, and purpose. Consider this:

- Information is purely content
- Knowledge is content understood
- Wisdom is understanding applied for what truly matters

This is what the great twentieth century poet T.S. Eliot was championing in his iconic poem "The Rock":

> *The endless cycle of idea and action,*
> *Endless invention, endless experiment,*
> *Brings knowledge of motion, but not of stillness;*
> *Knowledge of speech, but not of silence;*
> *Knowledge of words, and ignorance of the Word.*
> *All our knowledge brings us nearer to our ignorance,*
> *All our ignorance brings us nearer to death,*
> *But nearness to death no nearer to God.*
> *Where is the Life we have lost in living?*
> *Where is the wisdom we have lost in knowledge?*
> *Where is the knowledge we have lost in information?*[2]

In the Introduction, I argued that INFORMATION < KNOWLEDGE < WISDOM. Eliot's poem corroborates this. To become wise, we must better understand the various ways we can know and better apply them to what truly matters. In this chapter we will explore the ways in which we experience what we know—our perceptions, our analyses, our interpretations, and our responses to the knowledge. As you might guess, the Enneagram of Discernment helps us cultivate wisdom for this journey. We'll first start with an introduction to Divine Love as a way of knowing. Then we'll consider how all humans have three centers of knowing. Then we'll explore how the enneagram helps us make sense of it all.

Love as a Way of Being...and Knowing

At a fundamental level, I think the enneagram can illuminate pathways for us to the God who is Love. And, when we embark on this journey, we experience the most powerful, guiding, and animating force in the universe: Love. Think of Love as a way of knowing that cultivates the wisdom we need to live well.

Contemplative physicist Arthur Zajonc, in an interview with Krista Tippett, argued that "Love allows us gently, respectfully, and intimately to slip in the life of another person . . . In this way, love can become a way of moral knowing that is as reliable as scientific insight."[3] Love fuels our ability to know. This contrasts other understandings of knowing, which seek to rid the process of all emotion to elevate objective reasoning, to let the facts speak for themselves.

Consider the ways in which knowing is portrayed in the Christian Bible. In the New Testament, Jesus of Nazareth, when asked by the religious elite which commandment in the law is greatest, provides a two-part response. First, "Love the Lord your God with all your heart, with all your soul, and with all your mind" (Matt. 22:37, NIV). The original Greek terms used for "heart," "soul," and "mind" are insightful:[4]

- Heart—The Greek word used here is *kardia*. In ancient Greek, the *kardia* is the center of understanding, the fountain and seat of the thoughts, passions, desires, appetites, affections, purposes, and endeavors.
- Soul—The Greek word used here is *psuche*. In ancient Greek, the *psuche* is the vital force which animates the body and shows itself in breathing.

- Mind—The Greek word used here is *dianoia*. The faculty (the ability or power) to understand. This is the center of thinking.

Our minds, our hearts, and our souls are called to love God. In similar fashion, Jesus continues with the second part of his response, "Love your neighbor as yourself" (Matt 22:39). Our minds, our hearts, and our souls are likewise called to love others and ourselves, in the pursuit of flourishing. This *agape* love, or Divine Love, flows from God to creation as a sacrifice, ultimately expressed in Jesus's loving sacrifice on the cross of crucifixion.

Divine Love is pure and sacrificial. Thus, it's not selfish or self-serving. It's self-giving. It's a perfect love in that it is complete. Consider the times in your life where you felt particularly vulnerable, where your wounds or faults were laid bare. The most powerful love from others is when they truly *know* you, warts and all, and yet truly *love* you anyway.

This love is the very essence of God. Read the book of I John in the New Testament, and it's unmistakable. "God is love" (I John 4). Divine Love is who God is. Dr. David Benner wrote, in my opinion, one of the greatest treatises on Divine Love in print. In *Surrender to Love*, he reminds us that "the love of God is the most basic ingredient in the cosmos."[5] And, because God is love, and we are made in God's image, love is more than just a feeling or even an action. In the Vocation Triad (Chapter Two), we explored how love is core to who we are. In the Wisdom Triad, we now consider how love is core to how we know.

Thus, the "point of being human is to learn love."[6] It's to learn to be ourselves in the ways in which God intended. This doesn't solve the mysteries and complexities of calling, but it does give us a deep and rich place to start. We are knowers because we are lovers.

Divine Love that cultivates wisdom saturates the next three questions in the Way of Discernment:

- What am I doing?
- What am I feeling?
- What am I thinking?

Beneath these three "simple" questions are the riches of wisdom, a holistic intelligence that transcends intellect. Jesus's words convey this truth. The philosopher James K.A. Smith puts it this way: "Jesus is a teacher who doesn't just inform our intellect but forms our very loves. He isn't content to simply deposit new ideas into your mind; he is after nothing less than your wants, your loves, your longings."[7] Such "loves" are formed in our whole selves: gut, heart, and head. Divine Love is a *wise* love—one that forms and transforms us.

Thus, our loves and our intelligence are more intertwined than we're often willing to admit. Love and knowledge are in a close relationship in our very being, and they can either work to keep us trapped in our old habits and patterns, or they can cultivate wisdom to discern our path faithfully.

The Three Centers of Knowing

Jesus's call to love God and others employs a three-part framework (heart, soul, mind). Similarly, the enneagram teaches a triad of knowing, commonly referred to as the centers of intelligence: the head, the heart, and the gut (or body).

Most enneagram teachers who work with the centers of intelligence draw from the work of Scottish psychiatrist Dr. Maurice Nicoll who wrote at length on the importance of the three intelligence centers: the head, the heart, and the gut (or, the body).[8] Think of each as a hub of knowing, meaning-making and intelligence. We find explorations of these three centers in many streams of psychology, many ancient spiritual traditions, and more recently, in neuroscience.

We all have a head, a heart, and a gut, but we tend not to use all three as we should. As we discovered in Chapter One, each center suffers a dominant emotion (anger, shame, or fear) that impedes discernment. But it doesn't have to be this way. We are smarter than we think we are. We have three centers to perceive, interpret, and analyze our experience. These three centers provide important ways to love God, love ourselves, and love others well. When considered together, many enneagram teachers refer to these three centers as the triadic self. This triadic intelligence is vitally important in our discernment, starting with our ability to experience God.

When we use them well, in an integrated way, we can see and engage the fullness of our present experience. Many enneagram teachers will refer to the three intelligence centers as a three-legged stool.[9] We need all three legs in order to sit. That's a helpful image, but I'd like to propose another. I think of the intelligence centers as three persons in a beautiful, coordinated dance. Flow. Rhythm. Beauty. Together they create something more complete and beautiful than the sum of their individual efforts.

If we consider the three centers of intelligence as the head, the heart, and the gut, then we can begin to see what each center offers us. Enneagram teachers Kathy Hurley and Theodorre Donson have done some of the best work in this area, which has been more recently developed and expanded by Suzanne Stabile. The head center provides us "thinking intelligence," the heart center provides us "feeling intelligence," and the gut center provides us "doing intelligence."[10] When we employ these intelligence centers, we gain wisdom to discern our lives. We think about our experience, we feel our way through our experience, and we act upon our experience. Here's how:

- Thinking intelligence is used for retrieving and organizing information. It also helps us plan and analyze.

- Feeling intelligence is used for observing emotions in ourselves and others, interpersonal community, and relationship.

- Doing intelligence is used for the movement of our bodies and the body's desires for pleasure and achievement.

Without awareness, we spend much of our time in an over-reliance on one center, supported by another, and misusing or neglecting the third. The flow and rhythm of our ability to know becomes arrhythmic, awkward, and out of sync. In the ancient

Christian tradition, there is a Greek term that captures the essence of the Triune God: *perichoresis.* The term communicates a sense of flow and movement that theologians refer to as the "divine dance" of the three persons of the Trinity, saturated with self-giving love. It's a helpful framework in considering our triadic brain. We need all three to dance together to discern life's decisions effectively.

Our Beautifully Complex and Distributed Mind

Before you write off triadic intelligence as some new age garbage, neuroscience is providing some insight into our ability to know. The human brain is wildly complicated, comprising over 100 billion nerve cells making trillions of connections.[11]

William Schafer, a clinical psychologist, writes that "modern neurology would also tell us that the brain is not located solely in the head but is distributed throughout the body."[12] Scientific researchers, who long considered the brain as more of a central intelligence processing system, are increasingly referring to our brain as a Distributed Intelligence Processing System.[13]

According to scientists Soosalu and Oka, new research identifies neural networks not just in our heads, but also in our hearts and guts. And, they function in highly intelligent ways.[14] To give an example, scientists have identified a network of neurons lining our guts as our "second brain."[15] Such research gives us a lot of insight on what we typically refer to as butterflies in our stomach. According to an article in *Scientific American*:

> Technically known as the enteric nervous system, the second brain consists of sheaths of neurons embedded in the walls of the long tube of our gut, or alimentary canal, which measures about nine meters end to end from the esophagus to the anus. The second brain contains some 100 million neurons . . . [16]

Studies also indicate that our emotions are probably influenced by gut nerves. There's also some intriguing neuroscience work on the heart-brain connection. Neuroscientist Richard Davidson argues that "social and emotional learning can change brain function and actually brain structure and can produce adaptive emotional and cognitive functioning as a consequence."[17]

To be clear, there is much to learn and know about how our cognitive, emotional, and physical systems work together. In the meantime, a basic acknowledgement that our heads, our hearts, and our guts are critical ways of knowing is sufficient to develop a fuller sense of intelligence. Thinking, feeling and doing. Head, heart, and gut. When we learn to trust all three centers of intelligence, we cultivate wisdom.

What does all this have to do with the enneagram? As mentioned earlier a key feature of the enneagram is its perpetual triadic nature. As we consider how our dominant enneagram type impacts our employment of the three centers of intelligence, two specific triadic groupings are helpful: triads and stances. Triads are enneagram types that share a common dominant center of intelligence. Stances are enneagram types that share a common repressed center of intelligence.

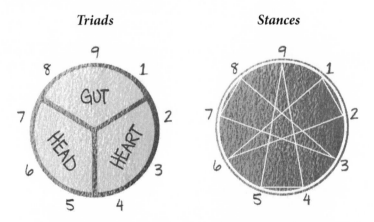

Let's start with the triads. I'll briefly introduce them, and then we'll explore each type in deeper ways in Part II of the book.

Enneagram Triads: Gut, Heart, and Head

Cognitive Behavioral Therapy is a prominent stream of counseling psychology. It is a psychotherapeutic tool that helps patients better understand the connectedness of thoughts, feelings, and actions. It's informally known as "talk therapy," where a counselor helps a client verbally process through negative, harmful, or disordered thoughts, feelings, and actions.

Thoughts. Feelings. Actions.

Thinking. Feeling. Doing.

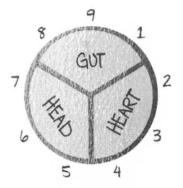

This triangle forms a basis of how we live in our world. Together they comprise the building blocks that help (or hinder) our ability to make wise decisions and achieve the results we want in life.

The enneagram similarly provides insight on our thinking, feeling, and doing. Many enneagram teachers begin workshops or trainings by teaching through the "triads," which group enneagram types by their common dominant center of intelligence. Every human being has access to all three centers. However, each enneagram type tends to prefer a center, support it with another center, and neglect or misuse a third center.

As we learned in Chapter One, types Eight, Nine, and One form the Gut Triad and lead with "doing" intelligence. Types Two, Three, and Four form the Heart Triad and lead with "feeling" intelligence.[18] Types Five, Six, and Seven form the Head Triad and lead with "thinking" intelligence. Each type resides in its preferred or leading center of intelligence, and has to more intentionally consider how it uses the other two.

By understanding a dominant personality type's triad and dominant center of intelligence, one gains significant insight into how one perceives their world. When we become more aware of our preferred ways of knowing, we can be more mindful of accessing all three centers more wisely. Neuroscience is now providing evidence of this through the phenomenon of neuroplasticity, the ability to change our brain. My friend Dr. Jerome Lubbe is a functional neurologist and has developed what he calls "The Brain-Based Enneagram." He writes: "Through neuroplasticity...you can reshape and remake how your brain not only functions, but how it continues to develop in the future."[19]

Another helpful way to consider the three centers is the Head Brain, the Heart Brain, and the Gut Brain.[20] To better understand, let's take a closer look at each center.

The Gut Center [Doing]

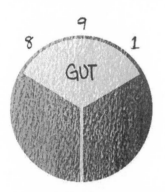

Types Eight, Nine, and One form the Gut Triad. These types tend to be more doing oriented, and let their gut lead in decision-making. Gut Types have loads of intuition and instinctual knowledge. They tend to be more aware of what's going on in their bodies physically, and they sometimes know before they *know*. We all have experiences where we knew something to be true before we had the facts and necessary information before us. As Schafer explains, "When you know something in the body, it seems beyond all doubt."[21] This type of experience is more common among the Gut Types, and is referred to by some as "GQ" or "gut intelligence."[22]

To a certain degree, we all learn by doing. Activity creates momentum. By engaging our bodies in activity, we open up our intelligence viscerally, utilizing sensations and instincts. Of the three centers of intelligence, the Gut Center is the one what helps us be present to what matters. Our minds and hearts can wander, but our bodies are where they are. When we say we can't be in two places at once, it's physically true. When it comes to decision-making, one of the most important strategies is to be present and focused on what matters most. The Gut Center helps us do this.

While the Gut Center helps us be present, this also comes with some challenges. Instinct and intuition can be powerful, but it's not foolproof. Gut Types can be prone to an overreliance on their instincts, forsaking thinking and feeling. They can also mistake gut-level intuition with feeling intelligence. This can truncate the emotional center to mere anger or frustration. In fact, many enneagram teachers attach a common response to anxiety (our common experience of stress) for each triad. For the Gut Triad, anger is that emotion. Each type experiences and responds to anger differently, but Eights, Nines, and Ones all are prone to anger when things go awry.

Gut Types, when not using their thinking and feeling intelligences effectively, can also fall into cycles of over-activity, reactivity, or over-planning. When this occurs, Gut Types often have high demands for themselves and others, and can become more hostile. Type Eights tend to excessively act at the expense of themselves and others. Type Nines tend to forget themselves and retreat to their inner landscape to plan and muse. Type Ones tend to be more reactive, often with a critical bent. Gut Types can be fixated on power and influence, and lose sight of their ability to rest in who they are.

However, when healthy, The Gut Center types are beautiful examples of how to be present, how to trust their own intuition, and how to take the next right step even if they don't have all the information others feel is necessary. This "Gut Brain" is where we find courage to move and act.

The Heart Center [Feeling]

Types Two, Three, and Four form the Heart Triad. These types tend to be more feeling oriented, and are more connected to the emotional world. This allows Twos, Threes, and Fours to access empathy and compassion more easily than other types. The Heart

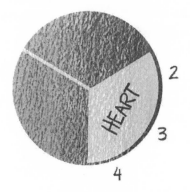

Types are highly relational and care deeply about connectedness. According to Hurley and Donson, for Heart Types, "the most important goal in life is understanding other people."[23] This ability to read people and connect with them conveys an emotional awareness or "EQ," and is described by Calhoun, et al. as "energized by the outer world of relationships."[24]

We can all let our feelings lead the way. Connecting with others in meaningful ways provides an important check to our instinctive reactivity. Instincts are powerful forces, and can sometimes lead to unintended harm to others. Such EQ also helps us more effectively apply our rational/objective thought by considering relational dynamics. We've all crafted ideas that seemed brilliant in our heads, only to fall flat when shared with others. By engaging our heart through listening to and exploring our emotional landscape, we rightly consider the impact we have on others, and the impact others have on us.

While the Heart Center helps us experience emotion, this also comes with some challenges. Feelings are not always the best barometer. Feelings can betray what is truly going on, and when the heart center feels threatened, shame can emerge. Shame is the common response to anxiety for the Heart Triad. Each type experiences and responds to shame differently, but Twos, Threes, and Fours are all prone to it. Type Twos tend to fixate on others' needs and how they can meet them. Type Threes tend to worry about others' perceptions of them as successful or attractive. Type Fours tend to be concerned about their distinctiveness or uniqueness.

Heart Types, when not integrating their doing and thinking intelligences effectively, can also image-craft, manipulate, or become overly sensitive. In a tragic irony, Heart Types can struggle with something they value deeply: authenticity. When their emotional world feels threatened, and shame creeps in, these types will focus too heavily on how others perceive them.

However, when healthy, The Heart Center types are lovely examples of how to connect with others, display empathy, and consider others in important decisions. This "Heart Brain" is where we relate to others and cultivate values to guide our decisions.

The Head Center [Thinking]

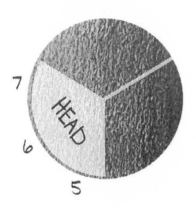

Types Five, Six, and Seven form the Head Triad. These types tend to be more thinking oriented, and tend to let their thoughts dominate decision-making. They are great at harnessing mental faculties to analyze and perceive information. Content is king for Head Types, and generally they don't let emotions or instincts get in the way of their objectivity. If Gut Types major in "GQ" and Heart Types in "EQ," Head Types major in "IQ." According to Calhoun, et al., "The safety and security of our world often ride on the shoulders of head people who know how to gather, analyze, and compute information into plans, strategies, and action."[25] In other words, when there's an important decision to make, Head Types can think their way through it.

The ability to think our way through problems is a critical skill for us all. By engaging our cognitive abilities, we test our feelings against reality. We also slow down our instinctual responses to consider our impulses and evaluate our activity. By employing our head, we learn, critique, consider, and develop important strategies.

Head Types must be careful not to solely rely on their IQ to make their way in the world. While we can think our way through much, we don't always have sufficient information for every situation. Demoting emotions can cause pain and frustration and neglect the wisdom of others. Overanalyzing instincts can delay important action. Head Types can then become anxious about their inability to think their way through. When this occurs, anxiety creeps in and Head Types become prone to fear. Fear takes on different forms for each Head Type. Type Fives tend to retreat and withdraw from others. Type Sixes tend to operate based on worst-case scenarios. Type Sevens tend to flee when things become boring or difficult.

Such fear-based reactions can cause Head Types to double-down on their thinking. Such overthinking is often poor thinking. According to Hurley and Donson, a persistent aspect of Head Types is "their deep-seated unwillingness to accept information from the other two centers."[26] Head Types must be careful to not feel superior to others who lead with GQ or EQ.

However, when healthy, The Head Center types are brilliant examples of how to employ our cognitive abilities to gather information and use it to make wise decisions. This "Head Brain" provides cognition, meaning, and creativity to aid discernment.

Our thoughts, feelings, and actions are powerful tools of discernment. When we lack self-awareness, we rely too heavily upon our dominant center of intelligence and tend to distort or misuse the other two centers. Without some serious work, we simply operate on a mechanical level. In other words, our intelligence is functional and not formational. When we consider vocation, our overuse and underuse of our three centers "distorts our ability to perceive or understand ourselves, others, and life in general."[27]

Our lives are too important to live on autopilot. The goal is to faithfully employ our thinking, doing, and feeling to cultivate wisdom in life. To depend too heavily on your preferred center of intelligence will distort our discernment. To underuse your full range of intelligence will also distort our discernment. This is where a different grouping of enneagram types can be helpful: the Stances.

Enneagram Stances: Aggressive, Dependent, Withdrawn

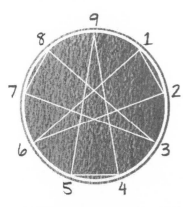

The Stances of the enneagram, sometimes referred to as "social styles" or "Hornevian groups" (a credit to psychologist Karen Horney),[28] provide further insight into how each enneagram type uses the three centers of intelligence. Remember, The Triads help us understand what center each type leads with: Doing Intelligence for Gut Types (Eight, Nine, One), Feeling Intelligence for Heart Types (Two, Three, Four), and Thinking Intelligence for Head Types (Five, Six, Seven).

The Stances of the enneagram are grouped by the center of intelligence that is misused or distorted. Some teachers refer to this as the repressed center of intelligence. I find it helpful to consider the three centers of intelligence playing a game of keep away, with two centers leaving out the third, who rarely gets the ball.

Consistent with the inherent logic of the enneagram's design, the three Stances form identical isosceles triangles, grouping two neighbor types with a third across the circle. Think of it as one edge of an intelligence center pairing with another edge to shoot across the frame to form the triangle.

The three Stances of the enneagram are the Aggressive Stance (types Three, Seven, Eight), the Dependent Stance

(types One, Two, Six), and the Withdrawn Stance (types Four, Five, Nine). Each Stance draws from two Centers of Intelligence to form a particular way of engaging their world, while neglecting or distorting a third center.

The Stances help us better understand how each type engages its world and tries to solve problems. By identifying each stance's distorted center of intelligence, we can notice the blind spots that inhibit our ability to make wise decisions.

The Aggressive Stance (Types Three, Seven, Eight)

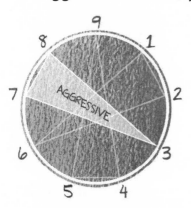

Those who lead from the Aggressive Stance, as the name implies, are more assertive toward others. They tend to "move against" others to get what they want (even if it's not apparent externally, it's often an internal move). Types Three, Seven, and Eight have abundant energy to gain what they desire. They are less affected by the attacks of inner critics, and portray a more defined sense of who they are in the world.

Aggressive Stance types *think* and *do* their way through life, and often neglect or misuse *feeling*. Types Three, Seven, and Eight are strategic, get-things-done people. They tend to look ahead (more on this in Chapter Three) and focus on what's next. This foresight and planning can be very helpful when discerning a path. They can make progress, forge ahead, and build momentum. But often looking ahead can come at the expense of our EQ (emotional intelligence).

When we quiet down our frenetic activity and let our hearts catch up to our bodies we can more fully assess the present. We can also better reflect upon the past. This raises up our EQ in ways that help us better read people and ourselves. When we do, we develop compassion and empathy to use the full range of our intelligence.

But this requires intentional work. Without such work, each type in the Aggressive stance represses or misuses feelings in unique ways. NOTE: This doesn't mean that Threes, Sevens, and Eights don't have feelings. Of course they have feelings. But these Aggressive types have tendencies to neglect or misuse them.

Type Three: Feeling Distorted

Type Threes are great at getting things done and looking good doing it. But Threes struggle to slow down the activity enough to truly engage their own feelings and the feelings of others. This can lead Threes to use people to achieve their goals. It can also prevent them from learning from past mistakes or failures. Such a dismissal of one's own feelings and the feelings of others can lead to a frenetic cycle of seeking value and worth from others rather than authentic connection. Type Threes can overvalue their own accomplishments as a means to compensate for under-valuing healthy relationships. In summary, the value and worth that Threes seek can be found within oneself and within vibrant relationships with others.

Type Seven: Feeling Distorted

Type Sevens thrive at moving from activity to activity. They tend to devote much of their thinking to planning what's next to keep up the adventure or intrigue. This is why Sevens are always up for just about anything. Such activity seems wonderfully (or terrifyingly) spontaneous to non Sevens. In reality, Sevens are quick thinkers and planners. To them, such a move to what's next isn't nearly as spontaneous.

Like Threes, Sevens often move about in the world too fast for their heart to catch up. They can jump quickly to the next thing, especially when the present environment feels boring, painful, sad, or awkward. With one eye perpetually on what's next, they tend to overlook their own feelings and others'. The satisfaction they seek in their activity is fleeting, which causes them to plan for the next, over and over again. If Sevens stick around long enough to acknowledge and engage their feelings and the feelings of others, they'll eventually realize that growth and contentment come from working through pain, not running from it.

Type Eight: Feeling Distorted

Type Eights often seem the most aggressive of the three Aggressive Types. Type Eights can be intensely focused on the task ahead and can bulldoze their way through it. When unchecked, others can feel hurt and discarded in the process. Unhealthy Eights may not care that others get hurt. Many Eights care, but simply don't notice.

This hard-charging nature of Eights tend to pursue activity at the expense of feelings. When feelings do occur in Eights, they can be dark or vengeful, which fuels their ability to operate in terms of conquest. Such a conquering posture maintains a false sense of protection and control. When Eights slow down enough to let their hearts catch up to their heads and bodies, they realize that projecting strength and control doesn't truly protect or control what matters most. By listening to the wisdom of their hearts and the feelings of others, Eights relinquish unnecessary control and feel more protected where they are.

Riso and Hudson tell us that Aggressive types must open their hearts.[29] Aggressive types fall victim to the myth that feelings aren't helpful in discerning the most important questions. They seem wasteful, unproductive, and inefficient. In reality, healthy engagement of our hearts draw us into deeper parts of ourselves, and nudge us toward others in community. When faced with life's most important questions, authentic emotional connections with ourselves and others are essential.

Discernment: What am I feeling?

For those who lead from the Aggressive Stance, restless hearts must become authentic places of emotion and connection. In a word, they must *OPEN* their hearts with vulnerability. Types Three, Seven, and Eight can intentionally form **Wise Hearts** to discern well. This requires intentional work exploring their emotional world, honoring it as a teacher (not just a drag).

The Dependent Stance (Types One, Two, Six)

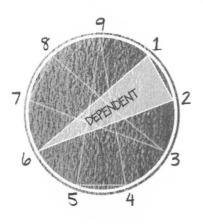

Those who lead from the Dependent Stance, are other-focused. They tend to "move toward" or come alongside others for affection, approval, or belonging. In this way, their sense of self is more flexible, looking to others for definition. These types are compliant to their inner critics, which tends to leave them conflicted internally. Types One, Two, and Six form this stance, and tend to be more dutiful in their engagement with others.

Dependent Stance types *do* and *feel* their way through life, and often neglect or misuse *thinking*. Types One, Two, and Six are often dependent upon others to get things done. They tend to look at what's right in front of them (more on this in Chapter Three) and focus on the here and now. This often thwarts productive foresight and planning that is essential when discerning a path. They can suffer from the tyranny of the urgent and often neglect their own IQ (thinking intelligence).

When we take a deep breath and assess what we truly want and need, we can more fully plan for the future. This accesses our IQ in ways that help us better plan and prepare. When we do, we develop a calm confidence and healthy ambition by using the full range of our intelligence.

Like most (if not all) worthwhile things, this takes work. Without some honest work, Dependent Types can neglect or misuse their thinking intelligence in some unique ways. NOTE: This doesn't mean that Ones, Twos, and Sixes are less intelligent than the other numbers. Rather, they have pronounced tendencies to misuse the IQ they possess. Here's how.

Type One: Thinking Distorted

Type Ones are in the continuous quality improvement business. They perpetually scan for ways to make things better. They are partial to practical ideas and solutions that just seem to make sense. They feel deeply about how to improve something, and set about the task of doing it. This can lead to a busyness that thwarts open-minded inquiry and self-care.

Ones tend to improve what's around them as a way to cope with their own feelings of deficiency. Thus, their thinking is often dominated by their own inner critic. By quieting the mind to think more productively and authentically, Ones can see that the goodness they care so much about is within.

Type Two: Thinking Distorted

If Ones tend to improve, Type Twos move toward others to help. They instinctively feel when someone has need, and set about helping. Riso and Hudson describe Twos as those who "do their feelings."[30] Those who lead with Type Two act almost instinctively upon their feelings, often without much thinking.

When Twos take the time to pause and think about what they feel before they act, they provide a clearer boundary between feeling and doing. Such thinking also helps Twos evaluate where and when to help others. When they do, they can more clearly experience love for who they are, not what they do. They can then employ their helping skills with wisdom.

Type Six: Thinking Distorted

Type Sixes are prone to move toward others to feel secure. This leads Sixes to depend on others for guidance and support. When the present environment feels at all threatening, Sixes are prone to focus on mitigating the threat. This "batten down the hatches" mentality prepares for scenarios that often are unlikely, and uses energy better served for more hopeful planning.

To get out of feeling insecure, doing-things-to-feel-more-secure cycle, Sixes must learn to trust their own thinking and intuition. They must decrease their tendency to think through threat-forecasting and instead trust themselves to be free to plan, dream, and strategize about good things.

Again, those who lead with One, Two, or Six are not dumb; not in the least. However, they tend to limit their thinking in ways that curb their ability to discern well. By opening their minds, Dependent Types find agency to lift their gaze out of the present deficiencies, needs, or insecurities to consider life with more vantage.

Discernment: What am I thinking?

Those who lead from the Dependent Stance must find ways to focus their racing minds into poised, salient thinking. In word, they must *TRUST* their heads. Types One, Two, and Six can cultivate **Wise Heads** to think creatively and strategically about important decisions. Deepen thinking beyond the tyranny of the urgent to discern what is truly needed.

The Withdrawn Stance (Types Four, Five, Nine)

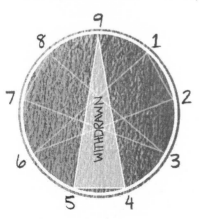

We all can point to times when we needed others to help us find our way. The important people in our lives inspire us to move and act. The Withdrawn Stance types are more distant from others, and often, distant from their authentic selves. They tend to move away from others, valuing privacy, space, and independence. This wariness can often be sold as solitude, but it's important to know that withdrawing is not the same as solitude. Karen Horney puts it this way: "They (withdrawn types) draw around themselves a kind of magic circle which no one may penetrate."[31] Their sense of self become defined by the barrier more than what it protects. A tendency to isolate can further thwart discernment and estrange those who lead with Four, Five, or Nine from others. Withdrawing on its own is a reactive act, and wisdom is rarely present in reactivity. Solitude has aspects of withdrawal, but is proactive. Wisdom is often cultivated in intention.

If the Aggressive Stance moves in the world with a ready, fire, aim approach to life, the Withdrawing Stance can operate from a ready, aim. . . approach. Sometimes in life, we simply have to discern as we go, something challenging for Withdrawn Types. These types often think and feel their way through life, at the expense of right action. This doesn't mean that they do nothing (although sometimes this is the case). Often, Withdrawn Types do everything BUT the very thing they should do. These types tend to long for what was and what could be, often at the expense of what is (Again, more on this in Chapter Three). They are astute in their reflection and their vision, but struggle to get started on the path. They often feel they need to work through their inner world before they can act. Here's how:

Type Four: Doing Distorted

Those who lead with Type Four have close and ready access to the full range of emotion. When confronted with seemingly overwhelming emotion, they tend to withdraw to think about their feelings, and avoid doing.[32] This thinking often leads to what is missing, or incomplete. These thinking-fueled emotions can bait the Type Four into traps of inferiority or superiority. With all this going on, it can be really challenging for those who lead with Type Four to move to action.

However, this ability to think and feel with such depth and richness provides the Type Four with deep wells of empathy, aesthetic sensibilities, and meaning. When they employ these gifts to what's right in front of them, present to what matters most, the spell breaks and they can fully engage the present moment with wisdom.

Type Five: Doing Distorted

Type Five is the most "heady" in the Withdrawn Stance. When Type Four engages in thinking-fueled emotion, Type Five employs emotion-fueled thinking.[33] Those who lead with Type Five are often described as always "in their heads." Their need for competency will compel them to retreat to a place where their minds can work, and they often won't emerge until they feel competent enough for what's next.

This causes those who lead with Type Five to struggle to initiate; there's always more to know first. It's important for the Type Five to embrace the learning and competency that comes from doing. Experience is a powerful teacher, often more so than study. Wisdom comes from being embodied and grounded in our worlds, rather than escaping from it to the palace of our minds.

Type Nine: Doing Distorted

Those who lead with Type Nine want peace, and they are so committed to it they will withdraw from disruption to maintain it. The Type Nine has an uncanny ability to be physically present in a room, but internally withdrawn to another place. Such a reaction isn't authentic peace. Rather, it's a version of calm that gets us through the momentary conflict.

For those who lead with Type Nine, this extends to even withdrawing from the possibility of disruption or conflict. Which, understandably, keeps a Type Nine right where they are: stuck at the starting line of the race they should be running. This doesn't mean Nines are sedentary. Often they are incredibly busy doing things that aren't all that important, but help them avoid the disruptive activity that awaits them. There's a deeper, lasting peace that is forged in the fire of well engaged conflict. By engaging in right doing, Nines can find it.

The Withdrawn Types are highly skilled at moving away from others and thus, not acting on what matters most. Sometimes the withdrawal is physical. Those who lead with Type Four, Five, or Nine can disappear from a party or meeting like a ghost. Sometimes the withdrawal is internal, physically going through the motions. By engaging the body in doing what needs to be done, Fours, Fives, and Nines access an active wisdom that helps them make sense of their thoughts and emotions.

Discernment: What am I doing?

Those who lead from the Withdrawn Stance must find ways to align their heads and their hearts in their bodies. In a word, they must *EMBODY* their environments. Types Four, Five, and Nine can cultivate **Wise Bodies** to listen to their instincts and act when necessary.

A Quick Aside: The Anchor Points

You may notice that my description of the Triads (types that share the same dominant intelligence) and Stances (types that share the same distorted intelligence) has some seeming contradictions. For those who lead with Types Three, Six, and Nine, the Triads and Stances tell us that these types lead with the very intelligence they distort. How can this be?

Some teachers refer to this triangle of types as the Anchor Points of the Enneagram. Each of these types is in the middle of its Triad. Type Three is in the middle of the Heart Triad, Type Six is in the middle of the Head Triad, and Type Nine is the middle of the Gut Triad. And yet, each distorts that same intelligence. There are a few theories as to why this is. Rather than taking the time needed to explore them all, consider how each distorts its own dominant intelligence:[34]

- *Type Three leads with* feeling, *but quickly converts it to intel to impress, achieve, and succeed (reading a room to determine who is most important or influential, rather than developing empathy).*

- *Type Six leads with* thinking *but quickly converts it to threat-forecasting, worst-case scenarios, and plans to secure (making safety plans rather than trusting their intuition that everything will be okay).*

- *Type Nine leads with* doing *but quickly converts it to doing all sorts of things but that which needs to be done (cleaning the bathroom instead of finishing that report for work, for example).*[35]

In other words, each of these types leads with a form of intelligence, but reject its appropriate use. In tragic irony, Threes become even more detached from their hearts, Sixes become even more detached from their minds, and Nines become even more detached from their bodies. The result is something they all share in common: a sort of conformist-people-pleasing to what each type feels is safest: to be impressive for Threes, to be safe for Sixes, and to be calm for Nines. For those who lead with these types, wise use of the very intelligences they distort is challenging, but essential work.

Conclusion:

The Wisdom Triad spans the full range of intelligence available to each of us:

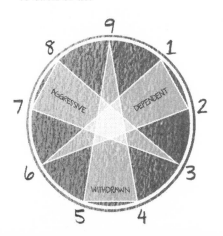

- What am I doing?
- What am I feeling?
- What am I thinking?

Discernment demands this full range: thinking, feeling, and doing. The good news is that we are smarter than we think we are. With intention and work we can employ our bodies, our hearts, and our minds to decisions big and small. The enneagram helps us see the ways in which our personality limits our ability to cultivate wisdom and apply it.

Riso and Hudson teach us that each center provides qualities of our essential and authentic nature that personality is simply trying to imitate.[36] For the Aggressive Stance, those who lead with Three, Seven, or Eight must find ways to open their restless hearts toward authenticity to develop *Wise Hearts*. For the Dependent Stance, those who lead with One, Two, or Six must find ways to trust their racing minds to develop *Wise Heads*. For the Withdrawn Stance, those who lead with Four, Five, or Nine must embody their world to develop *Wise Bodies*.

Many enneagram teachers who work with the intelligence centers talk about the need for balance. I find this problematic as it can create an unhealthy expectation to use all three centers all the time, full throttle. A healthier, more realistic approach to align the intelligence centers is to develop healthy rhythms of doing, feeling, and thinking. In this triadic dance, rhythmic alignment of all three centers cultivates the wisdom to discern.

Exercises:

Your Triadic Brain

- For three days in a row, track ways in which each intelligence center helps you know. Write down what you notice.
    - Day 1—What is my "Head Brain" telling me about my day?

    - Day 2—What is my "Heart Brain" telling me about my day?

○ Day 3—What is my "Gut Brain" telling me about my day?

- For day four, try to notice when your triadic brain is working together. For example, an upset stomach connected to anxious thoughts about an upcoming meeting at work. What do you notice?

Aggressive Stance (Threes, Sevens, Eights):

- An important word for those who lead from the Aggressive Stance is OPEN, specifically calling for an opening of the heart. Spend time throughout a day (or even better, a week), considering your feelings that emerge during your daily activities. Sit with those feelings for a bit (longer than you usually do). Find someone close to you (close friend, spouse, family member) and practice opening your heart by sharing what you notice.
- **Wise Hearts**—Find a few people you trust who aren't in the Aggressive Stance. Ask them the following questions: *How do your feelings help you make wise decisions?* Write down what you learn and try it.

Dependent Stance (Ones, Twos, Sixes)

- An important word for those who lead from the Dependent Stance is TRUST, specifically calling for a trust in sound thinking. Interrogate your inner critic (or, perhaps, committee). Ask questions, such as, is this critic trustworthy? If I don't trust in this inner voice, what would be more trustworthy? Also, consider your trust level of those around you compared to the level of trust you place in yourself. Are you giving yourself enough credit? Are you giving others enough credit?

- **Wise Minds**—Consider recent events in which you fully showed up and everything turned out okay. Consider recent events in which you didn't need others to be ok, finish the job, or find security. What can you learn from this?

Withdrawn Stance (Fours, Fives, Nines)

- An important word for those who lead from the Withdrawn Stance is EMBODY, specifically calling for full presence and participation in their world. Consider ways (even simple ones) in which you can use your body in a given situation. Before retreating from something difficult, painful, or awful, take stock of what your body is telling you before you get into a head and heart space.
- **Wise Bodies**—What physical activity can you engage (exercise, breathing, stretching, power poses) in that would help you develop a Wise Body?

Notes

[1]Serge Benhayon, *An Open Letter to Humanity: A Treatise on Energetic Truth* (Goonellabah, New South Wales, Australia: UniMed Publishing, 2013), p. 287.

[2]T.S. Eliot, *The Rock* (Boston: Harcourt Brace and Company, 1934), p. 7.

[3]Arthur Zajonc, interviewed by Krista Tippett in March 12, 2015, *On Being with Krista Tippett*. https://onbeing.org/programs/arthur-zajonc-michael-mccullough-mind-and-morality-a-dialogue/.

[4]Greek language help here from the NET Bible https://netbible.org.

[5]David Benner, *Surrender to Love: Discovering the Heart of Christian Spirituality* (Downers Grove: InterVarsity Press, 2015), p. 92.

[6]Benner, *Surrender to Love*, p. 93.

[7]James K.A. Smith, *You are What You Love: The Spiritual Power of Habit* (Grand Rapids: Brazos Press, 2016).

[8]Kathy Hurley and Theodorre Donson, *Discover Your Soul Potential: Using the Enneagram to Awaken Spiritual Vitality* (Lakewood, CO: WindWalker Press, 2012), p. 15.

[9]Suzanne Stabile introduced me to this concept in one of her workshops, for which I'm eternally grateful. I've heard other enneagram teachers use it since.

[10]Hurley and Donson, *Discover your Soul Potential*, p. 20.

[11]Kyra Ward, "Neuroscience the Enneagram Part 1: The Link Between Neuroscience and Coaching" (June 21, 2019), https://www.integrative9.com/.

[12]William M. Schafer, *Roaming Free Inside the Cage: A Daoist Approach to the Enneagram* (Bloomington: iUniverse, 2010), p. 6.

[13]For an example of a study of the brain as a Distributed Intelligent Processing System, check out https://www.ncbi.nlm.nih.gov/pmc/articles/PMC3057967/.

[14]G. Soosalu and M. Oka, (2012), "Neuroscience and the Three Brains of Leadership," http://www.mbraining.com/mbit-and-leadership).

[15]https://www.scientificamerican.com/article/gut-second-brain/.

[16]Ibid.

[17]https://www.edutopia.org/video/heart-brain-connection-neuroscience-social-emotional-and-academic-learning.

[18]By "feeling intelligence," I don't mean to include all feelings we experience. For example, the feeling of being cold, or constipated, is not directly tied to emotions. I consider feeling intelligence similarly to emotional intelligence. Feeling intelligence is used more broadly among enneagram teachers, so I use the term to maintain integrity within enneagram teaching.

[19]Jermoe Lubbe, *Whole-Identity: A Brain Baised Enneagram Model for (W)holistic Human Thriving* (Atlanta: Thrive Neuro Theology, 2019), p. 4.

[20]Anna-Rosa Le Roux, "Neuroscience and the Enneagram Part 3: Neuroscientific Evidence for the Enneagram Three Centers of Intelligence," July 25, 2019, https://www.integrative9.com/.

[21]William M. Schafer, *Roaming Free Inside the Cage: A Daoist Approach to the Enneagram*, p. 8.

[22]Adele & Doug Calhoun, Clare and Scott Lougrige, *Spiritual Rhythms of the Enneagram: A Handbook for Harmony and Transformation* (Downer's Grove: IVP, 2019), p. 18.

[23]Kathleen V. Hurley & Theodorre E. Dobson, *What's My Type?: Use the Enneagram System of Nine Personality Types to Discover Your Best Self* (San Francisco: Harper SanFrancisco, 1991), p. 73.

[24]Calhoun, Calhoun, Loughrige, & Loughrige, *Spiritual Rhythms of the Enneagram: A Handbook for Harmony and Transformation*, p. 74.

[25]Ibid, p. 130.

[26]Hurley & Dobson, p. 75.

[27]Ibid, p. 71.

[28]The Enneagram Stances or social styles are sometimes called Hornevian Groups because they derive from the work of psychologist Karen Horney, who theorized that children cultivated three distinct coping strategies: expansive, submission/self-effacement, resignation/detachment. Based off of her work, Enneagram teachers employed and mod-

ified Horney's typology to further understand how enneagram types engage others (aggressive, dependent, and withdrawn).

[29]Riso and Hudson, *Understanding the Enneagram: the Practical Guide to Personality Types Revised Edition* (New York: Houghton Mifflin, 2000), p. 277.

[30]Ibid, p. 258.

[31]Karen Horney, *Our Inner Conflicts: A Constructive Theory of Neurosis* (New York: W. W. Norton, 1945), p. 75.

[32]Risso and Hudson, in *Understanding the Enneagram*, have some really helpful content about the interplay of thinking and feeling in Type Four.

[33]Again, Riso and Hudson, *Understanding the Enneagram*.

[34]Thanks to the teachings of Suzanne Stabile and the written works of Kathy Hurley and Theodorre Donson for helping make sense of this. Note: Theodorre Donson has written under the surname "Dobson" and "Donson."

[35]Suzanne Stabile often uses similar language about the Type Nine throughout her writings and teachings.

[36]Riso and Hudson, *Understanding the Enneagram*, p. 250.

CHAPTER 4

The Practice Triad: Past, Present, Future

"All we have to decide is what to do with the time that is given us."
—J.R.R. Tolkien, *The Fellowship of the Ring*

It seems to hit me about once a month. Despite my best efforts to manage my calendar and leave some breathing room to avoid turning into some soulless worker-robot, I'll have a day where my schedule is packed from the beginning of the workday till the end. Inevitably, my first appointment of the day will run ten minutes late, forcing me to play a cruel and sadistic game of catch-up every hour on the hour. I enter each room breathless and apologetic, and end the day in a daze of frustration. The commute home causes me to wish "if only I had more time."

Western approaches to time reside in a place of scarcity. We're always running out of time. And yet, time is elastic: the days feel full but the years, in retrospect, are short. We often feel that we have too much to do in any given day, but we look back over the course of a year and wonder, "Where did all the time go?"

We live in a cultural moment in the West in which we have an abundance of technology to help us be more efficient and productive. Productivity seminars, techniques, apps, and the like all contribute to what Melissa Gregg referred to as "The Productivity Obsession."[1] Google "productivity" and you'll find about 18 million results. (Reading through them all doesn't seem that productive).

A century ago, Max Weber observed that the Protestant ethic believed that the "waste of time is the first and in principle the deadliest of sins."[2] Yet, this pension for productivity hacks and efficiency techniques seem to have the opposite effect.

We even subconsciously reveal the madness of our busyness obsession in our interactions with others. A simple, "How are you?" often results in: "I'm crazy busy." Our obsession with productivity is affecting us in profound ways.

We now are busier than ever, more stressed, and more connected to work through emails, messaging apps, and social media.

We haven't found a way to create more time. But we continue to find ways to spend it toward less important ends.

When we do this, we enter into a frenetic life guided by what our calendar apps tell us to do. We simply wander from event to event and lose a sense of wholeness. Our lives become a packed list of appointments and meetings on our calendar app. We search for meaning and significance in the escapes.

To take stock of how we spend the time that comprises our days and our weeks is a daunting task. When we do, we are confronted with two truths found in the arts:

Where you invest your love, you invest your life
—Mumford and Sons[3]

How we spend our days is, of course, how we spend our lives
—Annie Dillard[4]

While time machines and science fiction tales of bending the space-time continuum are tempting, we don't really need more time to live a good and faithful life. In fact, we have all the time we need. We have all the time we're going to get. What we need is greater depth in our time. What we need is better stewardship of our time...not to be more efficient or productive, but *to be more faithful.*

The Enneagram of Discernment encourages us to live life in the *fullness* of the time available to us. To discern deeply, we must have a full perspective of time. A full perspective includes engaging the following questions:

- *What am I remembering?* This question engages our past.

- *What am I experiencing?* This question engages our present.

- *What am I anticipating?* This question engages our future.

Minutes vs. Moments

This full perspective of time requires us to think less about quantity, and more about quality. The ancient Greeks have something to teach us on this. They had two words for time: *chronos* time and *kairos* time. *Chronos* time refers to ordinary, chronological time: seconds, minutes, hours, days, weeks, months, years, etc.

Kairos time is different. In the ancient Greek, the word refers to a right, critical, or opportune time.

Chronos time is essentially quantitative. It's finite. It's easily defined and measured...by minutes.

Kairos time is, in essence, qualitative. It's infinite. It's more easily experienced than defined. It's immeasurable...captured in moments.

In the New Testament, *kairos* is used 86 times, utilizing this expansive depth of time to refer to the appointed time in the purpose of God. [5]

Chronos is ordinary time.

Kairos is EXTRAordinary time.

We too often operate our lives in *chronos* time (minutes) in ways that thwart *kairos* time (moments).

But discernment and transformation occur in *kairos* moments.

Discerning cannot simply be done in *chronos* time. The moments of clarity, the glimmers of insight, and the rays of vision of our calling come in *kairos* time.

This isn't to say we can escape *chronos* time. Humanity is bound by it. It's irrefutable. But, we can use our ordinary time in more purposeful ways. We can make way for *kairos* moments when we utilize all three perspectives on time: past, present, and future.

When we have a deep understanding of how our past shapes us. . .

When we truly pay attention to our present . . .

When we do what is needed to be prepared for our future. . .

We make ourselves more available to the work of God in *kairos* time.

Etymological studies trace origins of *kairos* to archery; the moment when an arrow may be fired to hit a target. This minute, chronologically, is no different than any other minute in an archer's day. This minute contains that same amount of seconds as any other. But when an archer steadies her bow, pulls back the string to the "anchor point," and calms her breathing, this is the *kairos* moment. There's a weight and gravity in this moment. The attention, the focus, the steadiness, the wind, the force of the bow, the pointing of the arrow all create the condition for hitting the target.

Discernment is a lifelong practice of devoting our *chronos* time to listening to the call of God in the *kairos* moments.

Personality and Perspective on Time

How do we utilize all three perspectives on time to practice discernment? How do we listen to the past, stay present, and be prepared for the future? The Enneagram of Discernment provides insight into how each type utilizes time. Think of our overall perspective on time as another three-person dance, requiring alignment and rhythm; one dance partner is the past, one is the present, and one is the future. Each type has a tendency to put most of its focus on a dominant perspective to time, supported by another perspective on time, while neglecting a third. In other words, when we dance, we are prone to leave a partner out.

But, when we develop rhythms of practice in the fullness of time, seeking the wisdom of the past, the present, and the future, we make ourselves more available and ready for discernment.

In the last chapter, we looked briefly at triads and stances. Key to understanding your perspective on time are the enneagram's Stances (Chapter Three). Each enneagram Stance type has a dominant perspective to time, a supporting perspective to time, and a repressed perspective to time.[6]

Remember, there are three stances within the enneagram:

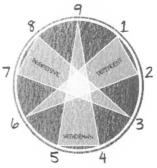

- The dependent stance (1, 2, 6)
- The aggressive stance (3, 7, 8)
- The withdrawn stance (4, 5, 9)

Each stance shares some common characteristics that we explored in the previous chapter. Each of us has all three intelligences (thinking, feeling, doing) available to us, but we're prone to lead with one intelligence center, support it with another, and distort the third.[7]

Stances are groups of types that share in common the ways in which they interpret their world, analyze it, and process it. In other words, stances are the primary postures we take when we engage the world and try to solve its problems. These stances are also marked by their posture in engaging others. This is not about introversion or extroversion. Rather, it's a posture toward others that flows from our internal motivations and can exhibit external behaviors, regardless of how outgoing you are.

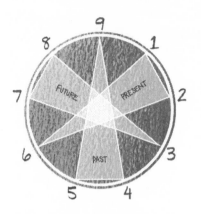

Let's begin with the Stances' dominant perspectives on time:

The types in the Aggressive Stances (Three, Seven, Eight) are future oriented. The types in the Dependent Stance (One, Two, Six) are present oriented. The Types in the Withdrawn Stance (Four, Five, Nine) are past oriented. Similar to the intelligence centers, each type tends to support this orientation with another perspective, while neglecting a third:

Enneagram Number	Dominant Perspective to Time	Supporting Perspective to Time	Neglected Perspective to Time
One	Present	Past	Future
Two	Present	Past	Future
Three	Future	Present	Past
Four	Past	Future	Present
Five	Past	Future	Present
Six	Present	Past	Future
Seven	Future	Present	Past
Eight	Future	Present	Past
Nine	Past	Future	Present

When we combine what we've learned about the intelligence centers with this approach to time perspectives, we begin to see some patterns that affect the ability to discern well.

Enneagram Stance	Distorted Center of Intelligence	Posture in engaging others	Neglected perspective to time
Dependent (1, 2, 6)	Thinking	Move toward	Future
Aggressive (3, 7, 8)	Feeling	Move against	Past
Withdrawn (4, 5, 9)	Doing	Move away	Present

The connections between a Stance's distorted center of intelligence and neglected perspective to time may not be apparent right away, but with some further explanation they make perfect sense. Let's explore each Stance to discover how.

Dependent Stance (One, Two, Six)

Enneagram Number	Preferred Perspective to Time	Supporting Perspective to Time	Neglected Perspective to Time
One (Reformer)	Present	Past	Future
Two (Helper)	Present	Past	Future
Six (Loyalist)	Present	Past	Future

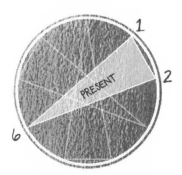

Remember, those in the dependent stance focus more on the external world and other people rather than themselves. This is also known as the "moving toward" stance. Those in the Dependent Stance rely primarily on doing and feeling intelligence and distort thinking intelligence.

In other words, they often struggle to productively think their way through a situation.

This is directly related to their orientation toward time. Ones, Twos and Sixes prefer to be *present* focused. They tend to fixate on what is presently before them either to improve (ones), help (twos), or secure (sixes). To support this present mindset, dependent numbers also rely on the past as their supporting perspective to time. The past informs the reforming motivation of ones, the helping motivation of twos, and the securing motivation of sixes as they move toward others.

What's great about this stance is that you typically don't need to worry whether or not dependent numbers will act in the present moment. They are highly responsive to needs in their midst. Also, they let the past inform their perspective on how to respond. They utilize the past as a teacher, which equips and empowers their present responses to situations.

However, the dependent numbers have a tendency to focus on the present, informed by the past at the expense of the future. When the future is repressed, they can be the ones rearranging the deck chairs on the titanic while it's sinking.

This tension is illustrated in Luke 10:38-42, where Jesus visits the home of Martha and Mary:

At the Home of Martha and Mary

[38]As Jesus and his disciples were on their way, he came to a village where a woman named Martha opened her home to him. [39]She had a sister called Mary, who sat at the Lord's feet listening to what he said. [40]But Martha was distracted by all the preparations that had to be made. She came to him and asked, "Lord, don't you care that my sister has left me to do the work by myself? Tell her to help me!"

[41]"Martha, Martha," the Lord answered, "you are worried and upset about many things, [42]but few things are needed—or indeed only one. Mary has chosen what is better, and it will not be taken away from her."

When not aligned or healthy, dependent numbers struggle to productively think what present needs are truly most important, and how tending to those needs will impact the future. Without a healthy and balanced perspective, dependent stances are prone to be like Martha, distracted by all that needs to be done. A more balanced perspective on time for dependent stances would be Mary: sitting at the feet of Jesus; a much more important preparation for the future.

In this way, dependent numbers are dependent on their response to others. This reactionary approach to life often leaves them trapped in the present.

More specifically, here is how each dependent number may neglect a future perspective to time.

Type Ones

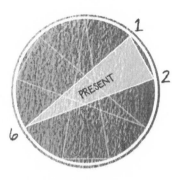

- "I can't plan for next week with my apartment in such disarray. I can't focus on what's next until I fix/solve the problems of right now."

Type Twos

- "There's just too much need around me right now to focus on what I need to get ready for."

Type Sixes

- "I can't focus on the future until I have my bases covered. Once I feel safe, secure and certain about right now I'll think about what's next."

Dependent numbers must realize that time and energy spent on the future is not wasteful or indulgent. Rather, a clearer vision of the future provides some healthy checks and balances to the present. It also provides an important avenue for the wisdom of past experience to be applied.

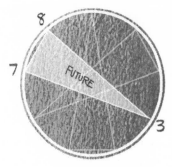

Discernment: What am I anticipating?

To bring their perspectives on time in balance, dependent numbers must cultivate a *Sacred Vision*; a Spirit-led look to the future that draws upon the wisdom of the past and the attention to the present. This requires an honest approach to anticipation.

Aggressive Stance (Three, Seven, Eight)

Enneagram Number	Preferred Perspective to Time	Supporting Perspective to Time	Neglected Perspective to Time
Three (Achiever)	Future	Present	Past
Seven (Enthusiast)	Future	Present	Past
Eight (Challenger)	Future	Present	Past

As we learned in Chapter Two, this stance is also known as the "moving against" stance. These types focus on gaining what they desire. They think clearly about what they want and then *assert oneself* (even if it's internal assertion) through action to get it. Those in the Aggressive Stance rely primarily on thinking and doing intelligence, and distort feeling intelligence. In other words, they often set aside or misuse feelings to get the job done or stay positive.

This repression of feeling intelligence impacts aggressive numbers' perspective to time by pushing feelings aside to focus on what needs to get done or what can be experienced. Reflecting on the past takes time and requires confronting feelings about the past, both good and bad. This gets in the way of efficiency and productivity. This distortion of feelings also impacts the present. To cope, aggressive numbers tend to only stay present enough to accomplish what they want to in order to get to what's next on the list of tasks, problems, or adventures. So, aggressive numbers prefer a future perspective to time in which they always have one eye on what's next. This future perspective is supported by a present perspective to time, devoting enough energy and focus to get the next thing done to move on. What's left behind (pun intended) is the past.

What's great about the aggressive numbers is that you don't have to worry about their lack of planning. They can be efficient, productive, and can conquer a to-do list. They can be decisive and can move quickly.

But this *ready, then fire, and then maybe aim* approach has consequences. An unwillingness to reflect or learn from the past will make aggressive numbers prone to repeat mistakes. This impulsivity can cause aggressive numbers to make rash decisions without properly tending to their own feelings and the feelings of those around them. In addition, aggressive numbers are present, but not fully so. They are present to the task at hand, but always gearing up for what's next. This often means that they struggle to stay focused and present in relationships with others.

This tension of dismissing the past is powerfully illustrated in a number of scientific studies of the brain that indicate that our ability to effectively imagine the future depends on the same neural parts of our brain that remember the past. In other words, our ability to store information from the past is critical to imagine future events.[8]

Aggressive numbers struggle to be honest with their feelings and the feelings of others. This leads them to shut off critical reflection of the past, which thwarts the past's ability to shape how aggressive numbers can live into the future. A more balanced perspective devotes time and energy to mining the riches of the past for wisdom to guide one into the future. This requires aggressive numbers not only to pause and reflect more, but also to be more honest and authentic with their feelings, both good and bad, suffering and joy, failure and success.

Eloise Ristad wrote, "When we give ourselves permission to fail, we, at the same time, give ourselves permission to excel."[9] Permission to fail requires risk, requires grace of ourselves, and requires an acknowledgment that we don't always measure up to our own high standards. Our past failures are teachable moments . . . opportunities for growth that are essential to our future achievement.

More specifically, here's how each aggressive type struggles to bring a past perspective to time into alignment with the present and future:

Type Threes

- "I can't dwell on the past. Don't have time. Look at this list! I need to get this one thing done so I can get to the six other things on the list before tomorrow."

Type Sevens

- "I begged my boss to let me take this project. I had no idea how long it would take. You know what, I need a breather. Wanna go get a cup of coffee with me?"

Type Eights

- "I don't have time to hear my coworker drone on and on about last week's meeting with corporate. Such a waste of time."

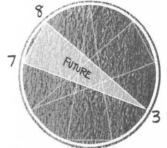

Aggressive numbers must realize that the past is a powerful teacher, with much wisdom to offer both the present challenge at hand, and the future ones ahead.

Discernment: What am I remembering?

To bring their perspectives on time in balance, aggressive numbers must cultivate the *Sacred Delay*, a proactive pause to wait and reflect upon the past and sit in the feelings that come with it. This requires an honest approach to remembering.

Withdrawn Stance (Four, Five, Nine)

Enneagram Number	Preferred Perspective to Time	Supporting Perspective to Time	Neglected Perspective to Time
Four	Past	Future	Present
Five	Past	Future	Present
Nine	Past	Future	Present

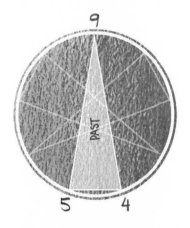

Those in the Withdrawn Stance are characterized by "moving away" from people. These types are highly imaginative, focusing on thinking and feeling. Those in the Withdrawing Stance rely primarily on thinking and feeling intelligence, and repress doing intelligence. In other words, they often struggle to initiate action, especially the most important thing that needs to be done. This doesn't mean they don't do anything. Rather, they are often very busy with anything and everything but the one thing they should be doing.

This distortion of doing intelligence directly relates to their preferred time perspective: the past. Withdrawing numbers can get stuck in the past, posing a significant challenge for the present. In fact, withdrawing numbers will very easily dwell on the past and then leap right over the present to dream about the future. This can cause these types to retreat into themselves in isolating and escapist ways.

What's great about withdrawing numbers is that they are able to see the complexity in any situation. Desire for uniqueness (fours), objectivity (fives), and peace (nines) compel them to take time to reflect, ponder, feel, and explore complexities. They are able to see things from many angles.

However, they can get caught in the vicious cycle of musing on what was and daydreaming about what could be. In so doing, they neglect what IS. When they neglect what IS, they neglect what can be done in the here and now.

It's important for withdrawn types to let the past shape, but not define. It's also important to know that engagement in the present is the best preparation for the future. To be fully present to the things that truly matter will prepare and equip you for the future. The present is the bridge between the wisdom of the past and the potential of the future.

More specifically, here's how each withdrawing type struggles to bring a present perspective to time into balance with the past and the future.

Type Fours

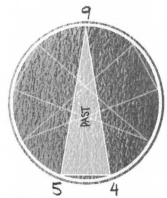

- "I don't think I'm up for going out. I need some more time to work through a few things. I don't really know some of the people anyway, so I'm not sure we'd click. Can we postpone?"

Type Fives

- "I don't have the time or energy to meet with you. I need to make some progress on this idea I've been working on. Lots of reading and researching to do. I need to find a quiet place to hole up and think."

Type Nines

- "Stressful meeting on the calendar today at work and I'm not feeling 100%. I really should be on top of my game, so it's probably better to take a day to regroup."

Withdrawing numbers must realize that the past and future are simply the abstract without the present; and the present provides essential context and meaning to our thoughts and feelings.

Discernment: What am I experiencing?

To bring their perspectives on time in balance, withdrawing numbers must cultivate a *Sacred Presence* which compels them to faithfully respond to what needs their attention in the here and now. This requires an honest approach to experiencing.

In summary, here are the time perspectives for each type:

Enneagram Number	Dominant Perspective to Time	Supporting Perspective to Time	Repressed Perspective to Time
One	Present	Past	Future
Two	Present	Past	Future
Three	Future	Present	Past
Four	Past	Future	Present
Five	Past	Future	Present
Six	Present	Past	Future
Seven	Future	Present	Past
Eight	Future	Present	Past
Nine	Past	Future	Present

Conclusion

Time can be a curse. It can also be a gift. There is a parable attributed to many coastal communities throughout Latin America that explores this tension. It's called "The Fisherman and the Businessman", and it generally goes something like this:

> There was once a businessman who was sitting by the beach in a small Brazilian village.
>
> As he sat, he saw a Brazilian fisherman rowing a small boat toward the shore having caught quite a few big fish.
>
> The businessman was impressed and asked the fisherman, "How long does it take you to catch so many fish?"
>
> The fisherman replied, "Oh, just a short while."
>
> "Then why don't you stay longer at sea and catch even more?" The businessman was astonished.
>
> "This is enough to feed my whole family," the fisherman said.
>
> The businessman then asked, "So, what do you do for the rest of the day?"
>
> The fisherman replied, "Well, I usually wake up early in the morning, go out to sea and catch a few fish, then go back and play with my kids. In the afternoon, I take a nap with my wife, and evening comes, I join my buddies in the village for a drink — we play guitar, sing, and dance throughout the night."
>
> The businessman offered a suggestion to the fisherman.
>
> "I am a PhD in business management. I could help you to become a more successful person. From now on, you should spend more time at sea and try to catch as many fish as possible. When you have saved enough money, you could buy a bigger boat and catch even more fish. Soon you will be able to afford to buy more boats,

set up your own company, your own production plant for canned food and distribution network. By then, you will have moved out of this village and to Sao Paulo, where you can set up HQ to manage your other branches."

The fisherman continues, "And after that?"

The businessman laughs heartily, "After that, you can live like a king in your own house, and when the time is right, you can go public and float your shares in the Stock Exchange, and you will be rich."

The fisherman asks, "And after that?"

The businessman says, "After that, you can finally retire, you can move to a house by the fishing village, wake up early in the morning, catch a few fish, then return home to play with kids, have a nice afternoon nap with your wife, and when evening comes, you can join your buddies for a drink, play the guitar, sing, and dance throughout the night!"

The fisherman was puzzled, "Isn't that what I am doing now?"[10]

It's a well-known story, typically used as a lesson on contentment amid our urge to strive. But I also think it has something to teach us about time. Given the same amount of time, people can perceive what we are called to do with that time in vastly different ways. Perspective is important. Discernment isn't so much about finding more time (*chronos*; quantity). It's more about stewarding the time (*kairos*; quality) more faithfully. We are all prone to consider time from only one or two perspectives, keeping the third at bay. Bringing all three to bear on our exploration of vocation will provide essential wisdom and clarity.

The enneagram teaches us that our dominant number doesn't change. I can't simply discard my own Threeness to be a Type Six. If our number doesn't change, then our stance doesn't change either. However, this shouldn't cause us to lose hope, shrug our shoulders, sigh, and carry on as we always have. You can work to unveil the patterns of your dominant type. You can work to access your neglected perspective toward time. Aggressive numbers (Three, Seven, Eight) can cultivate *Sacred Delay* (past). Dependent numbers (One, Two, Six) can learn to develop *Sacred Vision* (future). Withdrawing numbers (Four, Five, Nine) can learn to cultivate *Sacred presence* (present).

Delay. Vision. Presence. Past. Future. Present. Together they provide the environment for the very *kairos* moments to explore the depths and potential of vocation.

Exercises:

Minutes vs. Moments

- Track how you spend time in a 'typical' 24-hour day (that includes a normal workday). Mark down how you spend the time in 30-minute increments.
  - How much of your day was spent on 'autopilot'...just getting by?

  - How much of your day was devoted to reflection or spiritual practice?

- Reflect upon your life and list what you believe to be the *kairos* moments in your life; those important trajectory-shifting moments where you gained significant clarity or insight.
  - What were the circumstances or contextual factors around each of your *kairos* moments? Were you spending time intentionally searching for clarity? Or did the *kairos* moments sneak up on you?

Dependent Stance (Ones, Twos, Sixes)

- Schedule some significant time this week to foster a *Sacred Vision* for your future. Use this time to go to a place that is comfortable to you, but NOT your work or home (a coffee shop or bookstore perhaps). When you are there, use the time to think and dream about the future, unattached from all the i's you'd like to dot and t's you'd like to cross beforehand. Give yourself permission to engage in this even if it seems messy, selfish, or unsure. Overall, if it feels indulgent, you're on the right track.

Aggressive Stance (Threes, Sevens, Eights)

- Schedule some time this week to foster a *Sacred Delay* to learn from your past. Go airplane mode on your phone and laptop and spend some time reflecting upon your past day, week, month, and year. Spend time pondering the question: What can I learn from where I've been? Also, try to be more in tune with the feelings that emerge in this time. Write them down. To the best of your ability, let them surface and dwell on them. If it feels unproductive, you're on the right track.

Withdrawn Stance (Fours, Fives, Nines)

- Commit yourself to cultivating *Sacred Presence* through faithful action this week. Give yourself a defined amount of time (30 minutes perhaps), to look ahead at your week and its responsibilities. Write down the things you need to do this week and what it would look like to be fully present in each responsibility. Then, go do it. If it helps, use "Sacred Presence" as a mantra to bring your focus to the present throughout your week. If it feels a bit tiring, you're on the right track.

Notes

[1]Melissa Gregg, "The Productivity Obsession," in *TheAtlantic.com*, November 13, 2015.

[2]Max Weber, *The Protestant Ethic and the Spirit of Capitalism* (New York: Penguin Classics, 2002).

[3]Mumford and Sons, "Awake My Soul," *Sigh No More* (New York: Glassnote, 2009).

[4]Annie Dillard, *The Writing Life* (New York: Harper Perennial, 1989), p. 32.

[5]*The New Strong's Greek Exhaustive Concordance of the Bible* (Nashville, Thomas Nelson, 2010).

[6]The concept of orientation to time originally comes from enneagram teachers Hurley and Donson, from their book *Discover Your Soul Potential*. Types One, Two, and Six, they claim, are oriented toward the present, Types Four, Five, and Nine to the past, and Types Three, Seven, and Eight to the future. (Associated with your "stance"). I initially learned of time orientation from Suzanne Stabile.

[7]Many Enneagram teachers since Karen Horney teach this approach. I first learned it from Suzanne Stabile, and have developed my own understanding through the works of Don Richard Riso and Russ Hudson.

[8]Check out Daniel L. Schacter, Donna Rose Addise, and Randy L. Buckners article in *Nature Reviews Neuroscience (8)*, 657-661, 2007. Retrieved from: www.nature.com/articles/nrn2213.

[9]As quoted in Bobbi Govanus' *Breaking Through: Reinventing after Failure* (Morrisville, NC: Lulu Press, 2017), p. 132.

[10]This particular version of the story comes from Paulo Coehlo's blog, http://paulocoelhoblog.com/2015/09/04/the-fisherman-and-the-businessman/.

Part II

The Way of Discernment
for the Nine Types

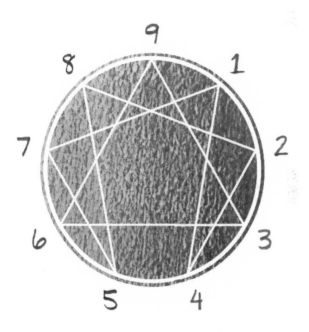

What I Mean When I Say...
(a brief review of key terms and concepts from Part I)

Adapted Self—an over-identification with our ego-centered personality. The persona we have developed to make our way in the world. Our adapted self helps us and hinders us. This is evidenced by our over-reliance on our enneagram type.

Authentic Self—the beloved self-in-God, made in the image of the Divine. Our authenticity reflects the *Imago Dei* (image of God).

Anger—a state of displeasure, annoyance, or hostility. The dominant emotion of the Gut Triad Types: Eight, Nine, and One.

Anxiety—the human response to stress in life. This is different than a clinically diagnosed anxiety disorder. Experiencing anxiety is a universal human phenomenon. Our responses to that anxiety vary by type, as evidenced by our dominant emotion.

Beloved—one who is completely covered and encompassed in love. By rediscovering our authentic self in the *Imago Dei*, we understand that we are beloved.

Discernment—the gift and practice of living our lives from a deep sense of vocation, with wisdom, in the fullness of time.

Ego—a psychological concept that is one of the three parts of psychoanalytic theory (along with the *id* and the *superego*). How you have learned to identify yourself. This when combined with our dominant enneagram type, forms the adapted self.

Fathom—The term "fathom" originally meant "outstretched arms," and was used in nautical contexts to measure the depth of where you were. Over time, "fathom" came to mean the way in which we understand a difficult problem or situation. It conveys a depth beneath the surface. We take the time to penetrate the surface, and, bit-by-bit, come to a place of deeper comprehension in order to better understand where we are going.

Fear—an unpleasant state caused by the belief that someone or something is dangerous, likely to cause pain, or a threat. The dominant emotion of the Head Triad Types: Five, Six, and Seven.

Flourishing—Our common purpose in the Vocation Triad. The proper translation of the ancient Hebrew concept of *shalom*. In the ancient Hebrew wisdom tradition, *shalom* means flourishing in the expanse of life. It's a call to live a life in right relationships with God, self, others, and creation.

Practice in Time—The Practice Triad in The Way of Discerning is an invitation to cultivate the fullness of time (*kairos* time) through wise engagement of the past, present, and future.

Shame—a state of painful negative thoughts about oneself; humiliation or distress caused by the experience of being wrong or foolish. The dominant emotion of the Heart Triad Types: Two, Three, and Four.

Vocation—The Vocation Triad in The Way of Discernment is an invitation to receive the Divine Call of identity, purpose, and direction.

Wisdom—The Wisdom Triad in The Way of Discernment is an invitation to engage and apply the three centers of intelligence: head, heart, and gut. This forms the holistic intelligence that guides us to engage our lives, and the many decisions therein.

CHAPTER 5

Type Eight: "The Challenger"

"Vulnerability sounds like truth and feels like courage.
Truth and courage aren't always comfortable,
but they're never weakness."
—Brené Brown, *Daring Greatly*

Eights want protection but settle for control.

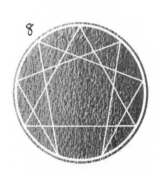

Type Eights are often labeled as "challengers." While this describes some common expressions of Eights, it doesn't capture what Eights are truly after. Eights, at their core, want protection. They want to be protected, and they want the world to be marked by protection. But when confronted with a world that isn't always protecting, the vulnerability feels threatening. They can see need for protection everywhere, and they see it most prominently within themselves. This leads Type Eights to feel anxious about

life, and that stress manifests as a particular type of anger toward vulnerability: controlling their environment on their terms. In order to keep the need for protection in check, Type Eights settle for the control they can manifest in their world. This pursuit of control can cause Eights to overlook the goodness of vulnerability in safe places.

The Way of Discernment for the Type Eight is to relinquish the compulsion to protect themselves as an outlet of their dominant emotion: anger. The anger that Eights carry is their most significant barrier. When Eights intentionally return to a place of vulnerability and tenderness, vocation, wisdom, and practice align to make good decisions.

When making decisions, Type Eights sense them in their Gut Center, and their intuition propels them into forceful action. They are living examples of those who believe "the best defense is a good offense." In their offensive posture, they chase the intensity of the moment. In fact, they thrive on it.

This is why Eights are often aggressive in groups. Their relational posture is assertive and declarative. Many Eights have been told throughout their lives that they are "too much" or "too intense." When not chasing intensity, they attempt to manifest it. They can be hard-charging, direct, and even forceful. One enneagram teacher, a self-identified Type Eight, describes the Eight in relational contexts as "stomping the ice between you and me to see if it holds."[1] Such displays of power are attempts at efficiency and control to protect themselves. In situations of conflict or disruption, Eights provide a charged emotional reaction to ratchet up the intensity and pace. Many types shrink in the intensity of conflict. Not Eights. They rise to the occasion, and often revel in it.

Strength - Self-Reliant Determination

When Type Eights discern, they have many skills in their arsenal. Eights have tremendous energy and focus to reach their goals. They march through life undeterred by obstacles that would stop most types in their tracks. When life becomes intense, Eights lean in. They thrive when the stakes are high, and are highly motivated. They approach life with strength, power, and determination.

Eights can seem tireless in their pursuits, and are shockingly decisive to those who need ample time in decision-making. They tend to move about their world with confidence and purpose. This results in a self-reliant determination to keep moving forward and doggedly reach the summit of whatever mountain they're climbing. When in situations that are unjust, Type Eights are often quick to challenge the status quo, uninhibited by others' expectations.

While all types develop "personas," the Eight persona is more of a battle mask, defined by strength and protection. All personas conceal, but the Eight persona has extra layers of protection. It is not easily shattered.

Eights' also have a high capacity to energize others. They have no trouble initiating and activating, often leading the charge to conquer what's before them. This is why Eights are often in positions of leadership. Their desire for protection is fierce, and compels them to be loyal and protective of those close to them. When they feel safe, they are our most fierce, yet tender allies.

Eights possess an intensity of focus. Eights can easily fix their jaw, furrow their brow, and grit their teeth as they move about their day. But don't mistake this intensity as simply negative. Eights embody an optimism that their power and determination will win the day. They will boldly risk, as risky endeavors provide the intensity of experience Eights crave. Seasons of discernment are often seen through this perspective: a series of risks full of the intensity Eights search for. As times of discernment can be lengthy and thorny, the self-reliant determination of the Type Eight is a great asset.

Type Eights Engage:

Write down a recent event in your life which demanded self-reliant determination to see it through.

List of few things worthy of your protection right now.

_____

Write down a recent event in which you came alive when things got intense.

_____

Challenge – Might Makes Right

A friend of mine once worked for a person who led with Type Eight. He described his supervisor this way: "My boss lives like he's driving a speedboat on a lake full throttle. He is always looking ahead at the water smooth as glass. His heart is pounding in the exhilaration of the pure power and speed. What he doesn't see is the carnage behind the boat; all the things he's run over that are now churning in the wake."

Of course, this isn't true of how all Eights' interact with others. But the capacity is there. The challenge for Type Eights lies in the temptation to be so forceful in their pursuit of protection and control that they become destructive. Eli Jaxon Bear refers to this as the Eights' "misusing the essence of power."[2] Their power can be wielded, fueled by anger, in explosive ways. This capacity for a scorched-earth approach to life can be a significant challenge to discernment. For those who burn the bridges of life (whether they be relationships, opportunities, etc.) eliminate the option to return to them.

In unhealthy seasons, this is done maliciously by Eights. But most of the time, it's accidental. Many Eights are surprised when they learn that their actions result in any form of destruction. Many are unaware of how they show up in the world with such power and intimidation.

In times of discernment, Eights must be aware that the intensity of the moment may not be shared by those around them. They should acknowledge their tendency to control and be honest about the ways in which their control has caused damage.

Might doesn't always make right, for wise decision making comes from a different sort of strength.

Type Eights Engage:

Think of a time in which you met a goal, but others felt hurt in the process. Did might make right in this case?

Think of an instance in which you took control. How did that impact those around you, positively and negatively?

Vocation – Identity, Purpose, Direction

Type Eights struggle with viewing vocation as something to conquer, rather than a gift to be received. A victory is the hopeful result of a battle. A gift is a way of being. To an Eight, identity, purpose, and direction are things to reach, win, and conquer in the future. The Way of Discernment for Type Eights requires a proverbial unclenching of the fist and jaw. Receiving the gift requires open hearts and open hands. For Type Eights any sort of letting down their guard can be terrifying. Such vulnerability feels like being naked and exposed. This is why, according to Claudio Naranjo, Eights "idealize autonomy."[3] It's a more preferable option than dependency. Healthy vocation "work" for Eights includes cultivating a deeper sense of dependency in the Divine and in those who steward one's hopes and fears with care. There the Eight will discover true identity, a sense of purpose deeper than life's battles, and look to the past for healing. There the Eight will transform.

Type Eights Engage:

What's a challenging season in your life that has shaped who you are?

Who am I?–Identity for Type Eight

The Way of Discernment Identity Statement for Type Eight is:

> *"I am made in the Divine Image,*
> *and in the Divine Image, anger is refined.*
> *My protection is in who I am, not simply what I control."*

To live from this place of identity looks different than the type of living Type Eights are used to. The journey from adapted self to authentic self (Chapter Two) provides insight for Eights to stop living from inside the fortress of their making to instead live from a Divine Image that is inherently protective and safe. Here anger is refined into righteous anger, a powerful force employed to fight injustice. In times of discernment, Eights must begin by asking the question *Who am I?* This is the very question that shifts the Eights' focus on their external battles to those within.

First, Eights must become more aware of their Eightness. As I mentioned above, Eights are often unaware of the "force of nature" that they are. Hearing that they are "too much" doesn't provide much clarity, only persistent feelings of insecurity. Those who lead with Type Eight must recognize the ways in which they battle their way through life to protect from anything getting too close. Eights: Consider the ways in which you challenge to keep your environment on its heels. Notice the ways in which you scan for intensity and then pursue it. Observe how you attempt to inject intensity into your world.

Second, Eights must acknowledge the Divine Voice that calls them beloved. Type Eights can be so protective and self-reliant that they neglect the God who loves them in their innermost being. Acknowledging the Divine Love is an important initial step for the Eight to open the gates of their fortress. In this inner place of love and protection from the *Imago Dei*, tender love flows.

Third, Eights must relinquish the adapted self. When those around us are kept at arm's length, we look elsewhere to feel alive. Notice the ways in which you reach for the intense in order to feel alive. Heed the words of Naranjo, who describes a common experience of Type Eight: "this reaching, substituted for being, leaves [Type Eights] forever dissatisfied, craving intensity."[4] For Eights, relinquishment means being more receptive than reaching.

Fourth, Eights must live from authentic self with humility. Eights project power and confidence, which to others seems void of humility. To live from an authentic humility, Eights must acknowledge their anger and its power; they must rely on others, and know their limits. This requires asking for help, deferring to others, and knowing when there are real battles to fight in their world (and when the battle is of their own making).

Fifth, Eights must befriend themselves. For Eights, this means that their vulnerability is not a weakness, but a strength. Constantly being on guard is exhausting. Self-care for Type Eights is authentic protection, intentionally quieting the body to let it heal and recover. This is a better safeguard then the battle mask they're prone to wear.

Sixth, Eights must live from authentic self with agency. From authentic identity, Type Eights can steward their natural capacity for power and protection for a common good, from a place of integrity. Their doing is aligned with being in flourishing, open expressions.

Seventh, Eights must intentionally continue to do all of the above. Remember, you can't rid yourself of Eightness. Eights must be careful not to let their intensity in battle turn them into the very thing they're fighting against. This is why they (unfortunately) are sometimes called "Eight-holes." But with vulnerability and tenderness, Eights can put the ego in its proper place, and flourish.

Why am I here?–Purpose for Type Eight

From this place of authentic protection, an Eight's purpose clarifies. When Eights discover their inner protection and tenderness, they live to recognize and engage the protection and tenderness of others. This is *shalom*. The Eight's fixation on control gives way to flourishing in relationships with God, self, others, and creation in pursuit of justice and truth. The Eight's adapted self seeks to maintain control to avoid vulnerability. The Eight's authentic self seeks to cultivate flourishing with others. Collective protection instead of conquer and control. Common good rather than personal victory.

When an Eight recognizes the *Imago Dei* within, and sees its inherent protection and purity, they're more likely to soften and open themselves up to others. In times of discernment, Eights can ask *Why am I here?* to remind them of this self-giving love and protection, rather than a compulsive self-serving control. Justice and truth are no longer weapons to be wielded in battle, but virtues to be embodied in community.

Where am I going?

The Way of Discernment cultivates a direction of depth (fathom). Eights struggle to fathom their lives because of their excess ways of living. They tend to overdo things. They can scrub the tub to the point of scratching it or overtighten a screw to the point of stripping it. Their fixation on the next hill to conquer impedes their discernment of the here and now. Depth requires a time and focus not marked by the intensity provided by external stimuli. Depth also must connect the head and body with the heart.

When Eights fathom and engage their Heart Center, they can encounter, rather than avoid, their vulnerability. They can relax in a world that doesn't require them to claw their way to control. Their power to destruct becomes power to construct. They steward their power, finding a magnanimity that recognizes the vulnerability and tenderness we all possess. Fathoming requires that Eights consent to stillness, an intentional restraint to conquer doing.[5] In beautiful irony, stillness conquers the Eights' compulsion to conquer.

Wisdom – Doing, Feeling, Thinking

In chapters three and four we explored the triads and the stances of the enneagram and how they each employ or distort the three forms of intelligence: thinking, doing, and feeling. Eights lead with doing intelligence in their Gut Center, supported by thinking intelligence, and yet distort their feeling intelligence.

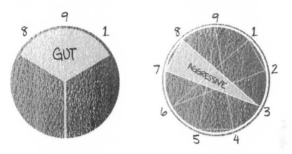

What am I doing?

The mountaineer George Leigh Mallory was asked by a reporter why he was preparing to climb Mount Everest. He replied, "Because it is there."[6] Such a statement is indicative of the way Eights evaluate their activity. Type Eights are the most energetic type in the Gut Triad, so there's tremendous capacity for doing. Like Threes, they are perpetually active, and struggle to be still. This question requires Eights to slow down and honestly assess their activity. Is the venture simply about reaching for intensity? The cycles of activity to feel alive can lead Eights to commit to activities and projects simply to maintain the feeling of intensity and keep a perception of control.

A healthier approach for Type Eights is to consider new opportunities through reflecting upon motivation. *What am I doing?* thus becomes a question about the *why* behind the activity. Is this enterprise congruent with the authentic self? Is it from a place of flourishing protection or about protecting my own vulnerability? This shifts the perspective from control to authenticity.

What am I feeling?

This is a challenging question for Eights to answer. They tend to struggle to know what to do with feelings. In this place of confusion, anxiety manifests as anger, often unfiltered. For the

Type Eight, the anger is expressed. Because of the Eight's lust for intensity, they are prone to equate intensity with emotion. Intensity brings focus and motivation toward a goal or project, but this isn't the same thing as emotion. The Heart Center of intelligence provides a depth and breadth of emotions, some are intensely felt, others are not.

Eights can have emotional blinders on that prevent them from taking the time to acknowledge their feelings. It's easy to understand why. Feelings are vulnerable. Feelings can signal weakness to Eights, which ramps up their defenses. If Eights seek to protect themselves from vulnerability, they will repress their feelings to get the job done. Without feeling intelligence, Eights are prone to some cyclical challenges. They can ignore the feelings of others, thwarting empathy.

For Eights to discern with wisdom, they must cultivate their feeling intelligence. They must commit to practices that engage their emotional self, and seek to honor and acknowledge the feelings of others. This doesn't necessarily mean they need to wallow in the dark emotions, but Eights cultivate wisdom by being honest with their vulnerabilities and allowing their inner tenderness to encounter others.

Type Eights Engage:

Describe your experience of encountering emotions without the lens of intensity.

_____

To whom or what are you tender and uninhibited in your love?

_____

What am I thinking?

Eights are quick and decisive thinkers. Their self-reliance and determination compel them to think and act swiftly. They're savvy at strategizing to maintain control in their environment and achieve their goals. Their "mind's eye" can quickly turn from their present responsibility to what's on the horizon.

The challenging work for an Eight when considering *What am I thinking?* is to allow their cognition to make space for complexity and nuance. According to Eli Jaxon-Bear, "Eights tend to see things in polarities. They have little tolerance for shades of gray."[7] It's easier to be quick and decisive when we consider situations in black and white. Complex issues, such as poverty, have many factors to consider. Nuance requires deeper reflection and contemplation, and can delay activity. To cultivate wisdom, Eights should consider the ways their ready, fire, aim approach to life thwarts good thinking.

Type Eight's Way of Discernment invites a cultivation of wisdom that considers the complexity that includes feelings in addition to activity and thinking. Integrated doing, feeling, and thinking provide a fuller picture of a world that allows Eights to relax into their inner protection and tenderness. This is a much better place from which to make decisions with integrity and authenticity.

Practice in Time

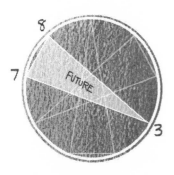

If you recall from Chapter Three, Type Eights are in the Aggressive Stance (with Threes and Sevens) and have a preferred future perspective on time, supported by the present perspective on time, while neglecting the past perspective. This results in Eights scanning their horizons, looking at what's ahead. In a way, it's a protective posture, for strategy and preparation hold the promise of keeping vulnerability at bay. Eights are skilled at gearing up for the next struggle, and are adept at finding the next battle to fight.

This future orientation is all supported by the present perspective. Eights' abilities to be quick and decisive thinkers allow them to approach the present with a forceful practicality. They know what it takes to get the job done.[8] Present projects provide opportunities to focus intensely, experience life, and feel the energy of the moment. What is astounding about Eights is that they can bring so much energy and focus to the present while also scanning ahead for the next intense experience.

In time, Eights struggle the most looking to the past. The past as a tool of discernment feels like a wasteful distraction to Eights. Many Eights are simply disinterested in looking back. The intensity has already been sucked out of past experience. More intensity lies ahead. But there's a deeper reason why Eights struggle with the past. For Eights, looking back can be particularly messy. The past often includes painful memories that legitimately cultivated their forcefully protective nature. It also includes instances in which they were caught up in the intensity of the moment and likewise caused pain. For the Eight to look back not only slows them down, but it forces them to confront times in which they've scorched their earth. To consider the implications of one's past behavior is a vulnerable thing for anyone.

In discernment, Eights must consider the past as a teacher. While it may be simple and efficient to look ahead, looking back helps Eights work through (rather than ignore) the past, and helps them realize that while the past shapes, it doesn't define.

What am I remembering? (Past)

The Type Eight persona is often built around profound past experiences of being weak or vulnerable, which instills a fear of being vulnerable and exposed. Their forceful presence in the world is a lifelong attempt to get it back. This is why the past is so difficult for Eights. To discern well, they must practice Sacred Delay. When they do, they engage the stem of their anger rather than externalizing it. They also can see a fuller picture of the past, including beauty, tenderness, truth, innocence, and healthy vulnerability.

Type Eights Engage:

What's your initial reaction to intentionally engaging your past?

_____

Think of a time in your life in which you felt safe in the midst of tenderness and vulnerability.

_____

What am I experiencing? (Present)

For Type Eights, this question should help discern the present by a barometer other than intensity. This requires Eights to unclench their proverbial fists and relax into the here and now. This is not easy, for their "moving against" often has them on guard in the present, oppositional by default. Asking this question in all three centers of intelligence gives us a better picture of what *is*. If there's not a battle here, what is there? This is good discernment work for Eights.

What am I anticipating? (Future)

This is the most compulsive time perspective for Eights. Anticipation is energetic when any type experiences it. It's electric in Eights. Once the energy is sucked out of the present, Eights are prone to move to the next intense experience, on their terms. Taking time to raise this question helps Eights become more aware of their fixation on future intensity and protection. This allows them to begin to see how their perpetual anticipation is often a result of the adapted self. Naming the things on the horizon help Eights with their tunnel vision, allowing them to widen their perspective and see their future with a softer gaze.

When Eights live from authentic identity, purpose, and direction, they can learn from the past (Sacred Delay), be more relaxed and grounded in the present (Sacred Presence), and consider a future (Sacred Vision) of tenderness, truth, justice, and protection for others. The search for intensity wanes, cultivating a grounded wisdom for the journey.

Discernment

Eights have no trouble making decisions. An Eight's ability to decide and then see a decision through with stamina can be helpful in discernment. But too often the Eight's decisions work because they approach life with a might-makes-right mentality. C. S. Lewis provides a good reminder to Type Eights that those with clenched fists "cannot open their hands to receive gifts."[9] The challenge of discernment for Type Eights is to unclench the fist and open the hand to receive the gifts of identity, wisdom, and time. Protecting oneself from legitimate harm and threat is something we all must do. But protecting oneself from nearly everyone thwarts our discernment. It's critical for Eights to be deliberate in the following when encountering important decisions:

- Identity Over Intensity: The journey to authentic self is terrifyingly vulnerable for Eights. Living from inherent protection, vulnerability, and tenderness is essential for Eights to inhibit their compulsion to march through life to obtain intensity. Make the identity statement for Type Eight a mantra: "I am made in the Divine Image, and in the Divine Image, anger is refined. My protection is in who I am, not simply what I control."

- Wise Heart: The Heart Center helps us identify ways in which our discernment considers not only ourselves, but others. Rather than viewing the heart as that which must be forcefully protected by quick thinking and forceful action, consider how your power and protective nature can be gifts stewarded for others. This requires an opening of the heart, an acknowledgement of the complexity of emotions, and befriending oneself.

- Sacred Delay: The Sacred Delay (Chapter Three) for Eights is critical for wise decision making. It prevents impulsive decisions that have long lasting consequences. By intentionally slowing down, looking to the past, Eights are less likely to make the same mistakes. This allows Eights to see things more clearly, and wisely pick their battles (instead of viewing everything as a battle).

Exercises for the Type Eight Within:

- The Trophy Case—It's been said that history is written by the victors. Make a list of your past conquests. This is your "trophy case." Eights often have many. Now look at each conquest on this list and consider this question: "Did my trophies give me what I was truly searching for?" Take time to sit with this question for each item on your list. Consider the implications of your answers for how you may approach your present and future differently.

- Practice Tenderness—Find opportunities to spend time with those who are truly weak and vulnerable. Be with those whose innocence and tenderness is on full display. For many, babies, puppies, or kittens do the trick. Holding them in your arms is an act of profound protection. The physical connection is tender and vulnerable. This is a safe place to let your guard down and be your authentic self to another.

- Rest in Stillness—The Ignation tradition teaches and practices a concept called "*Agere Contra.*"[10] It means "acting against": an intentional confrontation of our patterns of behavior that are not life-giving. For Type Eights, Agere Contra is resting in stillness, an intentional restraint that acts against impulsive and compulsive action. Practicing being still weans Eights off of their dependency on intensity, allowing them to simply be.

- Volunteer—Eights high capacity for action, justice, and power are beautiful gifts to be stewarded for the common good. Channel the protective and justice-seeking nature in spaces in which justice is needed for others.

Volunteering with non-profits or causes that advocate for justice for the vulnerable, disenfranchised, and silenced is a profound way for Eights to flourish and be about the flourishing of their world.

Questions for Discussion on the Type Eight Within:

- What is mine to control?
- When I'm in the world, how much is my true self?
- Do I like power more than my relationships with others?
- What around me needs protection that only I can bring?
- What am I protecting that doesn't need protection?
- What patterns am I in that keep vulnerability at bay?
- What is my true measure of victory?

Notes

[1]Christopher L. Heuertz, Biola University, June 20-18.

[2]Eli Jaxon-Bear, *Fixation to Freedom: The Enneagram of Liberation* (Ashland, OR: New Morning Books, 2019), p. 78.

[3]Claudio Naranjo, *Ennea-Type Structures: Self-Analysis for the Seeker* (Nevada City, CA: Gateways/IDHHB, Inc., 1990), p. 135.

[4]Naranjo, *Ennea-Type Structures*, p. 137.

[5]Christopher L. Heuertz, *The Sacred Enneagram: Finding Your Unique Path to Spiritual Growth* (Grand Rapids, Zondervan, 2017).

[6]This quote often incorrectly attributed to Sir Edmund Hillary, but Mallory said it decades before: https://www.forbes.com/global/2001/1029/060.html#76db11652080. Tragically, Mallory died in his attempt to reach the peak.

[7]Jaxon-Bear, *Fixation to Freedom*, p. 80.

[8]Hurley and Donson, *Discover Your Soul Potential*, p. 147.

[9]C. S. Lewis, *The Great Divorce* (San Francisco: HarperOne, 2015), Retrieved from https://www.biblegateway.com/devotionals/cs-lewis-daily/2054/04/03?show_return_link=true&highlight=.

[10]Read more about *Agere Contra* here: https://www.ignatianspirituality.com/acting-against/.

CHAPTER 6

Type Nine: "The Peacemaker"

"I think there are many people who bring a whole lot of baggage from their past and a whole lot of anxiety about the future to the present moment. What's so great is that people can be in relationship with each other for the now."
—Mister Rogers

"You are more powerful than you think you are. Act accordingly."
—Seth Godin

Nines want peace but settle for calm.

Type Nines are often labeled as "peacemakers." While this describes some common expressions of Nines, it doesn't capture all that Nines experience. Nines, at their core, want peace. They want peace within, and they want the world to be marked by peace. But when confronted with a world that isn't always peaceful,

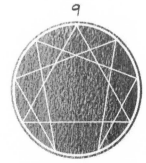

the vulnerability feels threatening. They can see need for peace everywhere, and they see it most prominently within themselves. This leads Type Nines to feel anxious about life, and that stress manifests as a particular type of anger toward disruption: passive aggression. In order to keep the need for peace in check, and to not disrupt with passive aggression, Type Nines settle for the calm they can maintain in their world. This pursuit of calm can cause Nines to forget themselves.

The Way of Discernment for the Type Nine is to awaken to their dominant emotion, anger, in order to resolve it. The anger that Nines carry (often unknowingly) is their most significant barrier. When Nines intentionally return to a place of peace and wholeness, vocation, wisdom, and practice align to make good decisions.

In decision-making, Type Nines tend to perceive the options in their Gut Center, and the disruption compels them to one of two responses: merge with their exterior environment or internally withdraw (or perhaps, a combination of the two). This is why Nines present themselves initially as being free of anger, often struggling to identify it. They often will expend great energy to maintain a sense of calm and equilibrium in their world. In reality, disruption triggers the anger within the Type Nine, which activates the responses of merging and withdrawing. The perpetual "going with the flow" builds over time, and anger often leaks out as passive aggression.

This is why Nines are often more withdrawn in groups and also quietly pragmatic. Their relational posture is conciliatory and deferential, for merging with others' desires is a relational strategy to maintain calm and comfort in their current state. Nines often hear from others throughout their lives that they are too lazy or conforming. This really isn't the case. Nines have immense capacity to act and to be resolute in their positions, but they often take more time in initiating and voicing their opinions. In situations of conflict, Nines often portray a positive outlook. They easily reframe the situation as if there is no conflict, an attempt that A.H. Almaas describes as the ability to "smooth the whole thing over acting as though everything's fine."[1] Smoothing over maintains the calm Nines value so highly.

Strength – Stable Consensus Building

In seasons of discernment, Nines should take heart that they have many skills to engage the disruption that comes with making any decision. Type Nines are effective consensus builders. When decisions need to be made in groups, Nines are adept at helping the group move together. They are highly attentive to others, empathetic, and supportive. As many decisions are interconnected with others, this is a valuable skill.

Nines build consensus so well because they have a distinct and pronounced ability to truly and purely see any issue from multiple perspectives. They are generally receptive to other's opinions and points of view and empathetic to their position. This openness can be tremendously helpful in times of discernment which requires input from others.

A core component of the Type Nine is stability. This comes from their tendency toward inertia. In physics, the law of inertia tells us that an object at rest stays at rest and an object in motion stays in motion, unless external forces show up. The inertia of a Type Nine is both a blessing and a curse. Typically, the Nine's inertia is presented in a negative light. But as a strength, if Nines commit themselves to the right thing, they are seemingly unstoppable. They don't possess the explosive force of the Type Eight, but they do possess the ability to be like a freight train. They may take some time to get to speed. Once a train reaches its speed, it's hard to stop. This stability makes them accountable and reliable.

Nines also exhibit immense patience that can be helpful in discernment. Many enneagram types want to force their way to the result of a decision. Nines have an ability to wait for the natural progression of life. They will not be rushed or hurried. This is its own stability.

Moreover, most Nines are simply pleasant to be around. They are often desired for their good-nature, their willingness to join the team, and their quiet strength. In a world often described by such words as "polarization," "incivility," and "entrenched," the Nine's mediating abilities are highly needed, and valued.

Nines embody a paced, relaxed approach to life, and this shouldn't be simplistically judged as sloth. Nines convey an optimism that everything's going to be OK. In times of discernment, this perspective can be a significant strength.

Type Nines Engage:

When has your stability been an asset in your life?

When is your patience helpful when making decisions?

Challenge – Showing Up, Fully

I have a friend who leads with Type Nine. He described his fellow Nines as those who "start slow and then taper off." It captures some of the challenging consequences of inertia. Inertia teaches us that it can be difficult to start. Inertia also helps us understand that once an object is in motion, it can be difficult to stop. For Type Nines, this is often the case. Nines suffer often from a struggle to get moving. Once they do, they struggle to know when to stop.

The difficulty in getting going for the Nine experience is a result of patterns of paying attention to others while forgetting themselves. The fear of disruption causes a sort of "closing in," an internal withdrawing into one's shell.[2] This is why Nines can be physically present in a room, but their eyes seem glazed over or focused on something in the middle distance. Many enneagram resources are quick to label this as "laziness" and stereotype the Nine as a couch potato. This is a harmful error. If the Nine is lazy, it's a laziness toward the self; a laziness toward what's going on inside.

This is why Nines can struggle mightily with discernment. When we lose sight of ourselves, we lose our bearings. It's less disruptive to simply merge with the surrounding environment. Thus, the Nine, according to Eli Jaxon-Bear, risks being "posed in ambivalence."[3]

This is the challenge for Type Nines on the Way of Discernment: to show up...fully. Nines are accommodating and compliant in physically being present. They are quite stubborn when it comes to engaging their world with their full selves. Some Nines refer to the experience as living life more like a gas than a solid.[4] Seasons of discernment require the wholeness of one's being. To acquiesce and merge is a form of abdication, an intentional subordination of the Nine's own discernment to the external world.

In times of discernment, Nines must show up as their full and authentic selves. They should acknowledge their allergy to disruption, and learn to engage the disruptive change that is inherent in making decisions. Merging is not discerning, for wise decisions come from carving one's own path and resolving, not simply suppressing, one's anger.

Type Nines Engage:

What was a time in which you simply went with the flow of what others were doing?

_____

Where in your calendar do you show up physically, but struggle to show up mentally and emotionally?

_____

Vocation – Identity, Purpose, Direction

Type Nines struggle to view themselves worthy of the gift of vocation, thus the practice of vocation seems self-aggrandizing. A gift is something marked with love and attention. Gifts mark the uniqueness of the occasion. Type Nines can view attention as another form of disruption, which risks perceiving it as negative and something to shy away from. Sandra Maitri describes this well:

> "Nines assume that they will not get love and attention, and also that they do not deserve it . . . they have great difficulty with attention being focused on them, with taking up their own space and other people's time, with asking to be seen or heard…"[5]

The Way of Discernment for Type Nines begins with believing they are worthy enough to receive the gift of calling. When they acknowledge their worthiness to receive, then the practice of vocation can begin. Healthy vocation "work" for Nines includes cultivating a defined and authentic sense of self rooted in the Divine Image. There the Nine will learn to show up fully, discover a sense of purpose distinct from others' agendas, and engage their present world with agency.

Type Nines Engage:

When in your life were you showered with love and attention? How did you respond?

Who am I?–Identity for Type Nine

The Way of Discernment Identity Statement for Type Nine is:

> "I am made in the Divine Image, and in the Divine Image, anger is resolved.
>
> My peace and wholeness is in who I am, not simply in what I keep calm."

To live from this place of identity requires the Type Nine to remember, not forget, who they truly are in the most technical sense. To "re-member" is to piece back together the various parts that have been fragmented, discarded, and forgotten. The Divine Image is inherently peaceful and whole, and rooting identity here allows for this re-membering to occur. Here anger is resolved, and there is no need to suppress desires, dreams, views, or beliefs. When discerning, Nines must begin by asking the question *Who am I?* This is the very question that helps Nines wake up to themselves.

First, Nines must become more aware of their Nineness. When Type Nines forget who they are, they're prone to be unaware of their egoic patterns. All types struggle with self-awareness, but the Nine's struggle to acknowledge their strengths and weaknesses is pronounced. Those who lead with Type Nine must embrace what Gurdjieff calls "self re-membering," being simultaneously aware of oneself and one's actions.[6] In the case of Type Nine, this also includes awareness of one's *in*action.

Second, Nines must acknowledge the Divine Voice that calls them beloved. Type Nines can be so committed to maintaining calm that they shut themselves off from listening. Entertaining the most significant of conversations is a form of holy disruption. Acknowledging the Divine Voice of Love confronts Nines' misguided belief that they aren't worthy of the gift. By showing up to the *Imago Dei* within, Nines are able to better understand themselves by better understanding the very nature of God.

Third, Nines must relinquish the adapted self. As Nines become more aware of their tendency to internally withdraw and externally merge, they must do that which is most terrifying: disrupt their patterns of avoiding disruption by relinquishing their fixation on calm. This requires Nines to see more clearly that their merging is its own form of stubbornness: a refusal to live from their authentic self.

Fourth, Nines must live from authentic self with humility. For Type Nines to live from identity with humility requires a subtle, but profound shift. Humility from the adapted self is believing the Nine isn't worthy of much (if anything). Humility from the authentic self believes the Nine is worthy, but this belief doesn't cultivate arrogance. Nines must not succumb to the first humility and must embrace the second.

Fifth, Nines must befriend themselves. As Nines are so focused on maintaining calm in their outer world, self-care seems absurd. When Nines struggle with disruption, they are prone to self-narcotize, engaging in soothing practices to dull the senses to the environment. There is a profound distinction between narcotizing and care. Narcotizing helps forget. Caring for oneself is a powerful antidote to the self-denial and self-neglect common to Type Nines.

Sixth, Nines must live from authentic self with agency. From authentic identity, the energy of the Nine isn't spent trying to maintain calm. It can be channeled into right action from an emboldened presence. Haphazard doing gives way to focused and profound agency, which comes at the expense of the calm Nines seek to maintain.

Seventh, Nines must intentionally continue to do all of the above. Type Nines are well-versed in patterns of forgetting. Remembering requires a stable, yet forceful intentionality. With wholeness and peace within, Nines can put the ego in its proper place, and flourish.

Why am I here?–Purpose for Type Nine

From a place of inherent peace, a Nine's purpose clarifies. When a Nine's inner world is at peace, they can see the inherent peace and wholeness in others, and are energized by the union and connectedness in the world. Their merging wanes, and makes way for them to emerge in their world. The Nine's adapted self seeks to keep whatever semblance of peace is left. The Nine's authentic self emerges to engage in peacemaking, an energetic, proactive pursuit of flourishing harmony.

When Nines recognize the *Imago Dei* within and live accordingly, they're more likely to show up with purpose. In times of discernment, Nines can ask *Why am I here?* To remind them of this self-giving peace and wholeness, rather than a compulsive commitment to the status quo.

Where am I going?—Direction for Type Nine

To fathom the direction of the Type Nine requires a depth of presence that engages, not withdraws. Nines struggle to fathom their lives due to their focus on maintaining calm. They tend to fade into the background of their world, for retreat is less disruptive than leaning in. Depth requires an energy and focus in the present that is not so concerned with the disruption or conflict that they may cause. Depth requires waking up the body, the heart, and the mind to the here and now in order to get moving forward.

When Nines fathom and engage their Gut Center, they can activate, rather than placate, their peacemaking. They can emerge in a world that doesn't require them to appease. Their energy to maintain becomes power to engage. They can see beneath the surface level disruptions of life to revel in the wholeness and harmony that exists. Fathoming requires that Nines *engage* in stillness to stop the drive to mediate. In a beautiful irony, such stillness is a proactive calming of the drive to calm.[7]

Wisdom—Doing, Feeling, Thinking

In Chapters Three and Four we considered the Triads and the Stances of the enneagram and how they use or misuse the three intelligence centers: thinking, doing, and feeling. Nines lead with doing intelligence in their Gut Center, but distort this doing, leading to an overreliance on thinking and feeling intelligence.

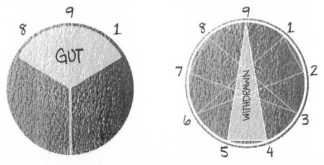

What am I doing?

Often misunderstood as lazy, Nines lead with their Gut Center by doing all sorts of things. If they are lazy, it's a laziness to prioritization. Eli Jaxon-Bear describes the Nine experience as often going "to sleep to the essential issues in their lives."[8] To ask *What am I doing?* awakens the Nine to their activity, so they can assess its importance. This helps Nines find healthier alternatives than their typical modes of activity: meandering or self-narcotizing. Both approaches open the door for vicariously living through the lives of those around them. Nines' inertia can keep them in perpetual busywork, and thus avoiding that which is most important. The activity becomes fragmented and scattered. Nines' repression of their anger and avoidance of disruption can cause them to self-narcotize, a series of numbing creature-comfort activities.

A much healthier approach for Type Nines is to consider their actions in terms of their priorities. This requires saying yes to engaging in right action, which inevitably requires saying no to other actions. *What am I doing?* thus becomes a deeper question about the motivation behind the activity. Is the Nine's activity representative of what matters most? Is doing emerging from a place of presence? This shifts activity from the path of least resistance to that which must be done.

Type Nines Engage:

When active, how many things are you doing at once?

_____

What is something you tend to procrastinate?

_____

What am I feeling?

When Type Nines awaken to who they truly are, they become more aware of their emotional center in a way that isn't regulated metrics of disruption. In the adapted self, the Type Nine's anger is repressed, denied, and seemingly forgotten. The Heart

Center provides an opportunity to resolve anger, and thus feel the range of emotions.

When Nines ask this question *What am I feeling?* they allow themselves "to feel the discomfort without needing to change."[9] More attention is devoted to what's going on within. From this place, real and right action can burst forth.

For Nines to discern with wisdom, they must beware of the tendency to merge as a defense against many things, including the engagement of their Heart Center. To acknowledge one's feelings is its own form of remembering. It's an intentional showing up within.

What am I thinking?

Nines tend to be methodical thinkers. Understanding multiple perspectives takes considerable time and energy. Their mediating nature works toward a cognitive consensus.

The challenging work for a Nine when exploring *What am I thinking?* is twofold. First, Nines are tempted to use thinking in the form of musing or ruminating as a socially acceptable withdrawal from disruption and avoidance of immediate action. When Nines muse or ruminate,[10] they tend to withdraw to another mental place, leaving their body in the room. It's easy for them to let their mind wander to calmer places and settle there. This is why Nines can appear distracted in a room.

The second challenge for Nines is thinking quickly enough to contribute to their world before others have moved on. Nines' methodical approaches to thought are sometimes too slow for a world that worships efficiency and productivity. This is a shame, for when Nines mentally arrive at a conclusion, it's often worthy of others' consideration.

The Type Nine's Way of Discernment invites a cultivation of wisdom that prioritizes doing to focus energy on right action. This involves integrating feeling intelligence and thinking intelligence in energetic rhythms with doing intelligence to fully show up in the world from a place of inner peace and wholeness. In this way, Nines don't just physically take space. They are fully alive, awake, and present.

Practice in Time

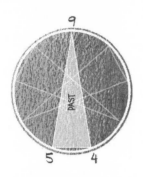

In Chapter Three, we considered the Type Nine's membership in the Withdrawn Stance (with Fours and Fives). Withdrawn Types have a preferred past perspective on time, supported by a future perspective on time, while neglecting the present perspective. This leads Nines to withdraw to past memories, by relishing in calmer memories or fixating on unresolved past events. The former is a proactive retreat. The latter is a failure to let go and show up to the present. Regardless, both experiences of the past perspective protect Nines from the disruption and conflict of the present.

This past orientation is supported by a future perspective. Nines have a way of jumping from the past to the future, which leapfrogs the present. A known past and an imagined future can conjure a sense of calm that avoids the disruption of the present. The future provides opportunities to long and hope for a resolution of conflict, something calmer than the present waters, without having to suffer through it. Such focus on the past and future expends tremendous energy, which is why Nines sometimes struggle to act in the present.

With regards to time, Nines struggle the most with showing up in the present. To show up fully in the present often seems too disruptive. But avoiding all disruption avoids good disruption, which is often a critical component to discernment. Nines struggle to believe that their presence is needed in the here and now, so they tend to conclude it's better to avoid initiating or simply go do something else somewhere else.

To show up fully for what matters most is a holy and right disruption, and one Nines must engage to discern well. While it may be tempting to look back or ahead, being fully present helps Nines clearly see what they have to offer, and glean from, the present moment.

It requires a more sophisticated feeling of our bodies, not simply occupying them.[11] By integrating the present experience into discernment work, Nines can better evaluate their present experience. For not all disruption is bad. If a Nine is experiencing disruption, asking these questions can help them name it and eventually, sit with it longer than their adapted self wants.

What am I remembering? (Past)

Nines' egoic patterns often cause them to look back. But it's another thing to look back and ponder this question. According to Hurley and Donson, "As long as they (Nines) cling to the past, failing to resolve its conflicts and letting them go, they will be walking backward..."[12] Nines remember all sorts of things: calmer settings, prior conflicts without closure, more serene days without disruption, etc. By further reflecting on their memory, Nines more deeply engage their compulsion to look back. What do these prior experiences offer the present? Are they escape routes or teachable moments? How can the past provide wisdom for the here and now?

What am I experiencing? (Present)

As I describe above, this is the most difficult question for Nines to engage. Nines often interpret present stimuli as disruption. They respond accordingly by finding ways to mitigate the disruption by merging, withdrawing, musing, etc. Nines often experience a "weight" of expectation that can often feel unbearable. Here Viktor Frankl is helpful: "Between stimulus and response there is a space. In that space is our power to choose our response. In our response lies our growth and our freedom."[13] Employing the power and freedom to choose a response is a profound way to more fully participate in the present.

Type Nines Engage:

What was a particularly disruptive event in your life? What was your common response?

What's your initial reaction to using power to choose your response to the present?

What am I anticipating? (Future)

When Nines engage the future, they tend to indulge a form of idealism. They can dream and muse about what might be. The challenge is to ground a vision of the future from the present reality. By engaging *What am I anticipating?* in the Nine's discernment work, daydreams can be integrated into vision. This form of discerning engages the present to work toward an anticipated future. Asking this question helps Nines gauge the coherence of their future-casting with their present realities.

Discernment

Type Nine's ability to truly see all sides of the issue and bring others together is valuable. This is undoubtedly needed now more than ever. Their empathic, adaptable approach can be helpful in their discernment work. But Nines must resolve their greatest challenge: a suppression of anger that leads them to self-forget. St. Augustine of Hippo is often quoted by praying, "Grant me God that I might know myself that I might know thee." This is true of all types. It's especially true for Nines. When Nines self-forget, they can lose their bearings. They can merge with others' perspectives and experiences, all the while failing to recognize their own. Avoiding disruption is avoiding discernment. It's important for Nines to be deliberate with the following when engaging the disruption of decision-making:

- Identity Over Diminishment: The journey to authentic self for Nines, in a word, is disruptive. The compulsion to suppress anger results in a diminishment of the self. Living from an inner peace and wholeness is essential for Nines to intentionally remember who they are. Make the identity statement for Type Nine a mantra: "I am made in the Divine Image, and in the Divine Image, anger is resolved. My peace and wholeness is in who I am, not simply the calm I maintain."

- <u>Wise Body</u>: The Gut Center helps us embody our existence. Through intuition, we activate our priorities of the heart and mind. Rather than viewing the body as a resource of distraction to stay busy, consider how your activity can be prioritized and oriented toward right action. This requires an "essentialism"[14] that often compels Nines to *do* the right thing, even if it's disruptive. A Wise Body doesn't simply take up space, but engages the environment.

- <u>Sacred Presence</u>: The Sacred Presence (Chapter Three) for Nines is crucial for wise decision making. It inhibits the Nines' tendency to vacillate from past and future. With intention and attention, Nines can show up fully in the present. When they do, they realize that peace is made, not simply maintained. This results in a shift for Nines from merely smoothing things over to truly smoothing them out.[15]

Exercises for the Type Nine Within:

- <u>Engage in Stillness</u>. At first, this seems confusing. If Nines suffer from inertia, why should they practice stillness? It's true that often they appear physically still. In reality, *engaging* in stillness is a growth posture. It's a proactive practice that keeps Nines in the here and now. When the flight response kicks in, engaging in stillness means sticking around. It's staying in the present in a way that doesn't placate, withdraw, or merge. It's quieting the mind's compulsion to try to mediate everything. Practice keeping your mind, heart, and body all present and still in an environment longer than you normally would. Let the disruptions be in your midst for a bit.

- <u>The Hardest-First Technique</u>. Over the course of a week, practice drafting a to-do list for each day. Begin with listing whatever comes to mind. Then reorder the list by placing the hardest thing at the top. Commit to doing the hardest thing first before moving to the easier tasks. This is the one Nines tend to avoid. By engaging it first, energy is spent resolving the disruption, not avoiding it.

- Self-Impose Deadlines. The inertia of Nines often results in leaving things undone. For Nines to arrive at a place of right action often requires self-imposed deadlines. Experiment giving yourself deadlines for the projects on your to-do list. Try imposing consequences for failing to complete and rewards for completion. Pay attention to how motivation enhances and wanes. Bringing trusted friends or relatives into this process can be helpful. What carrots or sticks would increase motivation for you to get things done in spite of their difficulty or disruption?

- Journaling as Preparation. Nines are deliberate and methodical in developing their own opinions or perspectives. This means they often enter and exit meetings or groups without sufficient time to express themselves. Before entering a group or meeting, journal through your thoughts and feelings clearly on paper. You'll have your bearings with you, and will be ready to offer the wisdom within.

Questions for Discussion on the Type Nine Within:

- What's mine to resolve?
- When I spend time alone, is it because I need rest or am I withdrawing from conflict?
- Where can I assert myself more?
- How can I communicate the time I need from others to make decisions and express opinions?

Notes

[1]A.H. Almaas, as quoted in Sanra Maitri, *The Enneagram of Passions and Virtues: Finding the Way Home* (New York: Tarcher, 2005), p. 41.

[2]William Schafer, *Roaming Free Inside the Cage: A Daoist Approach to the Enneagram* (Bloomington, IN: iUniverse, 2010), p. 61 discusses this "closing in" well.

[3]Eli Jaxon-Bear, *Fixation to Freedom: The Enneagram of Liberation* (Ashland, OR: New Morning Associates, Inc., 2019), p. 52.

[4]My good friend and Type Nine, Seth Abram, pointed me to this idea.

[5]Sandra Maitri, *Spiritual Dimensions of the Enneagram: Nine Faces of the Soul* (New York: Tarcher, 2000), p. 51.

[6]This came from the following paper on a site devoted to Gurdjieff: http://www.gurdjiefffourthway.org/pdf/SELF-REMEMBERING.pdf.

[7]Heuertz, *The Sacred Enneagram.*

[8]Eli Jaxon-Bear, *Fixation to Freedom*, p. 52.

[9]William Schafer, *Roaming Free Inside the Cage*, p. 64.

[10]Riso and Hudson consider "ruminating" to be the mental fixation of the Type Nine.

[11]Sandra Maitri, *The Spiritual Dimension of the Enneagram*, p. 46.

[12]Hurley and Donson, *Discover Your Soul Potential*, p. 171.

[13]Viktor Frankl.

[14]I highly recommend a book with this title. See Greg McKeown, *Essentialism: The Disciplined Pursuit of Less* (New York: Currency, 2014).

[15]This concept comes from Sandra Maitri, *The Spiritual Dimension of the Enneagram.*

CHAPTER 7

Type One: "The Reformer"

"I've spent my whole life searching desperately
To find out that grace requires nothing of me."
—Sleeping at Last, *"One"*

Ones want goodness but settle for order.

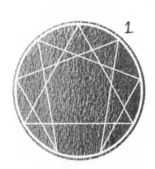

Type Ones are often labeled as perfectionists. While this describes some Ones, it doesn't capture what Ones are truly after. Ones, at their core, want goodness. They want to be good, and they want the world to be good. But when confronted with a world that isn't always good, it feels like a consuming wrongness. They can see wrongness every-where, and they see it most prominently within themselves. This leads Type Ones to feel anxious about life, and that stress manifests as anger. But because of their sensitivity to being good, they hold that anger down whenever possible. Anger then takes on a

more subtle and acceptable version: resentment. In order to keep the resentment in check, Type Ones settle for order in their world: self-improvement, rules, a sense of fairness, a sense of being right, ordering their environment, etc. Little releases of resentment help to keep things in check. Small attempts at improvement aim to satisfy the pursuit of goodness.

The Way of Discernment for the Type One is to acknowledge their dominant emotion, anger, in order to absolve themselves from the accusations of their inner critic. The anger that Ones carry is their greatest hindrance to wisdom. When Ones intentionally return to a place of goodness, vocation, wisdom, and practice align to make good decisions.

In decision-making, Type Ones tend to perceive the options in their Gut Center, and a nagging instinct of wrongness compels them to respond by tending to what can be improved. Ones expend much energy trying to suppress and hide their anger in hopes of maintaining a certain standard. The Type One believes that small doses of improvement will keep the anger tucked away in its proper place. They operate from a perspective that if they can just fix the one thing that's wrong, they'll be okay. This is an illusion, because life is rarely (if ever) perfect or complete. The suppressed anger thus builds over time, which is why it eventually leaks out as resentment.

Ones engage others by coming alongside them. They share this posture with Twos and Sixes. Often characterized by a dependency upon others, Ones', Twos', and Sixes' dependency is less about their dependency on others and more of a compliance to their superego, the part of the mind that is self-critical, responsible for regulating impulses, and conveys guilt. Type Ones often experience a powerful and overwhelming inner critic, which causes them to seek the company of others to silence it. By improving their world with others, Ones hope that the inner critic will give them a break.

Spend time with a One, and you'll notice that behind the high standards for excellence and improvement is an idealism. They truly see how things could be better, and this fuels their relational engagement. They possess a strong internal compass for how things should be. In times of conflict, Ones employ a competency that provides a rational, and reasonable way through. And when others don't see the One's competency, it adds to the One's irritation. Within the Gut Triad types, the Type One approach to life is clarified, distinguishing them from their fellow Eights and Nines. According to Eli Jaxon Bear, "Where Nines have lost the personal position, and Eights have a strong personal position on everything, Ones want the right position..."[1]

Ones rely upon their internal sense of integrity, morality, and distinction of right and wrong to convey what they believe to be the objectively right way forward. Not everyone wants to be good. Ones truly do. Behind their high standards, occasional rigidity, and commitment to the way things ought to be is a pursuit of all that is good and right.

Strength – Intuitive Improvement...with Integrity

In seasons of discernment, Ones have many skills to employ. Type Ones' sensitivity toward improvement fuels a strong work ethic. Ones are reliable and responsible. Important decisions often require discipline to see the choice through. Ones are naturally self-disciplined. Their self-control and hardworking nature allow them to be highly productive.

In addition, Ones also are adept at maintaining order, structure, and control in their environment. In the chaos that can come with times of discernment, these are helpful tools for the One to stay grounded and focused. Such skills are helpful in preventing the unknown from being overwhelming.

Type Ones are able to navigate decision-making with a strong inner compass. Ones are notoriously ethical. They're unwaveringly honest, and make decisions with a high level of integrity. Many types struggle to make decisions congruent with values and morals. Not Ones. They dare not violate their own sense of virtue.

Perhaps you're familiar with the conservation ethic called "Leave No Trace." It's a set of principles designed to help us leave an outdoor space like we found it. This is a good standard to set for most types. For Ones, it's simply a baseline. Their deep convictions compel them to leave a place better than they found it. When healthy and thriving, this comes from deep wells of righteous anger of the way things could be.

The One's intuitive improvement is inspiring. Riso and Hudson describe Type Ones at their best, saying they "embody true wisdom, especially in being able to discern appropriate and compassionate action. They radiate nobility and inspire others…"[2] In this way, they embody an inspiring blend of depth and action crucial for wise discerning.

Type Ones Engage:

When has your sense of integrity proven beneficial to you?

_____

When has your commitment to improvement helped make an important decision?

_____

Challenge – The Burden of the Unreachable Standard

Type Ones also suffer from some challenging patterns that inhibit their discernment. Their resentment at that which falls short of goodness often gets internalized. Those who know Ones can often spot when they are frustrated with something. What we sometimes miss is that Ones are typically projecting an inner frustration, a persistent anger of not measuring up to their own standards. The One's anger is usually not hateful or rude. It appears more in the form of critique or demand.[3]

Ones, when candid, are often frustrated that others aren't more frustrated when things are off, wrong, or incomplete. When something doesn't measure up to their standards, the anger builds until it reaches the mark. Ichazo, according to

Naranjo, defines anger as "standing against reality."[4] This is the essence of the One's challenge in discernment. The One's anger stands against the reality that *this* (whatever *this* may be) is good enough. This pertains to the One's situation in life, but it more directly concerns a One's understanding of themselves as being good enough for their life.

This is why Type Ones become known for their rigidity, criticism, and perfectionism. When unhealthy, they become domineering and controlling, critical of themselves and others. In this way, they can become fixated on certain things, and yet completely uninterested in others. Ones can exude an all or nothing mentality in life that can be confusing to those around them, but make complete sense to the Type One.

This is evidenced by their commitment to following rules, unless they feel the rules themselves are unjust. Ones are the consummate rule followers, but when the rules are unfair, they can be the first to rebel. When they find a set of rules that meet their standards, Ones can easily rely on rules rather than their intuition.[5]

A One's unreachable standards thus become a heavy burden. When standards are too high, life can feel like an ocean in which waves of wrongness continue to crash.

This is why Type Ones will often respond through a few defense mechanisms. The first is an attempt to conjure or manufacture virtue in places where it doesn't exist. In such an instance, The One can import a strong moral framework to something others see as amoral, such as picking out a paint color for the bedroom. This shortcuts the One's natural capacities for inherent goodness and instead tries to force it, "bringing forth a higher good through invoking a higher order."[6] Ones often couple this with another defense: a doubling down on their own self-discipline, inhibiting or civilizing any impulse or feeling that may hint at being wrong. This is where the One trips over themselves, undermining their own strengths of integrity and self-control by exaggerating them.

More specifically, this defense is known as "reaction formation" in which the One pushes their impulses forcefully down by creating and expressing the opposite impulse.[7] It's a way of turning something that feels threatening into its polar opposite, a pushing the bad down by over-compensating on the good. An example: Ones who place a high value on being polite possess people pleasing tendencies that can cause them to be excessively nice toward someone they don't really like.

In times of discernment, Ones must trust their inner goodness, integrity, and virtue. This requires them to acknowledge their anger so that they can learn to love and care for themselves. Reaction formation is not discerning, for wisdom comes from listening to one's anger and impulses, instead of stuffing them down.

Type Ones Engage:

Think of a time in your life when your standard was higher than those around you. What is this experience like for you?

_____

Where do you see evidence of reaction formation in your life?

_____

Vocation – Identity, Purpose, Direction

The loud inner critic within the Type One convinces them they are not worthy of the gift of vocation. To compensate, they can over-practice vocation. The Divine Voice of Love calls the One to their goodness. The inner critic reminds them of their faults and deficiencies. The Type One hates ambivalence, and strives to maintain a sense of right and wrong by developing an over-civilized or over-controlled persona.[8] By practicing their way into being controlled, appropriate, good, and right, Ones protect themselves from the critics of others. What they too often fail to realize is that these protective measures fail to protect themselves from their own inner critic.

The Way of Discernment for Type Ones begins with believing that the Divine Voice of Love is the voice worth listening to. It is good and right. This renders the inner critic a bald-faced liar. When they acknowledge their goodness and completeness, their practice of vocation emerges from a place of gratitude for the gift. Healthy vocation "work" for Ones includes an understanding of "good enough" being truly good. There the One will learn to cast a good and hopeful vision for their future and discover a sense of purpose that flourishes.

Type Ones Engage:

When in your life did you truly feel that you were good enough? How did that feel?

Who am I?—Identity for Type One

The Way of Discernment Identity Statement for Type One is:

"I am made in the Divine Image, and in the Divine Image there is no condemnation. My goodness is in who I am, not simply what I improve."

To live from this authentic identity requires the Type One to stop repressing and inhibiting who they truly are, out of fear that they don't measure up. Instead, they must learn to express themselves in the purest sense: uninhibited, without the self-restraint that holds them back. This comes from a Divine Image that is inherently good and complete. Here anger is transformed into righteous anger, and the One's integrity and virtue fosters flourishing. When discerning, Ones must begin by exploring the question *Who am I?* This is the very question that helps Ones learn to love themselves.

The Way of Discernment for Type Ones begins with trusting in that which God made and declared "good." When Ones can trust in the goodness of what is, they can stop "shoulding" all over themselves (I *should* do this…I *should* do that…), and instead engage their world with a deeper purpose.

First, Ones must become more aware of their Oneness. The One's cycle of repression, frustration, and resentment can spiral into a self-loathing. Those who lead with Type One must notice the ways in which they restrict themselves and engage in reaction formation. Ones must realize that the suppression of their anger results in a suppression of themselves.

Second, Ones must acknowledge the Divine Voice that calls them beloved. For the One, this is no small task. Eli Jaxon Bear describes the One's predicament well. He writes that while every type must deal with its super ego, "for the One it is the judge judging the judge."[9] In stark contrast with the inner critic, the Divine Voice speaks of goodness, wholeness, and completeness. Ones must engage and listen to this inner Voice without evaluating it. By engaging the *Imago Dei*, Ones counter the critical messages that swarm their minds, and better understand themselves by understanding the very nature of God.

Third, Ones must relinquish the adapted self. As Ones become more aware of their default patterns to inhibit and self-judge, they must do something which seems unthinkable. They must relinquish the adapted self by letting go of the unreachable standards by which they hold themselves accountable. Then, they can find joy in the inherent goodness and completeness. Here, Ones release the interior pressure and relax the tense watchfulness within.

Fourth, Ones must live from authentic self with humility. By disrupting the tendency to engage in reaction formation, Ones engage and confront their impulses, instincts, and desires. From a place of authentic identity, they can acknowledge them with honesty and humility. Humility from this authentic place believes that the One is good enough without having to prove it to themselves or others.

Fifth, Ones must befriend themselves. Here Ones can fall into a powerful trap, for they are skilled at self-improvement. The Type One can easily be convinced that self-improvement is self-care.

But self-care for the One is often less about improving themselves and more about nurturing themselves. Self-compassion is a healthier concept. It's an embrace of the self that requires the One to not only love themselves, but like themselves. When Ones befriend themselves, they can appreciate themselves for who they are and not beat themselves up for who they are not.

Sixth, Ones must live from authentic self with agency. From authentic identity, a One's energy isn't devoted merely to self-control. It can be fueled by a righteous anger to use their innate ability to improve their world from a place of integrity. The attempts to fix or improve everything give way to a deeper commitment to improve what truly matters.

Seventh, Ones must intentionally continue to do all of the above. Type Ones have well established tendencies toward inhibition, self-criticism, and reaction formation. They must be intentional, and yet kind, with themselves as they seek to live from authentic identity. From a place of goodness and serenity, Ones can integrate their ego and flourish.

Why am I here?–Purpose for Type One

From a place of goodness, a One's purpose clarifies. When a One believes they are good, they can begin to see the goodness in others, and the result is serenity: a state of being calm and untroubled by what is. Rather than noticing what is wrong or deficient, Ones can engage in the goodness of what is, and cultivate it for others.

When Ones recognize the *Imago Dei* and live accordingly, their skills of improvement and reformation build upon the good work of what's been done. In so doing, things are made better not just for themselves, but for those around them. In times of discernment, Ones can ask *Why am I here?* and distinguish between hosting and embodying hospitality. As a host, everything is in order and according to custom. As one who embodies hospitality, one makes room for whatever goodness is present to flourish.

Where am I going?–Direction for Type One

To fathom the direction of Ones requires a depth of presence that is at peace with what *is* as opposed to what is wrong. Ones struggle to fathom the goodness of their lives due to their compliance to the inner critic. They tend to focus on appeasing the inner critic, forsaking joy, goodness, and gratitude. Depth requires the One to focus not simply on what ought to be, but also on what *could* be. This requires a waking up to their bodies (not simply restraining themselves), integrating their embodied presence with the heart and the mind. This allows Ones to fathom the goodness of what, and to chart a good and right path forward.

When Ones fathom and engage their Head Center, they can cultivate habits of positive self-talk, a proactive measure that disrupts the patterns of listening solely to the inner critic. Listening to the inner critic animates the improvement and fixing egoic patterns of Ones. By bringing another voice to the table, the inner critic doesn't get the only and final say. Rather, Ones can invite the inner critic into a reflective conversation, where positivity plays a more prominent role. This allows Ones to lift their gaze up from fixing or improving the tyranny of the urgent, providing vantage for a direction of goodness and completeness.

This is why Ones practice resting in stillness, an intentional restraint to conquer the compulsion to improve or fix.[10] To rest in stillness is a difficult, but beautiful confession that what exists within and in the One's midst is truly good enough. In this way Ones can, with care, experience the type of rest that the poet David Whyte describes: "Rest is a conversation between what we love to do and how we love to be."[11]

Wisdom – Doing, Thinking, Feeling

In Chapters Three and Four we explored the Triads and the Stances of the enneagram and how they engage or misuse the three centers of intelligence: thinking, doing, and feeling. Ones lead with doing intelligence in their Gut Center, supported by feeling intelligence. They experience an over-reliance on these two intelligences, and tend to misuse thinking intelligence.

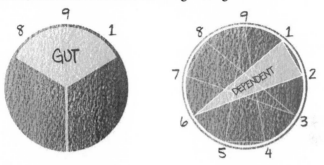

What am I doing?

As described above, Ones are often quite busy. From their residence in the Gut Triad, they have an instinctual energy toward action. The challenge for the Type One is recognizing that the impulses they experience from the gut and in the body are often coopted by their inner critic and translated as negative. In other words, Ones lead with doing intelligence but often from a negative orientation.

When a One views their body's impulses as wrong, their doing intelligence is deployed for regulation and improvement. Life is translated in terms of responsibilities and work at the expense of other important aspects. Their instinctual doing energy is devoted to what is right in front of them, an unfortunate bombardment of problems to be fixed, and situations to be improved.

The Way of Discernment provides an invitation for Ones to consider *What am I doing?* from a place of curiosity and wonder, not mere suspicion. This allows Ones to listen to what their body is telling them as opposed to automatically regulating their impulses. This allows Ones to engage their bodies in healthy and active ways. Is the One's activity a result of the demands of the inner critic? Is doing intelligence stewarded toward flourishing or is it simply an egoic pattern? This shifts the One's activity from rendering judgment to discerning what truly needs their gifts and abilities.

What am I feeling?

Type Ones have a complicated relationship with their feelings. Out of concern that they will present themselves inappropriately, they tend to keep a tight rein on their emotions. This is understandable, for Ones frequently feel anger, resentment, and negativity. This is intolerable when measured by the One's high standards, so they respond by constricting, regulating, and suppressing themselves.

In this way, the One hopes that through actions of improvement or restoring order, the negative emotions can diminish. This rarely works, for Ones experience an emotional attachment to their actions.[12] Every action has moral weight, and thus carries emotion from Ones. This is their superpower and their kryptonite. They can address the gravest injustices with integrity and passion. They can also get mired in "shoulding all over themselves." All of the *shoulds* become emotionally-saturated actions.

For Ones to journey through the Way of Discernment requires a look at *What am I feeling?* with a softer set of eyes. This allows them to enter into their emotional landscape and truly engage it. In so doing, they become hospitable to their emotions, positive and negative.

What am I thinking?

This is the most challenging intelligence for the Type One, not because they lack intelligence. On the contrary, Ones are quite smart. Their problem lies in misusing their thinking intelligence. Too much of the One's cognition is ceded to the inner critic. This causes unnecessary hesitation in the One for fear of making the wrong choice, upsetting others, or committing some other faux pas. Hurley and Donson capture this well: "Ones think nonproductively by looking at situations from all sides several times and overanalyzing them."[13]

Ones, due to their inner critic, have become accustomed to seeing their world as deficient.[14] And if deficiency can't be eradicated, it must be regulated and moderated. Consider how much brain power it takes for a person to engage in regulation and moderation. Ones experience a near constant applying of their mental brakes. This is wearisome work, the result of a struggle to use thinking intelligence to honestly evaluate.

The Way of Discernment invites the Type One to consider *What am I thinking?* In order to tame the inner critic to make way for discernment. This frees cognition from everything that is deficient toward things that truly need the One's integrity, excellence, and compassion.

The Type One's Way of Discernment is an invitation to wisdom that stewards their pursuit of the good. This involves disentangling the doing and feeling of the One's adapted state in order to align doing, feeling, and thinking from a place of serenity. Here the One can engage their present world in a way that doesn't wear them out. Energy is left in the tank to discern their future.

Type Ones Engage:

When have you experienced a feeling of exhaustion by all that is around you?

How would you categorize or describe the majority of your thoughts?

Practice in Time

In Chapter Three, we explored the One's membership in the Dependent Stance (along with Twos and Sixes). Dependent Types have a common preferred present perspective on time, supported by a past perspective, while neglecting the future. This compels Ones to

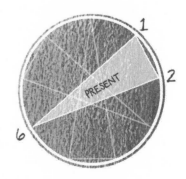

scan their present world for whatever needs to be fixed or improved. This present focus is a perpetually quick response to the "shoulds" of the inner critic, an attempt to protect the One from anything wrong, bad, or deficient.

This present orientation is supported by a past perspective. Ones in their adapted states have a way of carrying past resentment into their present situations. Prior instances of frustration, injustice, and hurt can shape the way Ones engage their present world. This is coupled with strong memories of a lifelong role of being the one expected to improve or fix. In these ways, the past provides vivid reminders of what "needs" the One's attention.

In terms of time, Ones are most challenged by the future. It's incredibly difficult for Ones to lift their gaze up from all that needs their improving skills in the present to take in the vantage of the future. Ones are well conditioned to see the wrong in their midst and focus on it until it is addressed. This presents a fixation that doesn't afford them the time and energy to look very far ahead. Consider William Schafer's take: "The root problem of the (One's) fixation does not lie in having inflexible standards; it lies in placing one's hopes in standards in the first place."[15]

This doesn't mean that the One should have no standards. But important time work for the One must include a widening of their scope to steward their hopes in something other than meeting a standard (that is often unreachable). When they do, Ones can relax their fixation on the present and find peace in the midst of its chaos.

What am I remembering? (Past)

Ones often hold on to memories of being the responsible one to show up and fix what needed to be fixed. These past actions can carry resentment that Ones bring with them to their present. Or, in times of enhanced chaos or disorder, Ones may reminisce about prior seasons free of the present condition. By engaging the Way of Discernment, Ones can reflect upon their past with greater serenity. By considering *What am I remembering?* Ones can consider past events in which they were free, uninhibited, joyful, and whole. This can help the One access a broader range of memories to help inform their present moment. Does the past only help us improve or fix? Or does it also help us experience the goodness of the here and now?

What am I experiencing? (Present)

If Ones are honest, their first answer to this question is simple, but profound: "A lot." The tyranny of the urgent can be consuming. A One can walk into a room, and sense proverbial arrows, light bulbs, and sirens alerting them to what is wrong and in need of attention. This, coupled with the One's perpetual patterns of regulation and inhibition, causes anger and frustration to be right beneath the surface. And, often, the inner critic is barking.

For Ones to engage *What am I experiencing?* on the Way of Discernment is an invitation to sense what is going on in their bodies in their present world. It's an opportunity to listen to the body, not simply keep the impulses at bay. And it's an opportunity to tell the inner critic to take a seat and even perhaps interrogate it. This creates space for the One to celebrate, practice gratitude, and shift to a place of serenity marked by an ease with "as-it-isness."

What am I anticipating? (Future)

As described above, this is the most challenging question for the Type One. The One's anticipation is often a bracing, a proverbial waiting for the other shoe to drop. Ones can worry about being let down, conjuring up negative scenarios in which they will have to step up and be responsible. This can breed a preemptive resentment. When particularly unhealthy, Ones can vividly imagine and long for a perfect world in the future, but convince themselves that they are the problem.

But when Ones follow the Way of Discernment and engage in Sacred Vision, they can relax their eyes, jaws, and bodies and imagine a goodness that leads to joy. They can envision an active role for themselves, in which they contribute from a place of authenticity. Here the One can ask, *What am I anticipating?*

and consider a future of flourishing, in which they bring their natural skills and abilities to be about the goodness of their future world.

Type Ones Engage

When your mind wanders to future scenarios, what do you tend to think about?

_____

What's your initial reaction to spending time thinking about a good future that includes you?

_____

Discernment

Ones' natural capacities to leave any situation they enter better than they found it comes with some helpful skills in discernment. Their intuition, integrity and commitment to justice and goodness are significant resources in decision-making. But Ones must relax their unreachable standards, especially when they apply it to themselves. This is their greatest challenge: They believe in a standard so high that they struggle to envision themselves ever meeting it. They must acknowledge and engage their anger that leads them to inhibit, regulate, and suppress themselves. In discernment, Ones find constructive ways to express their anger when they experience it. When Ones rediscover their inner goodness and completeness, they can harness their immense energy for improvement and direct it toward flourishing. They embody the very essence of flourishing: *right* relationships with God, self, others, and creation. The goodness they want is not manufactured and regulated, but cultivated and fostered from their inner goodness. It's critical for Ones to be mindful of the following when engaging decision-making:

- Identity Over (Self) Inquisition: The journey to authentic self for Ones can be chaotic and confusing. The One's compulsion to inhibit, regulate, and constrict leads to the inner critic calling the shots while resentment builds. Make the identity statement for Type One a mantra: "I am made in the Divine Image, and in the Divine Image there is no anger at oneself. My goodness is in who I am, not simply what I improve."

- Wise Mind: The Head Center helps us think through what our bodies are experiencing. The conversation between the mind and the body's intuition can be helpful or harmful. When harmful, the mind shouts over the body, rendering it suspicious. When helpful, the mind can help make sense of what the body is saying. Wise Mind helps Ones align and integrate their thinking with their doing in a way that empowers, not judges. A Wise Mind listens to the body without judging it, and integrates with it to let the One's intuition thrive.

- Sacred Vision: The Sacred Vision (Chapter Three) for the One is so important to experience freedom from their frustrating present. With intention and attention, Ones can lift their chin, relax their jaw, and soften their gaze toward the horizon. When they do, they experience a serenity in the here and now that grants them the permission they need to look ahead with hope and expectation.

Exercises for the Type One Within

- Rest in Stillness. Ones are known for active bodies and active minds. To rest in stillness is a tall order. At first it will feel like the restriction and inhibition common to the One experience. Over time, rest will become a proactive engagement. One of the most powerful resting in stillness practices for the Type One is Centering Prayer.[16] Centering Prayer is a silent, contemplative prayer in which one rests in the presence of God. When distractions come, Centering Prayer recalls a word or image (or takes a breath) to return to a state of contemplative rest.

- <u>Release the Anger</u>. Ones struggle feeling perpetually pent up. The only way to keep anger suppressed is to suppress just about everything. Finding healthy ways to release the anger is crucial for Ones to open up and relax. Physical exertion, especially activities such as kickboxing or punching (a bag, not a person), can release the anger. There is also research emerging showing the benefits of screaming as a healthy release.[17] Screaming into a pillow can achieve this without relational and social consequence.

- <u>Positive Self-Talk</u>. To quiet the inner critic, Ones can cultivate habits of positive self-talk to let grace abound within the self and with others. Positive mantras to counter the inner critic can be effective. Write such a message on your bathroom mirror with a dry erase marker. Place it as the wallpaper on your phone. This will help break the pattern of listening to your adapted self by talking to yourself with the truths you need to live. And then practice it in your engagement with others by approaching conversations and interactions from an *Imago Dei* perspective. Before any encounter, practice saying, "The image of God in me sees the image of God in you." This reminds you of your goodness and reminds you of others' goodness.

- <u>Play</u>. For the Type One, the *shoulds* and the *oughts* can dominate their time. Ones can really benefit from intentional time and space to play. It will feel indulgent for a while, but engaging in play relaxes the constriction and regulation. It effectively challenges the ever-present high standards that Ones carry with them. Play reminds Ones of a childlike purity, joy, and goodness. Play will often feel wasteful or wrong to Ones. But intentionally scheduling and committing to playful activity will help them embody and experience the goodness of what is.

Questions for the Type One Within:

- What is mine to fix?
- When is it truly good enough?
- When am I settling for order when I really need inner peace?
- Am I doing this because I think I should or because I really want to do it?
- Is this simply a right or wrong issue, or is it more complex?

Notes

[1]Eli Jaxon-Bear, *Fixation to Freedom: The Enneagram of Liberation* (Ashland, OR: New Morning Associates, Inc., 2019), p. 100.

[2]Don Richard Riso and Russ Hudson, *Discovering Your Personality Type: The Essential Introduction to the Enneagram, Revised and Expanded* (Boston: Mariner Books, 2003), p. 93.

[3]Claudio Naranjo, *Ennea-Type Structures: Self-Analysis for the Seeker* (Nevada City, CA: Gateways/IDHHB, Inc., 1990), p. 22.

[4]As described by Naranjo.

[5]William Schafer, *Roaming Free Inside the Cage: A Daoist Approach to the Enneagram* (Bloomington, IN: iUniverse, 2010), p 115.

[6]Beatrice Chestnut, *The Complete Enneagram: 27 Paths to Greater Self-Knowledge* (Berkeley, CA: She Writes Press, 2013), p. 391.

[7]Ibid, p. 394.

[8]Ibid.

[9]Jaxon-Bear, *Fixation to Freedom*, p. 100.

[10]Heuertz, *The Sacred Enneagram*.

[11]Quoted from a Facebook post by David Whyte himself, https://www.facebook.com/PoetDavidWhyte/photos/restis-the-conversation-between-what-we-love-to-do-and-how-we-love-to-be-restis/884555304903807/.

[12]Kathy Hurley and Theodorre Donson, *Discover Your Soul Potential: Using the Enneagram to Awaken Spiritual Vitality* (Lakewood, CO: WindWalker Press, 2012), p. 51.

[13]Ibid.

[14]Ibid, p. 50.

[15]Schaffer, *Roaming Free Inside the Cage*, p. 116.

[16] A great introduction to Centering Prayer can be found here: https://www.thecontemplativelife.org/introduction-centering-prayer.

[17] See the work of Arthur Janov, called "Primal Therapy."

CHAPTER 8

Type Two: "The Helper"

"Only when we give joyfully, without hesitation or thought of gain, can we truly know what love means."
—Leo F. Buscaglia

Twos want unconditional love but settle for niceness.

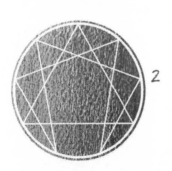

Type Twos are often labeled as helpers. While this describes some Twos, it doesn't capture what Twos are truly after. Twos, at their core, want love. They want to embody love, and they want the world to be marked by love. But when confronted with a world that isn't always loving, it feels like insufficiency. They can see need for love everywhere, and they see it most prominently within themselves. This leads Type Twos to feel anxious about life, and that stress manifests as shame. But because of their sensitivity to being loved, they hold that shame down whenever possible, and resolve

it through focusing on others' needs. This helps Twos experience a more subtle and acceptable version: pride in their sacrificial love. It is subtle and acceptable because Type Twos settle for being nice in their world: service, helping, other-focused acts, giving of themselves, etc. This results in Twos receiving flattery for being so sacrificial, kind, and thoughtful. These small doses of flattery can confuse the altruism of Twos, and feed their subtle pride. Twos' acts of helping are small attempts at giving love to try to satisfy the pursuit of unconditional love.

The Way of Discernment for the Type Two is to become more aware of themselves, specifically their dominant emotion: shame. The shame that Twos experience is their most significant barrier to discernment. When Twos turn inward to confront and engage their shame, they then can return to an authentic place of unconditional love and acceptance to make wise decisions.

In decision-making, Type Twos tend to perceive their options in the Heart Center, and often respond quickly through action: specifically embodying a loving and serving presence in the world. Their core desire for unconditional love, coupled with the shame they experience at often not feeling worthy of that love, compels them to perpetually give themselves for the sake of others. But when the gestures, the favors, and the sacrifices aren't reciprocated, the Two's perceived shame of being without love is enhanced. The Two then leans more heavily on being nice, sweet, accommodating, and helpful in hopes that appreciation will come.

This is why Twos engage others by coming alongside them. (See the Dependent Stance in Chapter Three.) They share this posture with Ones and Sixes. For Twos, their compliance to their ego compels them to be as helpful as possible. It's an attempt to receive love for what they do for others, even though they desperately want to feel loved for who they are. Twos in their adapted state believe that "to get, you must give. To be loved, you must be needed."[1] This activates great relational energy for Twos to engage others and work toward human connection through care, support, help, and kindness.

In times of conflict, Twos embody a positive presence in hopes of preserving and maintaining the relationship. They will often reframe the conflict, finding the bright side to protect the connection. This positivity often comes through action: "You're upset. Here, let me help you."

Twos rely on their kindness, sacrificial nature, and relational bonds to make their way through their world. They truly want others to thrive. But beneath their supportive effort is a longing for unconditional love that doesn't hinge upon their acts of service.

Strength – Strategic Relational Generosity

In seasons of discernment, Twos have many strengths upon which to rely. My friend Jerome Lubbe, who considers himself "most efficient in the Type Two space," writes that, "The innate human capacity reflected in Two nature is the energy of nurturing."[2] Twos are naturally loving, caring, empathetic, and attentive. Their orientation toward love fuels a relational approach to life, including discernment. Important decisions often require relational connection and support. The Two's reliance on a deep and connected relational world can be a valuable tool in discernment.

Certain enneagram types naturally are more enthusiastic. Sevens are enthusiastic in a way that recruits. Threes are enthusiastic in a way that inspires or impresses. Twos likewise are enthusiastic, but with a different expression. The Two's enthusiasm is characterized by a contagious sweetness. The Two's enthusiasm, according to Helen Palmer, results in making "difficult changes easier to undertake."[3] Seasons of discernment can sometimes feel like downing a poor-tasting medicine. It's difficult to swallow, but is important for health. Twos make such instances much more bearable. They are often the proverbial spoonful of sugar that helps the medicine go down.

This is evidenced by the Two's appreciation of others. Twos are often the first to honor and celebrate the accomplishments of others. Many are assertively nice, reminding others of their gifts, skills, and accomplishments.

Twos are excellent listeners. Their other-focused approach to life fosters an astute and finely-tuned ability to hear things most other types miss. This provides them the unique ability to hear needs and respond accordingly. When Twos translate this listening ability to their own Way of Discernment, it's a powerful skill. The honed ability to hear and respond quickly also cultivates an adaptability that can be helpful in the Two's discernment, especially when the unexpected occurs.

This develops the Two's innate ability to identify what motivates people, adapt sufficiently, and support it. In this way, they are strategically helpful, and are often the ones who can draw out the best in others. Perhaps their greatest strength in discernment is their kind strategy coupled with their generosity. Of all types on the enneagram, Twos are often the most generous, for they give what most types won't: themselves. When healthy, Twos embody a sacrificial life that invests in others. And here is what we know of investments: Over time, they earn a return. For the healthy, discerning Two, that return is often the love, support, and relationships needed to guide and animate good decision-making.

Type Twos Engage:

When has your generous spirit surprised you with an unexpected, but positive result?

How does your relational focus serve you well in life?

Challenge – The Only Need is to be Needed

While Twos' generosity toward others is a valuable asset, it can easily become a great challenge. Their other-focused sensitivity and sacrificial nature comes at a pricey cost: themselves. There is a line between healthy, sacrificial living and sacrificing at one's own expense. Twos struggle to see this line. They have a strong aversion to disappointing others. This, coupled with the suffering and need that they can see everywhere leads them to believe in what Ginger Lapid-Bogda refers to as a "false abundance."[4] Twos believe that their generosity is more abundant than it really is. When confronted with the dissonance of their false abundance and their own capacities, Twos can feel overwhelmed by so many needs and so many things to do. When Twos are overwhelmed, it's often because they are "compulsively preoccupied with what others need and almost incapable of noticing" their own.[5]

Initially, the Type Two just leans into their reserves of happiness and cheeriness, embodying the "grin and bear it" mentality. But over time, the Twos' pouring out of themselves for the sake of others can lead to feeling unappreciated or uncared for. In this space, they can easily cast themselves as a martyr, and vacillate between feeling superior (as the only sacrificial, selfless one) and inferior (why am I not more loveable?).[6]

Like all types, such inner conflict triggers a defense mechanism. For Type Twos, this is called "repression." For the Two, the repression takes on two primary forms. The first is a repression of certain feelings, specifically those that they fear are unacceptable, abrasive, or discomforting to others. Think of it as repressing anything that risks being emotionally needy, freeing the Two up to be fully available to others. The second form of repression is what Naranjo calls the "repression of neediness."[7] Twos tend to repress their own need to the point of pretending they don't have any.

In a tragic irony, the Two's efforts to repress all needs fosters their greatest challenge in discernment: The need to be needed. If Twos present themselves as being without need, they're fostering an unhealthy attachment to being needed by others. Let me be clear: Many Twos I know have awareness of their needs, but struggle in knowing how and when to communicate them to others. Their inability to communicate them is its own repression. The Two's other-focused nature causes them to value and prioritize other needs, and the relational connection, above their own needs.

Left unchecked, the seemingly unthinkable creeps into the Two's inner landscape: false pride. To many, this seems counter-intuitive. How can the most selfless enneagram type struggle with pride? Here we notice the sneakiness and subtleties of the Two's pride. Twos struggle with a pride based on what they do for others. When in repression mode, what other metric is there? The Two's helping thus hinges upon others' responses to their helping. In this manner, Twos in their adapted state don't exhibit a healthy pride we all should have in ourselves. Instead, they experience a false pride of "self-inflation."[8] The Two's self-inflating pride is a feeling of satisfaction in their ability to meet everyone's needs. In this way, unhealthy Twos can become manipulative. Their move toward people is less charitable than they present, in hopes that they will be liked and appreciated.[9]

The result of repression and pride is a forfeiture of many of Twos' natural discernment abilities, leaving them drifting and wandering from others' needs and wants, void of an inner compass that guides and directs their steps.

In times of discernment, Twos must trust that the love, care, and support they so naturally provide others is available to them. This means they must awaken to their needs, so that they can tend to them. This requires prioritization and trust that tending to their own needs won't break the healthy bonds they have with others. Repression is not discerning, for wisdom comes from listening to one's emotions and being honest with one's needs. Healthy Twos also allow others to help them. A commitment to self-care should not be interpreted as an isolated self-sufficiency. One of the most caring things a Two can do for themselves is to receive help from others.

Type Twos Engage:

Think of a time in your life when you exhausted yourself by helping others. What was the impact?

_____

Where do you see evidence of repression (of emotions or needs) in your life?

_____

Vocation – Identity, Purpose, Direction

Repressing one's needs can cause Type Twos to be unaware that the gift of vocation is available for them. Or, when they do encounter the gift, they often feel unworthy to receive it. Type Twos are far more comfortable helping others receive their gift of vocation. The Type Two desperately wants to be loved and appreciated for who they are, but yet compulsively tries to earn that love out of a fear of rejection. They are quite accustomed to operating from an unspoken assumption: "If I take care of you, you take care of me."[10] It's easy for Twos to project this assumption onto an exploration of vocation. They can struggle with believing it must be earned. And yet, the gift comes, free of any strings attached.

The Way of Discernment for Type Twos begins with believing that the Divine Voice of Love has a message for them. This is the grace that Twos often bestow to others and yet so rarely to themselves. When Twos acknowledge that they are loved for who they are, not what they do, they can receive the gift and cultivate the practice of vocation, without feeling guilty or selfish for doing so. Then the Two will learn to evaluate their helping and supporting nature in light of a deeper purpose and clearer vision.

Type Twos Engage:

When in your life have you experienced love for who you are, regardless of what you did? How did that feel?

Who am I?–Identity for Type Two

The Way of Discernment Identity Statement for Type Two is:

*"I am made in the Divine Image, and in the Divine Image there
is no shame of being unlovable.
I am loved and appreciated for who I am,
not simply what I do for others."*

To live from this authentic identity requires the Type Two to disrupt the cycles of repression that lead them to muster up a false sense of pride at what they do for others. Instead, they must be honest with their emotional and physical needs in order to love and care for themselves. From the Divine Image, this is not selfish or self-serving. Here, shame is transformed into a humility that the Two has limits, boundaries, and needs. From this humility, the Two is free to serve, help, and love. When discerning, Twos must begin by exploring the question *Who am I?* This is the very question that helps Twos reclaim their authentic identity.

The Way of Discernment for Type Twos begins with trusting in the God who is Love, and trusting in the natural generativity and reciprocity of love. When Twos can believe and experience that they are loved for who they are, they can stop serving others to receive love, compliments, flattery, and the like. Instead, they can engage their world as their healthiest self.

First, Twos must become more aware of their Twoness. The Two's concerns with being unloved leads them to repress key parts of themselves and replace them with an array of people pleasing skills. This is combined with a false sense of pride, masqueraded by niceness. Twos must become aware of how they attempt to earn love while trying to make it look effortless.[11] The subduing of their own needs results in subjugating themselves.

Second, Twos must acknowledge the Divine Voice that calls them beloved. This is what the Two wants to hear, and yet it's perhaps the most difficult message for them to accept. In their adapted egoic state, Twos believe the lie that they must *do* in order to be loved. Twos must learn to listen to the Divine Voice that calls them beloved for who they *are*. This will help the Two face their fears of rejection and inferiority, for real love begins when nothing is expected in return. Through a loving encounter with their *Imago Dei*, Twos counter the messages that exhaust them, and instead rest in their being, the very being that reflects the nature of God.

Third, Twos must relinquish the adapted self. As Twos raise their awareness of their patterns of repression, unspoken deal-making between others and themselves, and false pride, they must do that which is terrifying. They must relinquish their over-identification with being "helpful," in order to see how it comes at the expense of themselves. According to Hurley and Donson, "As perceptive and responsive as they (Twos) are to others, they are relatively blind to their own needs and weaknesses."[12] In the adapted state, asking what a Two "needs" is terrifying to them, perhaps because they are unaware of their needs. But it's also terrifying when Twos know their needs and yet don't know how to communicate them. When relinquishment occurs, Twos can begin to prioritize and engage their needs and begin to live more authentically with them.

Fourth, Twos must live from authentic self with humility. By reversing their patterns of repression, Twos can begin to see how their false pride "stands in the way of seeing things as they really are."[13] When Twos see themselves with greater clarity and definition, they can trade their false pride with a sense of grounded humility. This humility is marked by self-acceptance, not repression. This humility is shaped by a recognition of boundaries and limits. The Two's humility makes space for gratitude. The compulsive serving diminishes, allowing others to give and serve. Here the Two can embody how Helen Palmer defines humility: "The ability to look into a mirror and feel grateful for exactly what one sees."[14]

Fifth, Twos must befriend themselves. From a place of self-acceptance, the Two's limits and needs become places of care and loving maintenance rather than points of shame. A Two's authentic identity allows them to engage in self-care without feeling selfish. Here the Two's greatest act of self-care comes by establishing appropriate boundaries. Suzanne Stabile, a Type Two, wisely teaches her fellow Twos that, "I can't take care of myself if I can't say no."[15] When Twos say "no" from an authentic identity, the "no" is self-care, not a self-imposed rejection of love from others.

Sixth, Twos must live from authentic self with agency. From authentic identity, a Two's energy isn't completely spent on others. Rather, the Two can develop a will for oneself. Their agency emerges from a defined sense of self that includes their helping, but isn't determined by it. When Twos discover their inner significance, discover their belovedness, and awaken to their needs, they can employ their helping skills in a more natural, generative, and unfolding way.

Seventh, Twos must intentionally continue to do all of the above. Type Twos are quite comfortable repressing their own needs and emotions for the sake of others, convincing themselves it's the better way. Twos must be intentional advocates for themselves in order to know who they truly are. From a place of unconditional love, Twos can enter into loving relationships, without emptying themselves by trying to invent the love they need. Twos can then integrate the ego, and steward their capacity for helping and serving toward flourishing.

Why am I here?–Purpose for Type Two

From a place of love, a Two's purpose clarifies. When a Two lives as if they are loved and appreciated, they can begin to see the belovedness in others more clearly. This is freedom. Rather than worrying about being liked, needed, or favored, Twos can serve and engage others from a true sense of freedom and cultivate that same freedom for others. Twos live free to serve, not bound to serve.

When Twos recognize the *Imago Dei* and live accordingly, their helping and relational skills align with more natural rhythms of giving and receiving in healthy human interaction. This is flourishing: When unconditional love is given and received in right relationships with those in our midst. In times of discernment, Twos can ask *Why am I here?* to consider their engagement in their world. Is the Two's intent to serve really about receiving flattery, praise, or connection based on their servitude? Or is it about the mutual, reciprocal flourishing of all involved?

Where am I going?–Direction for Type Two

To fathom their direction, Twos must engage a depth marked by humility and self-awareness. Twos can lose themselves in their helping activities. The result can be a haphazard bouncing from need to need, never attending to their own. At some point, exhaustion sets in, and the Two can feel aimless, unnoticed, and underappreciated. Depth requires the Two to focus not simply on what others need, but how others' needs unite and align with their authentic identity, purpose, and direction. This requires the Two to awaken to their own experience of necessity in an embodied way. They must show up to themselves with appreciation before taking the next right step. When they do, Twos can integrate their bodies, their hearts, and their minds into the journey ahead.

When Twos embody their authentic self in the world, they are less prone to compulsively reach for others. This allows them to more deeply engage their Head Center to evaluate their activity before they're already in the midst of doing something. One of my enneagram teachers, Lynda Roberts, provides a powerful statement for Twos to help them fathom. She said, "Love shouldn't be a transaction. It just is."[16] This is a profound message for Twos to fathom as they discern the road before them.

An important practice for the Type Two is consenting to solitude:[17] saying yes to being alone. Here we find a challenging, but beautiful growth trajectory for Twos. To say "no" to others is brutally difficult. Perhaps it's a bit easier to say "yes" to something that includes an unspoken "no" that is so hard to say out loud. By consenting to solitude, Twos can experience a love and appreciation of *being* (void of doing for others) that helps them carve a healthy and flourishing path forward.

Wisdom – Doing, Feeling, Thinking

In Chapters Three and Four, we explored the enneagram's Triads and the Stances and how they employ (or misuse) the three centers of intelligence: thinking, feeling, and doing. Twos lead with feeling intelligence in their Heart Center, supported by doing intelligence. They often experience cycles of feeling and doing that tend to misuse their thinking intelligence.

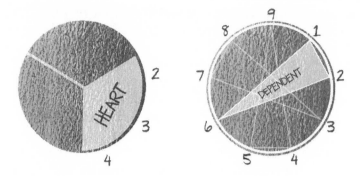

What am I doing?

Type Twos are active and busy. Their adaptability and other-focused orientation typically leads them to be spontaneous for the sake of others. Twos will often drop whatever they are currently doing to go and do what they feel needs to be done. The challenge for Twos is to recognize that their feelings of shame and desire for love often instigate a compulsive doing that leads them to do all sorts of things for others, leaving insufficient time and energy to do anything for themselves. It's important for Twos to pay attention to when they are uncomfortable in their bodies. This provides an opportunity to authenticate their body's messages to decide if they are legitimately telling them to reconsider their activity or if they are preemptively worried about their relational world.

When Twos don't evaluate their activity, their doing can become scattered and disorganized. Hurley and Donson capture this well: "Their emphasis on the interpersonal dimension can not only lead to dependent relationships, but it can also distract Twos from completing projects or meeting necessary deadlines."[18] Without reflection there can be no prioritization. The urgency of every other need is deemed important, sometimes at the expense of what truly is important.

The Way of Discernment offers an invitation for Twos to consider *What am I doing?* from a grounded, defined, and authentic presence. Activity that unfolds from identity, purpose, and direction leads to wise doing. This frees up the repression, sheds the false pride, and helps Twos consider: Is this thing that I'm doing the thing I truly should be doing? Is my activity congruent with my own sense of self? Am I tending to my own physical and emotional needs? This shifts the Two's action from a compulsive reaching to a wise stewardship of their abilities.

What am I feeling?

From their residence in the Heart Triad (with Threes and Fours), Twos are fundamentally oriented toward others.[19] In this way, Twos are often more comfortable describing how others are feeling, and how they can support and respond. This can create confusion for the Type Two, especially if they have repressed their own negative emotions in order to adapt in helping others.[20]

The Two's initial responses to this question convey this other-focus: feeling tenderness toward others, feeling sad for them, feeling sympathy or empathy. Or perhaps they are inspired by others, and feel enthusiasm to support the cause. This is a blessing and a curse. Their empathy and concern for others is a profound gift. But it also can mask what's truly occurring within the Two's emotional world. Beneath the surface, Twos can experience conflict with their own sadness of not being loved for who they are.[21]

For Twos to embark on The Way of Discernment requires an honest, reflective engagement with *What am I feeling?* without always linking it to the relational sphere. This question gets beneath the image crafting, delving underneath the presentation of being "fine" or "okay." In so doing, the seal of emotional and need repression is broken, allowing Twos to be more honest with themselves in a loving way.

What am I thinking?

Given their membership in the Dependent Stance, thinking intelligence is the greatest challenge for the Two. This doesn't mean they are less intelligent. Rather, Twos misuse the vast thinking intelligence they possess. Too much of the Two's cognition is ceded to others. Their minds are bombarded by others' needs, of which nearly all seem urgent and pressing.

This ceding of the Two's cognition is its own form of repression. Thinking for oneself gives way to thinking for others. The Two's thinking therefore becomes unproductive, as described well by Beatrice Chestnut: "When a Two experiences an internal conflict between what they are feeling or thinking and what they believe they need to form a connection with an important person, they will repress their real thought."[22] The practical implications are damaging. Twos tend to struggle sorting out the many issues in their head and struggle in prioritizing life's many responsibilities. Planning, schedules, and goals can be tossed when presented with unexpected or anticipated need.

The Way of Discernment for Twos provides the opportunity to consider *What am I thinking?* in order to take time and space to sort through all that is going on in their heads. Employing the Two's cognition for wisdom cultivation provides freedom from all the need that surrounds them, and stewards the Two's thinking toward that which is truly important and pressing. This clarity of thought also helps Twos step back from their situations and consider instances of false pride or shame from when they've been overlooked.

The Type Two's Way of Discernment is a hospitable call to wisdom that disentangles feeling from doing in the Two's adapted state. This makes room for the Two's thinking intelligence to be integrated in healthy rhythms of feeling, doing, and thinking. Then the Two can discern their engagement in the world more effectively.

Type Twos Engage:

When have you experienced seasons of frenetic helping of others? What have been the implications?

___

When you consider your thought life, how would you describe it?

___

Practice in Time

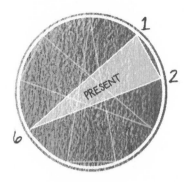

In Chapter Three, we considered the Type Two's experience in the Dependent Stance (along with Ones and Sixes). These types share a common preferred present perspective on time, supported by the past, while tending to neglect the future. This looks like the Type Two scanning their present environment for whatever needs can be met, helped, or served. This present orientation is an effort to keep the shame at bay by tending to others in their midst.

This present perspective is supported by a view to the past. Twos in their adapted state tend to bring past rejections, hurts, and unloving experiences into their present world. Such past encounters can inform the way Twos approach the present. When combined with a lifelong experience of being a "go-to" person to step up and help when needed, the past provides clear indicators of the needs that the Two interprets as their responsibility to address.

The most challenging time perspective for Twos is the future. Given the pervasive need, coupled with the Two's repression of their own needs, it's incredibly difficult for Two's to rise above the urgency of their world to look ahead. In this way, the tyranny of the urgent is truly tyrannical, a sort of prison of the Two's own making, keeping them locked in their present state.

This shouldn't cause Twos to neglect their present world and the needs before them. However, crucial time work for Twos should include taking time and space to cast a hopeful vision of the future. This is an act of freedom. When they do, Twos will not be so exhausted by the present and can develop a will to look into the future with hope and expectation.

What am I remembering? (Past)

As indicated above, Twos use the past to support their engagement in the present. They often have vivid memories of being the persons who help, even perhaps save the day. They can look to these instances with a nostalgia: "Back then, I was needed. Back then people recognized and appreciated my efforts." The Two's past also contains stark mental images of rejection, sometimes betrayal, and needs not met. This can stir a Two up inside, redoubling their efforts to find a place to serve, help, or engage in the present. This is done in hopes that the connection will result in acceptance, fidelity, and reciprocity.

By embarking on The Way of Discernment, Twos can reflect on their pasts with greater clarity. Through engaging *What am I remembering?* Twos can identify the impact memory has on their present. They can also recall times in which they were loved for who they are, not simply what they do. Does the past provide insight into what present engagement is appropriate? Does the past affirm the Two's authentic identity?

What am I experiencing? (Present)

Twos, like their fellow Dependent Stance Types, often find the present overwhelming. They have a sixth sense for sensing the needs and priorities of others. Their ability to read an environment is powerful, and the impulse and urge to engage it all is strong. This, combined with the Twos' patterns of repression and reaching out to others, causes the Two to experience some unpleasant emotions beneath their typically pleasant personas.

Exploring the question *What am I experiencing?* on the Way of Discernment can help Twos engage their embodied presence before impulsively reaching out to others and losing sight of themselves. By listening to their bodies, their hearts, and their minds, Twos can disrupt the cycles of self-diminishment for the sake of others. It's an opportunity to listen to legitimate and honest need, properly prioritizing themselves. Here the Two creates space and acknowledges the temptation to orient themselves toward others in the pursuit of being as "fine" and "okay" as they often present.

What am I anticipating? (Future)

As outlined above, this is the most challenging question for Twos. Their anticipation is truncated, for they only have so much time, energy, and attention left from their fixation on the present. When Twos anticipate, it's often scenarios in which they are without love, appreciation, or connection. It's often an anticipation of relational scenarios. This can be terrifying, reinforcing the need to manifest love, appreciation, or connection right now. In this way, Twos can anticipate the shame of being unlovable.

But when Twos embark on the Way of Discernment and engage in Sacred Vision, they can get off their proverbial treadmills and imagine a loving, gracious, and kind future. They can also open themselves up to whatever the future holds, for they will enter it from an authentic identity, a defined purpose, and a confident direction. Here the Two can ask *What am I anticipating?* and envision a future of flourishing that includes their full and true selves. Twos then worry less about whether or not they'll be loved when they show up to it.

Type Twos Engage:

When you let yourself consider the future, what does it look like? How would you describe it?

What emotions, thoughts, and sensations occur at the prospect of a good and loving future of which you are an active part?

Discernment

The Type Two's natural abilities to relate to others, encourage them, and give of themselves are inspiring. Their sacrificial nature can cultivate a wisdom that comes by entering in the messiness of life with others. But Twos must relinquish their need to be needed and find an inner assurance in their belovedness.

This is their greatest challenge: They believe that their need to be needed will assure them of the love we all desperately want to experience. They must acknowledge and engage their shame that compels them to reach toward others regardless of their own needs and limits. They must find ways to stop repressing parts of themselves for the sake of being liked. When Twos rediscover that they are loved for who they are, they can steward their profound gifts of helping and service toward flourishing. In so doing, Twos can experience what they often believed to be impossible: They can serve from their authentic sense of self. In so doing, others flourish, but so does the Two. The love they want isn't manipulated or coerced, but authentically nourished. It's important for Twos to be mindful of the following when engaging decision-making:

- Identity Over Repression: The journey to authentic self for Twos can be formidable. The Twos' compulsions to repress negative thoughts and emotions, and deny their own needs cede control to others. Make the identity statement for Type Two a mantra: "I am made in the Divine Image, and in the Divine Image there is no shame of being unlovable. I am loved and appreciated for who I am, not simply what I do for others."

- Wise Mind: The Head Center is helpful for Twos to think through what their hearts and bodies are telling them, BEFORE they act. The conversation between the mind and the heart is so important for Twos, for the mind can help the heart make sense of the emotional landscape and filter through the options for action before wearing themselves out and losing their sense of direction. Wise Minds help Twos align their thinking with their feeling and doing in a way that frees the Two to love. A Wise Mind listens to the body and the heart without repressing it.

- Sacred Vision: The Sacred Vision (Chapter Three) for Twos is important to experience freedom from their consuming present. With intention and attention, Twos can rise up from others' needs, take a deep breath, and tend to their futures with the care they bring to others. When they do, they will experience a freedom that at first feels lavish and indulgent. But with time, this freedom gives permission to consider their own legitimate needs and concerns about their futures.

Exercises for the Type Two Within

- Consent to Solitude. Perpetual activity on behalf of others is a default setting for many Twos. To the Two, choosing solitude feels like a rejection of everyone else. Consenting to solitude is a form of helping detox in which you say "yes" to being alone. In this way, it is an invitation to be present with yourself. To plan for your time in solitude, consider how you could employ your natural hospitality toward yourself. How can you make room and space to simply be for yourself? Initially, this could be engaging in a form of physical activity by yourself, like hiking in nature. The activity of the hike can seem less daunting than simply being still AND alone somewhere.

- Envisioning a Fulfilled Future. Often Twos are encouraged to simply respond to the question "What do you need?" My Two friends are adamant that this is a terrifying and debilitating question on its own. Instead, take a pen and paper and consider the following: If all the needs around me were met, how would I spend my time? What would I devote my energy to? How would I understand my role and place in the world? If I am not needed by others, what do I appreciate about myself? Take some time to truly ponder these questions, and write down whatever arises.

- Quality Time. One of my enneagram teachers, Nan Henson, is a Type Two who once told me, "How do you spell love for a Two? T-I-M-E."[23] Twos can struggle to allow themselves to simply "be" in the presence of others. They can often compulsively go help those in need while ignoring those closest to them. Plan to spend quality time with those who don't need you for something, but simply enjoy being around you. Spend quality time with those who love you best. Let this be an exercise in cultivating the love that IS.

- Assemble an Advisory Board. When Twos struggle to prioritize and say no at the expense of themselves, a few other trusted voices can be helpful. Find a few friends who know you well and who can steward your hopes and fears with love and care. Bring opportunities, requests, and invitations to them to help you decide whether or not a) you have the time, b) you have the energy, or c) the opportunities are aligned with your values.

Questions for the Type Two Within

- What is mine to do?
- At what point am I helping others to feel needed?
- Am I being realistic about what I can truly offer?
- What would happen if I put my desires first?
- What do I have to offer besides my help?
- When do I act lovable to get a certain result instead of trusting love to act?

Notes

[1]David Daniels & Virginia Price, *The Essential Enneagram: The Definitive Personality Test and Self-Discovery Guide* (San Francisco: HarperOne, 2009), p. 26.

[2]Jerome B. Lubbe *Whole Identity: A Brain-Based Enneagram Model for (W)holistic Human Thriving, Volume 1* (Atlanta: Thrive Neuro Theology, 2019), p. 56.

[3]Helen Palmer, *The Enneagram: Understanding Yourself and the Others in Your Life* (San Fransisco: HarperOne, 1988), p. 130.

[4]Ginger Lapid-Bogda, *The Art of Typing: Powerful Tools for Enneagram Typing* (Santa Monica, CA: The Enneagram in Business Press, 2018), p. 10.

[5]Schafer, *Roaming Free Inside the Cage*, p. 96.

[6]Sandra Maitri, *The Enneagram of Passions and Virtues: Finding the Way Home* (New York: J.P. Tarcher, 2005), p. 119.

[7]Naranjo, *Ennea-type Structures*, p. 43.

[8]Chestnut, *The Complete Enneagram*, p. 359.

[9]Palmer, *The Enneagram*, p. 101.

[10]Chestnut, *The Complete Enneagram*, p. 353.

[11]William Schafer in *Roaming Free Inside the Cage* writes about this experience of trying without appearing to try well.

[12]Hurley and Donson, *Discover Your Soul Potential*, p. 62.

[13]Maitri, *The Enneagram of Passions and Virtues*, p. 121.

[14]As quoted in Schafer, *Roaming Free Inside the Cage*, p. 98.

[15]As quoted from "The Enneagram, Trauma, and Adoption with Dr. Barbara Rila," *The Enneagram Journey Podcast*. January 3, 2020. https://www.theenneagramjourney.org/podcast/2019/episode73.

[16]I wrote this quote down from Lynda during Module I of my *Enneagram Applications Certification Progam—Module* in Atlanta, September, 2019.

[17]Heuertz, *The Sacred Enneagram*.

[18]Hurley & Donson, Discover Your Soul Potential, p. 62.

[19]Schafer, *Roaming Free Inside the Cage*, p. 96.

[20]Palmer, *The Enneagram*, p. 10 describes this well.

[21]Chestnut, *The Complete Enneagram*, p. 354.

[22]Ibid, p. 358.

[23]I wrote this quote down from Nan during Module I of my *Enneagram Applications Certification Progam—Module* in Atlanta, September, 2019.

CHAPTER 9
Type Three: "The Achiever"

"The consummation of work lies not only in what we have done,
but who we have become while accomplishing the task."
—David Whyte, "Crossing the Unknown Sea"

Threes want worth but settle for image.

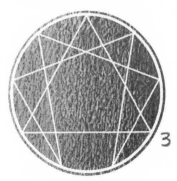

Type Threes are often labeled as achievers. While this describes common behaviors of Threes, it doesn't capture what Threes are truly after. Threes, at their core, want worth and value. They want to be worthy, and they want the world to be marked by the inherent value of all. But when confronted with a world that doesn't always value the good, the right, and the beautiful, it feels threatening. They can see need for value everywhere, and they see it most prominently

within themselves. This leads Type Threes to feel anxious about life, and that stress manifests as shame. But because of their sensitivity to being valued, they hold that shame down whenever possible. Shame then takes on a more subtle and acceptable version: image-crafting to impress and prove their worth. In order to keep the need for worth in check, Type Threes settle for the image(s) they create in their world: accomplished, polished, goal-oriented, and determined. This results in Threes receiving accolades and compliments for being so driven, focused, and successful. These small doses of recognition can confuse the inherent value and worth of threes, and feed their sense of vanity. The Three's ability to get-things-done are small attempts at seeking the validation we all need.

The Way of Discernment for the Type Three is to relinquish the need to image craft as a defense against their dominant emotion: shame. The shame that Threes carry is their most significant barrier. When Threes intentionally return to an authentic place of inherent worth and value, vocation, wisdom, and practice align to make good decisions.

When making decisions, Type Threes tend to perceive them in their Heart Center, which quickly engages a shift to one of two modes of activity: productivity or distraction. In productivity mode, Threes quickly feel motivation and excitement about the result of a decision. Threes may activate distraction mode when they experience onset shame and failure, quickly diverting their energy to other pursuits. This often leaves the Three in a perplexing state of polished, productive procrastination—an impossible combination to most other types. Both productivity and distraction modes are quick ways to short-circuit the Heart Center.

This is probably why Threes are both assertive and pragmatic in groups. They tend to have the energy to get what they want, but in a practical and sustaining manner. They exhibit a strong sense of self to their world, in hopes that the projected confidence will help it all work out. In situations of conflict or disruption, they appeal to competency to blaze an efficient trail through the chaos toward the goal.

Strength – Getting Stuff Done…and Looking Good Doing It

Threes possess a skill set to accomplish much, with seemingly limitless energy. These are enviable assets when discerning. According to enneagram teacher Beatrice Chestnut, Threes possess the ability to "make things happen by finding the most direct path to their goal, removing obstacles that get in the way—and looking good the whole time."[1]

Threes' work ethic reveals an inner drive to excel. They tend to thrive in competitive environments. In their world, they are efficient and savvy. Threes have an uncanny ability to size up what others see as admirable, and then become that very ideal. They can quickly read what others want and present themselves accordingly. This is why Threes are often described as chameleons or shape-shifters. They can work a room effectively, and present themselves to a world as having it all figured out.

Recall our exploration of the *persona* in the Introduction. While all types develop a "persona," Threes have a sophisticated and finely tuned one, which often places them in favorable positions to succeed. They have the ability to inspire others, get the right people on board, and ask the right questions. Their combination of getting things done and looking good while doing it often make them an excellent face of a company or organization.

These experiences cultivate a consistent optimism which encourages Threes toward calculated risks. Seasons of discernment are often thrilling to Threes, as they provide an opportunity to do what they love: dream, set goals, organize, and network with others. When discerning what's next, Threes should employ their ability to get things done and navigate networks well. Significant transitions, whether they be in work, family, geography, etc. require a lot of work. They demand focus, goal setting, follow-through, and charisma. Threes have this and more at their disposal. When exploring important questions of discernment, Threes must rely upon these abilities, for they are the greatest tools in their toolbox.

Type Threes Engage:

Write down a recent project or accomplishment (could be at work, home, church, community, etc.) in which you exhibited sustained focus and energy.

_____

List a few goals you currently are pursuing right now.

_____

Write down a recent event in which you 'shape-shifted' to be more effective or impressive in that environment.

_____

Challenge – Fake It Until You…Fake Yourself

Threes' shape-shifting skills can be tremendously helpful, but they come with some serious risk. The keen ability to "fake it till you make it" can become a crutch. Employed too often, Threes run the risk of not only fooling others, but also of deceiving themselves. Such deception is a significant hindrance to the gift and practice of discernment. Deception and discernment, like oil and water, don't mix.

When Threes devolve into deceiving others AND themselves, their integrity is diminished, and they are prone to make unwise choices. V.S. Naipaul wrote, "The only lies for which we are truly punished are those we tell ourselves."[2] When this occurs, the persona ceases to become an asset at all, and instead becomes only a liability.

This challenge is pronounced in a Western context, particularly North America and Europe, which exalts many aspects of Threeness. According to Chestnut,

> Type Threes' natural strengths align with Western ideals of what it means to be successful, so it can seem to others like the Three has no internal challenges. But the biggest

challenge for a Three is recognizing the difference between their authentic self and their image or role or job. . .[3]

An overemphasis on identifying with a particular role or job can lead to some dark places. When unhealthy, Threes can be narcissistic, vain, and superficial. They can be too competitive and vindictive. Relationships become simply a means to an end, and thus, discardable.

The Three's chameleon-like tendencies can also lead to an existential crisis when encountering important forks in the road of life. Because Threes desire to shape reality for themselves (and are often effective in so doing), they can imagine themselves successful at just about everything. In many respects, they are right. However, a Three who can see themselves succeeding at many things can easily suffer from a paradox of choice. If you can do anything, what should you do? If you spend your energy fashioning yourself in the favorable image of others, who are you truly called to be?

To cope with this fake-it-till-you-make-it tendency, Threes will often bury themselves in work and tasks to avoid the difficulty and the pain that lurks around the corner. They crank up their efficiency and productivity to just keep moving. Richard Rohr calls efficiency "the three's greatest temptation."[4] This can lead a Three to strive and push beyond what is healthy, keeping their "motor" running without rest. Along the way, Threes can become increasingly impatient with the inefficiency or incompetency of others. This all fuels their competitive drive in unhealthy ways, neglecting self worth for the sake of competition and comparison.

In times of important decision-making, Threes must be aware of the temptation to settle for information and accomplishment when they truly need wisdom and authenticity. Threes must be aware of their tendency to deceive themselves by ramping up their efficiency and achievement skills to push aside the time-intensive, emotional inner work they need to make wise decisions.

Type Threes Engage:

Think of a time where you had to "wing it" and it worked out. Write it below.

_____

Can you think of an instance in which you were so focused on accomplishing something that you neglected those closest to you?

_____

Vocation – Identity, Purpose, Direction

Type Threes struggle with viewing vocation as a goal rather than a gift. A goal requires much to do. A gift is a way of being. To a Three, identity, purpose, and direction are often cast using active verbs (obtain, strive, discover, pursue, etc.) with a future focus. The Way of Discernment for Type Threes must include disentangling achievement from the questions of vocation. This is no small thing for a Three to do. For a Three to consider identity, purpose, and direction apart from accomplishment can be terrifying, perhaps (initially) impossible. Threes must learn to heed the words of Carl Jung: "The greatest questions and most important problems of life are in a certain sense insoluble… they can never be solved, but only outgrown."[5] Healthy vocation "work" for Threes includes cultivating a deeper sense of true identity, a sense of purpose that transcends projects, and letting the past be a teacher. This leads to growth, maturity, and transformation in vocation.

Type Threes engage:

How would you describe yourself without including the things you do?

_____

Who am I?–Identity for Type Three

The Way of Discernment Identity Statement for Type Three is:

"I am made in the Divine Image, and in the Divine Image there is no shame of being worthless.
My worth and value are in who I am, not simply what I do."

To live from this place of identity requires a different sort of work than Type Threes are accustomed to. The journey from adapted self to authentic self (Chapter Two) provides insight for Threes to stop living from an image crafted to produce value and worth and instead live from an Image that is inherently valuable and worthy. In times of discernment, Threes must begin by asking the question *Who am I?*. To do so engages an inner conversation that should lead to authenticity.

First, Threes must become more aware of their Threeness. Noticing and naming the ways in which the adapted self controls the narrative of your life reveals much. Threes: Notice the ways in which you strive to accomplish things that seem incongruent with other parts of your life. Observe the ways in which you shift your persona to impress others. Notice the ways in which you commit to things that you eventually regret. These are all indicators of your adapted self.

Second, Threes must acknowledge the Divine Voice that calls them beloved. Remember that the question *Who am I?* inevitably raises the question *Whose am I?* Consider the God who calls you beloved. When tempted to craft an image because the authentic self seems too elusive, consider the essence of God. This assuages the Threes' fear of taking the mask off. Exploring the Divine Image helps us understand a sense of identity apart from accomplishment.

Third, Threes must relinquish the adapted self. When Type Threes relinquish their egocentricity, they learn to trust in their identity as a human being, not simply as a "human doing."

Worth and value are found in the self-in-God, not in what is accomplished.

Fourth, Threes must live from authentic self with humility. Threes often suffer from a contrived confidence, and rely upon their skills and hard work to keep the contrived from being exposed. The journey to authentic self requires humility to acknowledging shortcomings, pitfalls, and deficiencies.

Fifth, Threes must befriend themselves. For Type Threes, this often means dismissing the belief that any time they say "no," it's a form of failure. Overachieving will inevitably lead to burnout. Self-care is rest, not another concept to be achieved. It's a loving embrace of limits.

Sixth, Threes must live from the authentic self with agency. From authentic identity, a Type Three can steward their natural capacity to accomplish for a common good, and do so from a place of integrity. Doing is aligned with being in beautiful expressions. Overachieving will diminish, and in its place a common good achievement flourishes.

Seventh, Threes must intentionally continue to do all of the above. Remember, you can't rid yourself of Threeness. Its place is secured in your ego. However, with intention and attention, Threes can put the ego in its proper place, and let the authentic self flourish.

Why am I here?– Purpose for Type Three

From a place of authentic self, a Three's purpose clarifies. When Threes are able to live from a place of authentic worth and value, they live to recognize and engage the value and worth of others. This is *shalom*. The Threes' tendencies toward accomplishment give way to flourishing in relationships with God, self, others, and creation. The Threes' adapted self seeks to discover what would impress others and strive toward it. The Three's authentic self seeks to cultivate flourishing with others. Collaboration instead of competition. Common good rather than personal good.

Remember the purpose mantra from Chapter Two: *The image of God in me sees the image of God in you*. If Threes recognizes the *Imago Dei* within, and sees its inherent value and worth, they're more likely to recognize this value and worth in others. This is the type of sight discernment provides, a way of seeing beneath and through the opportunities for accomplishment. In times of discernment, Threes can ask *Why am I here?* to remind them of their self-giving, rather than self-serving purpose.

Where am I Going?–Direction for Type Threes

The Way of Discernment cultivates a direction of depth (fathom). Threes struggle to *fathom* their lives a few distinct ways. Their fixation on what's next impedes their ability to engage in the deeper work of discernment. Depth requires time and focus, free from the tyranny of endless possibility. Depth also inevitably engages the heart. When we regulate our activity long enough to engage our heart center, we encounter a fuller range of emotions that can seem scary to a Three (or, at least, a drag).

But when Threes intentionally fathom life, their need to move ahead to earn approval wanes. Threes grow when they engage in solitude and intentional withdrawal to conquer this compulsion to seek approval.[6] It's hard to impress others when you're intentionally by yourself.

Francis Bacon wrote that it's a sad fate for someone to die well known to everybody else and still unknown to themselves.[7] This is the danger of all Threes: living a mile wide but an inch deep. The wisdom of the enneagram can help Threes avoid this common pitfall, and provide a path to understanding their true selves: who God created them to be. By reflecting on the pages above and engaging in the suggested practices, Threes can move more deeply and authentically in the world, not simply for their own gain, but out of a faithful response to God's call upon their lives. In times of discernment, considering *Where am I going?* is a helpful check for Type Threes to truly fathom their direction.

Wisdom – Doing, Feeling, Thinking

In Chapters Three and Four we explored the triads and the stances of the enneagram and how they each employ or distort the three forms of intelligence: thinking, doing, and feeling. Threes, lead with feeling intelligence in the heart center, and yet distort this, developing an overreliance on thinking and doing intelligence.

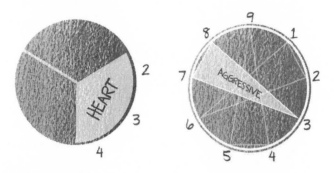

What am I doing?

Ask a Type Three what they're up to and they'll likely provide a lengthy list. Threes often find themselves in a perpetual state of activity. To consider this question requires a basic level of reflection that many Threes fail to employ. For most Threes, this question arises in the midst of an activity, project, or work that they regret agreeing to. Threes struggle with over commitment, and often regret when those commitments pile on one another.

A healthier approach for Type Threes is, when new opportunities arise, to be slower to say "yes" and more authentically consider *What am I doing?* This allows them to better gauge their capacities to commit time and energy. This question also helps Threes discern whether their activity is aligned with their authentic self: Is my activity from a place of inherent value and worth, or is it in pursuit of external value and worth? This shifts the reflection on activity from mere efficiency (how activity leads to accomplishment) to authenticity.

What am I feeling?

The tragic irony of Type Three is this: Though it is in the Heart Center, it is most disconnected from the heart. Threes have developed an over reliance on their thinking intelligence and doing intelligence to make their way in the world. They are assertive (even if it's an internal assertion) in accomplishing their goals, whether with projects or people. This assertion is often a proactive defense against engaging the Heart Center. They will repress their feelings to get the job done, stay positive, and maintain efficiency. Without feeling intelligence, Threes are prone to some common challenges. Threes can read a room of people effectively and are even able to clue in on others' general emotional states. However, they struggle to develop sincere empathy, often discarding this wisdom for the sake of the project or task. Feelings to Threes can be "intel" and research. In addition, Threes' need to impress and feel worthwhile to others leads them to be quick to repress their own feelings for fear of rejection. Such fear of failure is a powerful motivator in life and helps Threes get many things done. However, it thwarts the many valuable and important lessons we can all learn from our failures.

Wisdom in discerning must include healthy feeling intelligence. Threes must intentionally develop habits and practices to honestly encounter their feelings, as well as honor the feelings of others in order to better understand the various roles to which they are called.

This also means that Threes need to move more honestly in the world with a greater awareness of how they feel about situations and relationships, as they are prone to evaluate them based off of their sense of achievement.

Type Threes Engage:

When did you last spend time intentionally celebrating and savoring something good in your life (before moving on to the next task)?

When is the last time you had a good cry?

What am I thinking?

Threes are quick and complex thinkers. They are clever problem solvers and have loads of strategy. They're effective at creating mental structures to maintain productivity and focus toward their goals. These thought patterns also make room for the Three to think about where they stand with others as well as future-casting hopes and goals.

For a Three to consider *What am I thinking?* raises other important evaluative questions about the stewardship of their thoughts. In what ways are strategy and efficiency hindering good discernment? What are the implications when my mental energy is spent considering one's standing with others? What is lost in the present when I focus my thoughts on the future?

The Type Three's Way of Discernment requires a cultivation of wisdom that more thoroughly questions doing and thinking, and properly recognizes feelings as intelligence. This is a wise use of doing, feeling, and thinking, and provides a holistic intelligence that guides us to engage our lives, and the many decisions therein, with integrity and authenticity.

Practice in Time

As we explored in Chapter Three, Type Threes are in the Aggressive stance (with Sevens and Eights) and have a preferred future perspective on time, supported by the present perspective on time, while neglecting the past perspective. In other words, Threes are future-focused because they are often primed and ready for the next step, the next promotion, or the next phase in life. They always have the road ahead in their view, and can clearly articulate plans for what's next.

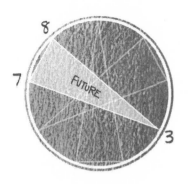

All the while, Threes are supported by a present perspective on time. They can be keenly aware and focused on the task right in front of them. They are energized by something to achieve in the here and now. They are also perpetually calibrating how they are engaging and presenting themselves to others.

What Threes struggle to incorporate in their use of time is the past. To include the past in discernment is messy, inefficient, and tough to control. Turning a Three's attention to the past causes them to slow down, reflect, feel, and ponder. These are not essential practices in a world that values image and getting things done. To cultivate wisdom in discernment, Threes must learn to develop healthy rhythms of learning from the past to inform their present and future perspectives. Practices that require inner work, slowing down, reflection, and contemplation are critical to Threes' healthy use of the past. It also means honestly confronting their failures to learn from them, heal from them, and grow from them.

In discernment, Threes must, counterintuitively, turn to the past. For us all, the past is a sorted and mixed tale, full of highs and lows, successes and failures. It's much easier to not look back, because that's where unresolved pain and grief reside.

What am I remembering? (Past)

In seasons of discernment, this is the most difficult time-based question to answer. It requires a Sacred Delay that with honesty and courage includes the past as a teacher. Including memory in the discernment causes the Three to confront their shame, rather than avoid it. Listening to the past, and learning from it, reduces the chance of repeating it.

Type Threes Engage:

When is the last time you spent significant time reflecting on the past week, month, or year?

What's your initial reaction to incorporating intentional, sustained time thinking about your past?

What am I experiencing? (Present)

It's important to ask this question to each of your intelligence centers. What am I experiencing in my body? This helps us be more aware of our intuition. What am I experiencing in my heart? This opens us to our emotional state. What am I experiencing in my head? This increases our capacity for reflection. For a Three to "scan" in this way takes a more thorough read of the present moment. It deepens the cursory glance Threes often give to the present as they cast their gaze on the future.

What am I anticipating? (Future)

This question explores the most compulsive time perspective for Threes: the future. Ask a Three what's on the horizon and they'll have a definitive answer (or three). Taking time to acknowledge anticipation helps us become more aware of the Threes' fixation on the future, and how this anticipation may be tied to unhealthy expressions of the adapted self. When Threes arrive at decisions, big and small, rooted in authentic identity, purpose, and direction, they can reflect upon their past (Sacred Delay), consider their present (Sacred Presence), and cast a healthy vision for their future (Sacred Vision). The frenetic striving to achieve gives way to wisdom for the journey.

Discernment

Confident decision-making appears natural for Threes. A Three's assurance can be helpful in times of discernment, but too often a Three's decision-making can be a "polished impulsivity." Challenge comes when Threes must make faithful decisions amid so many good options. Saying "yes" to them all eventually catches up to you. It's important for Threes to be intentional with each of the following when it comes to important decisions:

- <u>Identity Over Image</u>. The journey to authentic self is sacred and profound for each type, but it's harrowing for Threes. Living from inherent value and worth is essential for the Three. It's also terrifying. Make the identity statement for the Type Three a mantra: "I am made in the Divine Image, and in the Divine Image there is no shame. My worth and value is in who I am, not simply what I do."

- <u>Wise Heart</u>. Listen to your heart, for in it is wisdom that you'll need for discernment. Instead of viewing empathy and compassion as hindrances to discernment, consider them opportunities for wisdom. Instead of discarding your feelings so you can more efficiently think and do, take stock of how you're feeling in important decisions. Be honest with yourself. This requires Threes to first acknowledge that they indeed fail, and practice befriending themselves in the midst of their failures.

- <u>Sacred Delay</u>. Suzanne Stabile reminds us that "you can't discern while moving. You have to be still."[8] The Sacred Delay (Chapter Three) is so helpful in decision-making, providing space for the past to speak its wisdom. Also, proactively build in delays. I've heard contractors say that it's wiser to build in a cushion of 20% more time to finish a project and 20% more budget to pay for it than you initially think. This is wise advice for Threes who often assume that the most efficient and smooth process will always occur. Their optimism and efficiency can be blinders to reality.

Exercises for the Type Three Within:

- <u>Let the past guide you</u>. As a Three, looking back in order to see where you are going is counterintuitive. However, taking time to reflect on the past and seek the wisdom that it provides is a helpful practice. Experiment with the Prayer of Examen, an Ignatian prayer method that spiritually explores the past day through guided prompts. The Ignatian Spirituality website (www.ignatianspirituality.com) has a helpful introductory guide to this ancient practice.[9] Spend time reflecting on the past week, month, and year.

- <u>Fail for growth</u>. Risk doing something in which you're likely to fail (at first). You'll learn more from one failure than a handful of successes, and you'll be better equipped to navigate the future. One idea is to pick up a difficult or time intensive hobby. Threes struggle with failure, and hobbies that provide opportunities for failure to teach Threes a valuable lesson: If you fail, it's not the end of the world.

- <u>Rest in solitude</u>. Take the vacation time you are given, and don't bring your work with you. Threes can be workaholics, and vacations can simply be remote working environments. Take the vacation time you've earned and use it to recharge. Beyond time off, intentionally withdraw from your environment to relinquish your need to impress. Such solitude is not a measurable achievement, but it may be the most important "work" you do.

- <u>Redeem the list</u>. Threes carry and monitor lists. Some carry them physically, others carry them internally. These lists are almost always lists of things to-do. But other lists can be made that cultivate a Threes' growth: lists of feelings, lists of ways to show love and care for others, lists of lessons learned from past events, etc. Take time to create and ponder such lists. Another list worth writing: Answer the question "Who am I?" by writing down anything that comes to mind. Next, place a check by anything you write that is a role/responsibility. Then honestly consider the question: "If these roles go away, who am I?"

Questions for Discussion on the Type Three Within:

- Are my expectations realistic? Do I have realistic expectations of what I'm capable of? Do I know my limitations?

- When I present myself to the outside world, how much of this is self-deceit? How much is my true self?

- To what extent do I like my image more than my true self?

- When do I prioritize works, tasks, and goals to the exclusion of other elements of life?

- In what ways do I develop patterns and habits to protect me from my emotions or the emotions of others?

- What do I (really, truly) mean by success?

- What do I push aside or leave out when I'm striving to achieve?

Notes

[1]Beatrice Chestnut, *The Complete Enneagram: 27 Paths to Greater Self-Knowledge* (Phoenix: She Writes Press, 2013), p. 312.

[2]As quoted in Judith Levy, *V. S. Naipaul: Displacement and Autobiography* (New York: Routledge, 2015), p. 72.

[3]Chestnut, *The Complete Enneagram*, p. 325.

[4]Richard Rohr, *The Enneagram: A Christian Perspective* (New York: The Crossroad Publishing Company, 2001), p. 84.

[5]Carl Jung, "Commentary by C. G. Jung," in *The Secret of the Golden Flower: A Chinese Book of Life* (Orlando: Harcourt, 1931), p. 92.

[6]Heuertz, *The Sacred Enneagram*.

[7]Francis Bacon, "Of Great Place," *Essays* (New York: P.F. Collier and Son, 1909), p. 30.

[8]Suzanne Stabile, *Enneagram and Discernment Audio CDs*, Life in the Trinity Ministry, 2009.

[9]Here's a helpful introduction to practicing the Prayer of Examen: https://www.ignatianspirituality.com/ignatian-prayer/the-examen/.

CHAPTER 10
Type Four: "The Individualist"

"Empathy is the antidote to shame."
—Brené Brown

Fours want belonging but settle for longing.

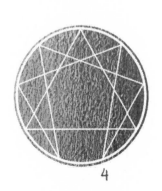

4

Type Fours are often labeled as individualists. While this describes some expressions of Fours, it doesn't capture what Fours are truly after. Fours, at their core, want belonging and connection. They want to belong, and they want the world to be marked by connection. But when confronted with a world that doesn't always make space for all as they are, it feels threatening. They can see need for belonging and connection everywhere, and they see it most prominently within themselves. This leads Type Fours to feel anxious about life, and that stress manifests as a particular type of shame: deficiency. Because of their sensitivity to being truly known and accepted, deficiency takes on a more subtle and acceptable version: deep and extraordinary longing for connection. In order to keep the longing in check, Type Fours settle for secondary longings they conjure in their world: the extraordinary, the creative, and the unique. This results in Fours shunning the ordinary and mundane in search of re-establishing depth and connection. These small doses of uniqueness can confuse the inherent belonging of Fours, and feed their sense of deficiency or inadequacy. Fours' attunement toward being misunderstood drives this pursuit of the unique.

The Way of Discernment for the Type Four is to engage their dominant emotion, shame, in order to reconcile it. The shame that Type Fours carry is their most significant barrier. When Fours intentionally return to a place of belonging, significance, and wholeness, the components of the Way of Discernment (vocation, wisdom, practice) align to make good decisions.

In decision-making, Type Fours tend to perceive the options before them in their Heart Center, and feel a persistent sense of loss. The shame of what's missing compels them to respond in a few ways. First, they tend to isolate and retreat into the depths of their emotions. A Four's shame often arises when they don't feel that they belong, which can result in a turning inward, where they see more lack within. Second, when they reemerge from their cocoon, they present a uniquely crafted persona, much like a butterfly, that distinguishes them from the crowd in which they withdrew. In this way, their distinct presence in their world masks a self-consciousness about how they appear to others. Both responses are defenses against the anxiety that manifests as shame for Type Fours.

According to Beatrice Chestnut, Fours "have a natural gift for understanding the deeper emotional level of experience and seeing the beauty in darker emotions that other types would rather not feel, much less acknowledge."[1] The vividness of their emotional world, coupled with their shame, often leads Fours to feel like outsiders in their world. This is enhanced by a pronounced sense of idealism that saturates the Four's experience. They want to be in an ultimate and ideal world in which nothing is missing and everything belongs. My friend Seth Creekmore relayed to me a description of the Type Four he heard from enneagram teacher Leslie Hershberger: "Fours see the best of what's missing and the worst of what is present."[2] When integrated, Fours see the best of what is here and the form and shape of what's to come.[3] This develops a sort of push and pull dynamic in relationships, a tension of what is and what could be. Fours often draw people in on deep emotional levels. They also can push away out of fear that others can't handle or understand them. While confusing to other Types, this push/pull approach is a relational expression of the Four's living in the tension of belonging and longing.

This inner intricacy in Type Fours is one of the reasons why they are perhaps the least understood type of the enneagram. Often typecast as the "overly dramatic," they are simply better able to access the depth and breadth of their emotional world than the rest of us. In times of conflict, Fours can be emotionally reactive and wonder why other types aren't following suit. Relational tension can bring up shame and question their sense of belonging, which stirs the Four's emotional wells. When we question if Fours are being "too dramatic," perhaps we should question whether we are being dramatic enough. Beneath their expression is a deep ache to be known and understood.

Strength – Beauty and Meaning in the Journey

In seasons of discernment, Fours should be encouraged, for many of the skills and practices required for wise discerning are quite natural for them. Fours, when healthy and thriving, are attuned to their inner world in a way that naturally discerns. Their ability to plunge the depths of a situation allows them to see beneath the surface and through the superficialities of their world.

In this way, they have a way of recognizing, perhaps even manifesting, the beauty and meaning of the journey. This is why David Daniels describes Fours as having "a knack for making the ordinary extraordinary."[4] Seasons of discernment can be intense, saturated full of meaning and significance. Fours are poised for times such as this. They can naturally attach deep symbolism to things that other types wouldn't. They possess an aesthetic sensibility that appreciates and cultivates beauty in their midst. Fours are deep souls that long for the depth that discernment requires.

Because of their deep emotional wells, Fours often have a high capacity for empathy. As discernment often includes invitations into communal wisdom and insight, the empathic ability of the Type Four provides important opportunities for connected, generative belonging. This allows Fours to be safe, trusted confidants. In empathic modes, Fours can gain clarity about their own lives. There is a beautiful reciprocity in love: When we help others, we too are helped. Fours embody this.

Fours also have the ability to arrive at a place of unique illumination and clarity about decisions because of their inclinations toward imagination and creativity. They have an uncanny ability to let their idealism motivate them toward that which can seem impossible to other types. Their aesthetic sensibilities aren't simply for creating a unique look for themselves. They have an eye for the good and beautiful, and thus can tap into creative energies and pursuits that can unlock insight and wisdom.

A healthy Four is a wise, discerning person. Fours can access the depths of their emotions, connect emotionally with others, and imagine a good and beautiful future. Recall the difference between *chronos* time and *kairos* time (Chapter Four). Fours provide a unique and clear insight into how to live in *kairos* time. Trace a Four's longing to its source, and you'll find a desire to experience *kairos* moments. In these moments, Fours embody a sense of belonging and with equanimity, a calm and composed state that engages the ups and downs of life without being swept to places where they get stuck.[5]

Type Fours Engage:

When has your appreciation of beauty led you to a surprising place?

_____

When has your search for meaning helped you make a wise decision?

_____

Challenge – Stuck in a Drama that Never Unfolds

The longing that Fours experience in their adapted state is a perpetual focus on what's missing, a thirst that is never quenched. When their environment reveals what's presently missing, Fours will withdraw in an attempt to chase down the longing. For most Fours, this is a complicated experience, for the longing they experience has a certain attraction and repulsion.[6] They are simultaneously captivated and offended by it.

This leads to an unhealthy dependency on the experience of longing. Left unchecked, the longing becomes an end unto itself, rather than an invitation to reflectively listen to want and desire. When Fours retreat into their own shadow world, they develop an attachment to the emotional experience that prevents them from fully living in the present. The push/pull nature others experience when in relationship with Fours is thus a reflection of what's occurring within. This is enhanced by the phenomenon of _introjection_, an unconscious adoption of the ideas or attitudes of others. Fours succumb to introjection in a particularly unfortunate way. When unhealthy, their capacity for empathy shrinks. They assume that the void and the lack of belonging is really within. Ginger Lapid-Bogda describes this as "fully absorbing and internalizing negative information about themselves without discerning if the data is accurate."[7] This is the temptation of the Type Four: to internalize perceived negativity.

This is the challenge of the Four's emotional world. While they have a distinct ability to wade into the depths, they can easily remain there at their own detriment. The introjection hijacks external negativity and finds ample room within, resulting in unhealthy patterns and cycles of shame. This ramps up the Four's longing and further distances themselves from engaging the present.

Left unchecked, Fours can become embroiled in a drama that never unfolds, a life lived one climactic scene to the next, while the overarching narrative never advances. Darkness becomes more comfortable than light. It's thus understandable why Fours are drawn to experiences of melancholy, the sweet but unquenchable longing for what could be. Introjection convinces the Four that the sweetness of melancholy is all there is. Inclusion and satisfaction are seemingly unattainable to the unhealthy Four, for they believe that they are the ones who are missing, lacking, and deficient. The stagnant drama festers an envy that comes from a comparison trap: Unhealthy Fours view others in a more positive light than they view themselves.

The challenge for Type Fours on the Way of Discernment is to engage the drama of life with equanimity, a calm and composed state that doesn't require the roller coasters of life to feel alive. The unfolding nature of life is inherently dramatic, full of intensity, surprise, and emotion. Fours must be careful in absorbing that which is missing in their world, and viewing it as their own void. Wise decision-making requires the ability to see what is missing, and then fully show up to the present and engage any lack with clarity of identity, purpose, and practice.

Type Fours Engage:

Where in your life do you feel stuck in a drama that won't seem to end?

When do you tend to absorb the negativity of the surrounding world?

Vocation – Identity, Purpose, Direction

Type Fours struggle with viewing vocation as a sufficient call to action. To borrow from a parable of Jesus in the New Testament, Fours may receive the extraordinary gift of calling and "hide it under a bushel," (a bowl or basket), rather than let light shine throughout their world.[8] Receiving the gift and committing to the practice of vocation are intertwined and interdependent. The Fours' inward focus can be helpful in receiving the gift, but Fours must be careful that their inward focus doesn't come at the expense of outward practice.

Vocation also compels the Type Four to engage their tendency to self-scrutinize. Hearing the Divine Voice of love allows them to confront self-loathing. Shame dissolves in the face of love. If Fours' enter into activities of self-scrutiny, they have little energy left for discernment from a place of authenticity.

This disconnect between gift and practice is enhanced by the Four's tendency to operate in their world from a perspective that people don't understand them and therefore don't know them. This is why many Fours play to their uniqueness as a doubling down on their perceived difference. And all the while the voice of introjection can drown out the Divine Voice. The *Imago Dei* is a redemptive rebuttal to introjection, for if we are created in the Divine Image, we are understood and known from a place of goodness and wholeness. Internalized negativity is drowned out by the Voice of God.

The Way of Discernment for Type Fours begins with returning to an authentic identity which believes that they inherently belong for who they are. The Divine Voice is calling Fours to the ultimate place of belonging: love. When Fours acknowledge their inclusion, they can embrace their authentic being. Here the Four shows up fully in their world, for they no longer have to *do* authenticity (cultivate a unique persona) because they *are* authentic.

Type Fours Engage:

How do you let your perception of difference thwart your activity?

Who am I?–Identity for Type Four

The Way of Discernment Identity Statement for Type Four is:

> *"I am made in the Divine Image, and in the Divine Image there is no shame of being unknown or excluded. My belonging and significance is in who I am, not simply what I uniquely express."*

To live from this place of identity requires the Type Four to align longing with the truth of inherent belonging. Longing and belonging are linguistically similar, deriving from the same root. And, the only difference between belonging and longing is "be."[9] Longing conveys desire. Belonging conveys affinity. Longing is directed toward that which is beyond our grasp. Belonging is experienced in that which is in our midst. In the call of the Divine, shame is brought into the light and exposed for the lie that it is. Belonging counters inner scrutiny and perceived difference. When discerning, Fours must engage the question *Who am I?* This is the very question that cultivates their empathy from an authentic place of belonging.

First, Fours must become more aware of their Fourness. The Four's tendencies to withdraw, disengage, and introject lead toward inaction that keeps them stuck and can thwart discernment. Type Fours must acknowledge the persistent longing in order to begin the journey toward belonging. Their over-reliance on their uniqueness in comparison to others is a proactive defense against exclusion.

Second, Fours must acknowledge the Divine Voice that calls them beloved. That which is created and unique comes from a source. Fours can be so consumed with the tension of belonging and longing that they lose sight of the Divine Source of all belonging. From this source, our differences and unique expressions are not proof of our separation from others, but show the beautiful diversity in creation. You do belong. By showing up to the *Imago Dei* within, Fours are better able to reconcile their uniqueness and belonging.

Third, Fours must relinquish the adapted self. Fours, in their adapted state, can overplay uniqueness as a way to engage their longing. Here we encounter the difference between longing and letting go.[10] Longing is a refusal to let go of what might have been or what could be. In this way, the adapted Four is a fantasy self. Relinquishing this adapted self is terrifying, for it ramps up the shame that whispers that they are ordinary at best, inferior at worst. Relinquishing confronts the Fours introjection and opens them up to their authentic identity. Here the Four must practically and physically learn to listen to their longings to gauge whether their responses are from an adapted or authentic place.

Fourth, Fours must live from authentic self with humility. For Type Fours, humility from authenticity requires a relaxing of sensitivity toward being misunderstood. Left unchecked, the growing perception of being misunderstood can foster aloofness. True humility engages others with the Four's natural capacity for empathy rather than envy, which embraces the presence of uniqueness and common ground. Humility holds difference and belonging in tension. Here the Four can raise their awareness of how their body communicates this sensitivity (and needs to engage in relaxation).

Fifth, Fours must befriend themselves. For the Type Four, befriending the self means stopping cycles of self-frustrating. When Fours become entrenched in their longing, their attraction to melancholy becomes an imitation of self-care. In this way, they trade self-care for a form of frustrating self-indulgence. Self-care is a willingness to be happy and pursue joy, which is an affront to the Four's tendency to remain in the shadows, stuck in cycles of darkness as a defense against the fear of being happy.[11]

Sixth, Fours must live from authentic self with agency. From authentic identity, a Type Four's energy is redirected toward activity. From an inherent place of belonging, agency is activated. This authentic agency can reverse what Sandra Maitri calls the Four's tendency toward the "extinguishing of gratitude."[12] Instead, they live purposely from the generative gratitude of their inherent belonging and significance.

Seventh, Fours must intentionally continue to do all of the above.
The Type Four patterns of longing and withdrawing are well-established. Fours must be intentional and even vigilant in reclaiming their sense of belonging. With belonging and significance within, Fours can put the ego in its proper place, and flourish.

Why am I here?

From inherent belonging and significance, a Four's purpose in life clarifies, fostering a concern about the belonging and significance of others. Their introjection wanes, and makes way for them to be fully present in their world. The Four's adapted self seeks to remain in the shadows of life in a fixation on suffering. The Four's authentic self emerges to engage others as they work through their own shadows. Here the Type Four can channel their empathy toward flourishing to help others work through their suffering.

When Fours recognize the *Imago Dei* within, they live with purpose. In seasons of discernment, Fours can ask *Why am I here?* to remind them of their self-giving belonging, significance and empathy.

Where am I going?

Fathoming the depths of the Type Four's direction comes naturally. The Four's challenge lies in fathoming from a place of presence, not withdrawal. The tendency to retreat to their inner sanctum replaces the essence of fathoming: to measure the true depth of where you are in the world. This requires the Four to align their body, heart, and mind to the present to set a healthy trajectory.

When Fours fathom and engage their Gut Center, they can animate their presence in the world. They can show up fully in a world in which longing doesn't hold such power. Rather, the longing can become an embrace of the lack, freedom from the tyranny of what was or what could be. Their intuition is engaged, and their energy is focused toward action. They can use their ability to navigate the depths of their emotional world, and cultivate a beautiful and beloved community. To fathom this way, Fours should rest in solitude[13] to quell the persistent longing.

In this way, rest and solitude transform the compulsion to withdraw and craft an authenticity. The image crafting gives way to a more authentic being.

Wisdom – Doing, Feeling, Thinking

In Chapters Three and Four we considered the Triads and Stances of the enneagram and how they employ the three centers of intelligence: doing, feeling, and thinking. Fours lead with feeling intelligence in their Heart Center, supported by thinking intelligence in their Head Center, but distort or misuse doing intelligence in their Gut Center. This leads to an overreliance on feelings and thinking.

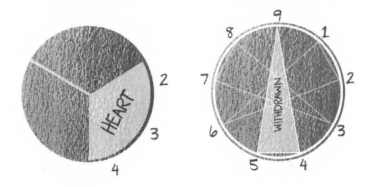

What am I doing?

Fours are keenly aware and interested in the depth and significance of their world, so it makes sense that they can struggle to see worth in the practical and mundane. Yet, most of our doing is engaging in practical and mundane matters. This affects Fours' motivation to do the routine. To ask *What am I doing?* helps Fours reflect upon their activity, or inactivity, to assess whether they are sufficiently showing up in their world. This helps Fours develop a check on their inaction, which often comes from a belief that they don't feel they can affect their environment.[14]

A much healthier approach for Type Fours is to activate their presence in the world by bringing their emotional depth with them and seeing it as a resource for their activity. This busts Fours' myth that they must work through their emotions before they can act. *What am I doing?* confronts this false dichotomy, and fosters healthy rhythms and alignment of doing intelligence with feeling and thinking.

Type Fours Engage:

What conditions typically need to be met before you act on something?

_____

In what settings do you feel the most resistance to act?

_____

What am I feeling?

Of all nine questions in The Way of Discernment, this is often the Type Four's favorite. Of all nine enneagram types, Type Fours are most aware of their emotional state.[15] Fours feel intensely. Many Fours describe their emotional state as feeling everything and yet also nothing. One Four I know, in a recent conversation, expressed, "When I want to feel sad, I listen to sad music, read dark poetry, etc." multiple times. The Type Four is not afraid of the emotional world, even when it leads to darker emotions.

When Fours ask the question *What am I feeling?* in The Way of Discernment, they must come to terms with their experiences of longing for what's missing, often that which they cannot name. Discernment raises this question in hopes of working through, rather than getting stuck in, the emotional space. This fosters a wise listening of the Four's longing, rather than a more compulsive submission to it.

For Fours to discern with wisdom, they must be aware of their attraction to experiences of melancholy. Their willingness to engage and explore their shadows is tremendously helpful in discernment. However, their comfortability in making a home there can be dangerous. For the Four, courage is evident when they are willing to leave the confines of their shadow world and step into the light of the here and now. Only then can the Four *integrate* dark and light.

What am I thinking?

Type Fours are prone to use thinking intelligence to analyze their feelings. This feeling-thinking combo fuels their tendency to withdraw, for analyzing the depths of the emotional world takes significant time and energy.

When a Four explores *What am I thinking?*, they assess the objectivity of the present use of their thinking intelligence. Fours have high capacities to employ their thinking toward what might have been and what would be. Riso and Hudson refer this to compulsion as "fantasizing."[16]

This causes Fours to struggle with objectivity. Their thinking is so closely tied with their feelings that sound judgment can be clouded. Left unchecked, a Four's thinking intelligence can be used to habitually intensify feelings.[17]

The Way of Discernment for Type Four is to disentangle their thinking from feelings in order to develop healthier, more objective rhythms of thinking intelligence. It's an invitation to the integration of thinking and feeling, as opposed to a form of enmeshment. From this integration, doing intelligence can be employed to enable the Type Four to engage with an active, grounded presence.

Practice in Time

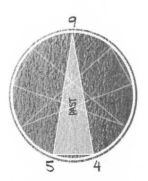

Type Four is a member of the Withdrawn Stance (See Chapter Three) along with Types Five and Nine. Withdrawn Types have a preferred past perspective on time, supported by a future perspective on time, while tending to neglect the present. This is evidenced by Fours willingness to withdraw to work through their feelings, longing for what was (past) or what could be (future). Both are compulsive reactions to longing, and a defense against engaging the present. Type Fours can translate the felt experience of something missing as a form of abandonment. This means that the searching for what is missing is more pressing than just about anything else in the present. Through practice, the Type Four can listen more attentively and objectively to the longing, in order to consider how to embrace the here and now (even when it lacks.)

This past orientation is supported by a tendency to circumvent the present to look into the future. In this way, the longing of a Type Four seems like an infinite line, extending into the past and future simultaneously. A nostalgic past and an idyllic future are comfortable ways to avoid engaging the present. Type Fours can cling to past events they believe were extraordinary, significant, or safe. They can also struggle to move on from past hurts. Fours also dream of fantastical futures rich in meaning, marked by belonging, free of shame. They are also just as able to imagine future scenarios marked by lack. The Four's ability to look back and ahead is sophisticated and complex.

Fours struggle the most to be fully present. In a way, showing up fully is a confession of belonging. One's presence is evidence of their perceived acceptance, that they are known and understood enough to feel safe and contribute. This is why Fours question whether or not they can truly affect their present environment. It's not so much a question of power, but membership.

To show up fully as one's true self in the here and now is a vulnerable and courageous act, one that Fours must engage to discern well. The temptation to look back or ahead is strong and often consuming. Intention and attention in the present helps Fours see the ways in which they belong, matter, and have power to engage the here and now.

What am I remembering? (Past)

The egoic patterns of the Type Four are dominated by a past perspective, so much so that Fours often fail to consider *What am I remembering?* Like a fish describing water, it may be difficult for a Four to reflect on this question. While it's accurate to say that Fours are prone to look to their past, it is also accurate to describe Type Fours as often being stuck in the past. This is especially true of painful past experiences. Fours can over-identify with past sufferings.[18] When unhealthy, Fours "may replace old hurts and disappointing experiences over and over again..."[19] How have these past experiences shaped who I am in the present? Am I clinging to things I should be letting go? How can my past sufferings cultivate empathy and love for those around me?

What am I experiencing? (Present)

If the Four's past is compulsive, the present can be overwhelming. If longing cannot be satisfied in the present, a Four can be quick to retreat. If being present is experiencing pain that is residual from the past, this is understandable. But from an authentic place of identity, a Four can honestly assess their experience, whether it be painful, exhilarating, boring, or extraordinary, and show up in their environment with agency and purpose. In this way, Fours can access their natural abilities of illumination and clarity. They can experience their present world with a depth and sight that discerns well.

To do so, the Type Four must experience the present not just in their Heart Center, but also in their bodies. By aligning their physical experience, their emotional experience, and their mental experience from identity and with wisdom, Fours can more keenly assess their present experience. At times, the present is marked with a noticeable lack, a missing piece of the puzzle. Often the missing piece is you. Belonging and significance are sometimes actualized by showing up and engaging as a leap of faith. Here longing actually can be a nudge to be present here and now.

Type Fours Engage:

What's your initial response to being fully present in an unknown situation?

How do you typically respond to situations in which you aren't sure you belong or fit in?

_____

What am I anticipating? (Future)

When Fours consider their anticipation, they often can describe vivid narratives of what might or could be. It is here that the Fours' fantasizing tendencies tend to animate, imagining negative scenarios marked by lack (or even shrouded in darkness). Fours also develop ideal futures that help them escape from the present. The Way of Discernment invites the Four into a future grounded in reality, in which the past informs and the present activates. *What am I anticipating?* weaves the future together with the present in ways that minimize both extremes.

Discernment

Fours' abilities to see textures of life are a profound gift to discernment. Their appreciation for depth, beauty, and meaning are powerful resources. Their capacity for empathy gives them a unique ability to hold and steward others' pain. But these gifts are hindered when Fours experience shame as what they perceive they lack. Their sensitivity to difference and distance can isolate, further diminishing wisdom. When Fours cater to their perpetual longing, they can lose sight of who they are and *whose* they are. They can double-down on difference, discarding connection. Tragically, this can result in self-selecting out of groups, pre-determining that they don't belong. To discern well, Fours must be intentional with the following:

- Identity Over Insufficiency. The Type Four in an adapted state of persona is characterized by deficiency. It's what fuels the longing. The Type Four in an authentic state of identity is characterized by sufficiency. It's what eradicates shame and allows Fours to see their inherent belonging and significance. Make the identity statement for Type Four a mantra: "I am made in the Divine Image, and in the Divine Image there is no shame of scrutiny or lack. My belonging and significance are in who I am, not simply what I uniquely express."

- <u>Wise Body</u>. By intentionally engaging doing intelligence, Fours listen to their intuition to be actively engaged in their world. Living from Wise Body grounds Fours' feeling and thinking in their body rather than fantasizing in the past or future. In the Way of Discernment, the Four's feeling, thinking, and doing are integrated and aligned to engage the present with the many gifts they have to offer.

- <u>Sacred Presence</u>. Fours must practice Sacred Presence (Chapter Three) in order to discern their lives well. To show up fully is a bold admission that you belong and are significant. It acknowledges the role that the Four plays in satisfying the longing ever-present in our world.

Exercises for the Type Four Within

- <u>Consolations and Desolations</u>. In the Ignatian tradition (a stream of Catholicism) consolations and desolations are practices that cultivate deeper listening to the Divine. Consolations are those things that orient us toward God. Desolations are those things that orient us away from God.[20] Find helpful guides on this ancient practice from the Loyola Press website: www.loyola-press.com. Categorizing our life experiences in this way helps us more objectively discern our lives in light of the good and bad. Contemplatively spend a day or two in this framework. Next, take another two to three days considering the interplay of your consolations and desolations. How do your consolations and desolations each (or together) help you embrace lack (longing) and practice gratitude (belonging)? How do dark and light invite and teach?

- <u>Practice Gratitude</u>. Gratitude enhances a sense of belonging, for we develop connections to that which we are grateful. Take a week and commit to verbally giving thanks for anything worthy of it. Your gratitude should extend from the smallest of joys to the most extraordinary. If possible, keep a journal with you to document all that you are grateful for.

- <u>Incremental Habits</u>. The struggle to be fully present and employ doing intelligence poses a sometimes overwhelming challenge for Fours. Pick one or two habits that would increase your doing intelligence. Employ what James Clear refers to as the Atomic Habits technique,[21] incrementally increasing your doing in these one or two habits by 1% every day or two. Small wins will snowball into more complete action.

- <u>Invert the Understanding Gap</u>. Fours fall victim to the myth that others simply don't understand them and therefore can't really know them. This kicks the door open for introjection. Instead of focusing on other's lack of understanding, consider your own lack of understanding in a way that cultivates curiosity. Commit to two or three conversations with people which begin with you acknowledging, "I don't fully understand where they are coming from. How can I learn more?" This will foster the inherent empathy within you, and reveal how curiosity and connection can develop your own sense of belonging.

Questions for the Type Four Within

- Is this thing I'm doing now the thing I really should be doing?
- What emotions are warranted for this situation?
- What's mine to long for?
- How can my deep emotional wells be employed toward empathy for others?

Notes

[1]Chestnut, *The Complete Enneagram*, p. 268.

[2]Seth attributes this idea to enneagram teacher Leslie Hershberger.

[3]Thanks to my friend and Type Four K. J. Ramsey for this depiction.

[4]Daniels & Price, *The Essential Enneagram*, p. 33.

[5]Schafer, *Roaming Free Inside the Cage*, p. 106.

[6]Ibid, p. 104.

[7]Lapid-Bogda, *The Art of Typing*, p. 14.

[8]See Matthew 5:15 in the New Testament.

[9]Thanks to my buddy Seth Creekmore, who leads with Type Four, for this gem.

[10]Carolyn Bartlett, *The Enneagram Field Guide: Notes on Using the Enneagram in Counseling, Therapy, and Personal Growth* (Fort Collins: Nine Gates Publishing, 2003), p. 72.

[11]Chestnut, *The Complete Enneagram*, p. 280.

[12]Maitri, *The Enneagram of Passions of Virtues*, p. 141.

[13]Heuertz, *The Sacred Enneagram*.

[14]Hurley & Donson, *Discover Your Soul Potential*, p. 92.

[15]Riso and Hudson, *Discover your Personality Type*.

[16]This is Riso and Hudson's term for the mental fixation of Type Fours.

[17]Suzanne Stabile introduced this idea to in her compact disc recordings entitled *Enneagram and Discernment* (Dallas: Life in the Trinity Ministry).

[18]Calhoun, Calhoun, Loughrige, & Loughrige, *Spiritual Rhythms for the Enneagram*, p. 114.

[19]Chestnut, *The Complete Enneagram*, p. 276.

[20]You can find a good introduction to the Ignatian concept of con-

solation and desolation here: https://www.loyolapress.com/our-cath-olic-faith/ignatian-spirituality/discernment/discernment-consola-tion-and-desolation.

[21]Learn more about atomic habits from James Clear's website: https://jamesclear.com/atomic-habits.

CHAPTER 11

Type Five: "The Investigator"

*"It's not that I'm so smart, it's just that
I stay with problems longer."*
—Albert Einstein

Fives want competency but settle for knowledge.

Type Fives are often labeled as "investigators." While this describes some common expressions of Fives, it doesn't capture what Fives are truly after. Fives, at their core, want competency and sufficiency. They want to be capable, and they want the world to be marked by sufficiency of understanding. But when confronted with a world that doesn't always makes sense, or in which they don't feel prepared, it feels threatening. They can see need for competency everywhere, and they see it most prominently

within themselves. This leads Type Fives to feel anxious about life, and that stress manifests as a particular type of fear: being useless and empty. Because of their sensitivity to competency, this fear of scarcity takes on a more subtle and acceptable version: depth of knowledge and insatiable curiosity about complex things. In order to keep the need for competency in check, Type Fives settle for the knowledge they acquire in their world: deep dives on complex topics, ideas, or hobbies. This results in Fives' allergies to superficiality, small-talk, and high-energy social engagement. This pursuit of knowledge can cause Fives to withdraw to their safe places to study or tinker, which can further isolate and feed their fear of being useless or incompetent.

The Way of Discernment for the Type Five is to recognize their dominant emotion, fear, in order to fully engage their world. The fear that Fives carry impedes wise decision-making. When Fives intentionally discover a place of inherent competency and sufficiency, vocation, wisdom, and practice align for discernment.

In decision-making, Type Fives perceive the options before them in their Head Center, and fear of incompetency and depletion often compels them to withdraw and isolate. For Fives both fears feel like failures. Withdrawal and isolation preserve the knowledge Fives have, and preserve their energy to collect and gain more knowledge. The acquisition of knowledge is the Five's chief strategy to stave off fear.

This is why Fives tend to withdraw from social spaces as a way to maintain firm boundaries and sufficient distance from others. Relational interactions can pose a threat to Fives' competency and energy levels, so they deem it preferable to limit interactions to instances that allow them to provide reason and perspective (or receive them). In social environments, you'll often find Fives on the periphery, as if they have one foot in the room and the other out the door. This can be interpreted by others as arrogance or aloofness, which isn't accurate. Fives' seemingly stoic approach to others can mask their capacities for humility, generosity, and connectivity. In times of conflict, Fives work very hard to push feelings aside to remain analytical, objective, and level-headed. They value objectivity and rationality in conflict above all else. And often, their ability to think their way through conflict is effective. It's also effective at protecting and managing their inner resources.[1]

Strength – Deep Calls to Deep

In seasons of discernment, Fives should trust in their many skills of focus, research, and analysis. These can be used effectively to work through the fear that can otherwise paralyze a Type Five when making a decision. Type Fives are calm, perceptive, and curious. They can maintain a simplicity of focus on one thing and sustain that focus with depth and time. Fives are highly cerebral and thorough in their approach to whatever they are committed.

Fives have a unique capacity to explore the depths of any topic or project. They embody the poetic description in Psalm 42:7 of the Hebrew Bible: "Deep calls to deep in the roar of your waterfalls." When the surrounding noise is overwhelming, Fives have the ability to find the depths. This is a way of knowing that Fives seem to uniquely possess. Whether it be a hobby, a current event, or a work project, Type Fives can engage with an intense focus and a level of depth that provides tremendous insight and perspective.

When discerning, focus and depth are valuable. In fact, they are necessary. Type Fives can approach life with a Spartan-like simplicity. They move through life in a self-contained, primitive manner. Their focus and energy are directed at what matters most to them.

Fives are not swayed by the whims of the surrounding culture or environment. They value privacy and space, and are willing to set and maintain boundaries. Their non-conformity can be helpful in preserving a sense of integrity that guides wise decision-making. Contrary to simplistic takes about Fives' stinginess, they are very giving and engaged. They simply want to know what the expenditure of their time and energy will be before they engage.[2] They only commit to what they truly believe is worth their time. A Five's inner circle tends to be small.

But for those in the inner circle, they are fully engaged with their intensity and focus.

Important decisions require sufficient time and energy. Fives have no problem spending both. This allows Fives to consider and study something fully before rushing to a decision. Important matters require sufficient information. Like the Type Nine, they will not be rushed or hurried when making a decision. Fives are willing to wait until they have enough information to make a wise decision. Consider this description by Riso and Hudson: "Fives will stay with a problem or a question that fascinates them until it is solved, or until they discover that it is unsolvable. Boredom is unimaginable to them because there are so many fascinating things to explore, understand, and imagine."[3] When healthy, Fives commit to decisions from a depth beneath rationality. They become more comfortable with the unknown nature of some things, and trust intuition.

In seasons of discernment, Fives are not swayed by the tyranny of the urgent or the whims of those around them. A healthy, engaged Five is a wise soul, with an immense capacity to explore the depth of a situation, with an intense focus and a sustaining energy.

Type Fives Engage:

What's a recent project or interest that captivated your focus and attention for a sustained period of time?

_____

When have your research and analysis skills helped you make a wise decision?

_____

Challenge – Nested in a Jail of Information

The knowledge acquisition that Fives energetically pursue can eventually lead to what is described by the law of diminishing returns.[4] More information is helpful to a point. Beyond this point, it can be detrimental and foster a perpetual state of deficiency. Fives' fear of depletion and incompetency develops some unhealthy patterns of withdrawal, isolation, scarcity, and a lack of engagement.

The Type Five's fear can activate a withdrawal from the present environment. They become fearful that their energy will be depleted, and their knowledge will likewise run out. This is why Fives often are perceived as private and distant, and at times, socially awkward. Even when Fives do engage their world relationally, they often present themselves as detached. This is in order to provide perspective from a more objective (read: safe) place. This detachment is its own compulsion, a clinging to a sense of boundaries and safety. The buffer becomes essential.

While Fives engage a withdrawn posture like Fours and Nines, the Five's withdrawal can be more persistent and safeguarded. Fives suffer from a tendency to not only withdraw, but isolate. A Five's isolation can be self-perpetuating to the point of not believing that you are an individual, but in fact an *isolated* individual.[5] Isolation thus becomes part of the Five's adapted identity. This fosters an emotional isolation in addition to the physical. Fives tend to compartmentalize their emotions from their thoughts, because they view emotions as potential threats of depletion.

Over time, the cycles of withdrawal and isolation can foster a misguided belief that no provisions can come from the outside. The Five thus looks within for the necessary resources for survival, through a lens of scarcity. They tend to buy into a false dichotomy: They must either conceal themselves and give nothing away or open themselves and offer everything.[6] Maintaining the little that they have left becomes a preferable option. This is what is driving the "greed" and "avarice" that many enneagram teachers ascribe to the Type Five. They are not greedy for money or possessions, but of their time and energy. Type Fives react to their fear through "a defensive expectation of impoverishment."[7] Naranjo, who writes at length of the Five's avarice, refers to it as a compulsive "holding back and holding in."[8]

The Five's withdrawal, isolation, and scarcity mindset results in a perpetual and practical challenge, their thirst for learning can occur in a vacuum, void of engagement. Type Fives have learned to live so simply that they can remain too long in their vacuum. For as long as they are learning, they don't need much to survive. But information without places of application (such as problem-solving, teaching, or sharing) can lead to an analysis paralysis, an overindulgence in data to the point of being overwhelmed. The distance they've established between themselves and others becomes its own comfort, for they easily can adopt a role of observer rather than participant.[9]

This is the persistent impediment for Type Fives' discernment: They become comfortable in a jail of their own information. When they become too detached, too distant, too comfortable in their isolation, they over identify with their knowledge and intelligence. If you recall, Nines are known as the merging types. They tend to merge with others and the external environment. Fives suffer a merging of their own sort—a merging with an idea or concept.[10] Fives must be careful not to lose themselves in their ideas. Good discernment doesn't happen in isolation. It is refined, animated, and tested in community. Wise decision-making requires engagement in the world, applied thinking, and the insight of others.

Type Fives Engage:

When in your life have you researched and studied something and struggled to act?

_____

What type of situation causes you to withdraw from others?

_____

Vocation – Identity, Purpose, Direction

In Chapter Two, we explored that vocation is both a gift and a practice. This requires shifts from receiving the gift to engaging the practice. Type Fives struggle with this shift, as practice requires application, often before one is proficient or competent. Fives are hesitant to practice, for it stokes their fears of depletion.

Fives may very well have received, pondered, and studied the gift, but struggle to implement their knowledge. This is the Five's tragic irony: They have immense capacity for discernment, and yet when not applied, their discernment is left on the shelf. Receiving the gift and committing to the practice of vocation are both essential.

Hearing the call of the Divine also compels Fives to consider the role that ideas play in their discernment. Are they a means to an end, or an end in and of themselves? Fives' tendencies to dive deeply into something are valuable and helpful, to a point. When they get to the point of being lost in their own ideas, they are not discerning from an authentic place of identity, purpose, and direction. They are simply nurturing their own isolation with ideas.

The Way of Discernment for Type Fives begins with believing that they've received a Divine Gift, reflected in the *Imago Dei*, which provides them the competency and energy needed to live their lives. God's call is inherently wise and invigorating. When Fives discover this, they can embrace their authentic place in the world and show up fully.

Type Fives Engage:

What's your response to *practicing* your calling?

Who am I?—Identity for Type Five

The Way of Discernment Identity Statement for Type Five is:

"I am made in the Divine Image, and in the Divine Image there is no fear of incompetency or depletion. My competency and viability are inner renewable resources to be shared with others."

For a Five to live from this place of authentic identity requires an integration of knowledge and information with their inherent competency and sustainability. When this occurs, Fives live with a sense of generativity as opposed to finitude. Knowledge and information should be an energetic extension of authentic identity. When discerning, Fives must engage the question *Who am I?* by relaxing their firm boundaries that not only buffer the Five from others, but from their true selves in the Divine Image.

First, Fives must become more aware of their Fiveness. When Fives become more aware of their tendencies to withdraw and protect their reserves, they can begin to see how their retentiveness hinders their discernment. They can then consider how their capacities for study, analysis, and insight can be applied. Type Fives must acknowledge their tendency toward isolated knowledge acquisition to begin their journey back to their true selves. Then they can see how to integrate their learning with living.

Second, Fives must acknowledge the Divine Voice that calls them beloved. In reality, the move from withdrawal to isolation is a myth. For we are never truly alone. The Divine Voice calls, even in our isolation. For a Five to acknowledge this Voice is to acknowledge the Five's false sense of their own autonomy and self-sufficiency. Hearing the voice welcomes an invitation into the interdependency of the Five and the Divine.

Third, Fives must relinquish the adapted self. In their adapted state, Fives over-rely on their knowledge and intellect to assuage their fear of depletion and incompetency. By preserving and maintaining their knowledge, and their ability to acquire more, they have developed patterns of energetic withholding. Relinquishing the adapted self requires relaxing this more forceful withholding, what Beatrice Chestnut refers to as "a fearful grasping of time, space, and energy, motivated by an underlying, unconscious fantasy that letting go would result in catastrophic depletion."[11] This relaxing counters the Five's isolationist disposition, emboldening them to bring their full selves into their world.

Fourth, Fives must live from authentic self with humility. Many enneagram resources begin the Type Five path to humility with an encouragement for Fives to admit what they don't know. This isn't very helpful, as most of the Five's egoic patterns already reveal a fear of not knowing. Rather than giving into their fears, it is healthier for Type Fives to explore the humility that is required in interdependency. Fives have developed ways of living within the illusion that they don't need others. Authentic humility opens us to others.

Fifth, Fives must befriend themselves. For Fives, befriending the self begins with a defined self that transcends ideas. Self-care is caring more for the self than the idea. This may result in setting aside an idea to socially engage, exercise, or even sleep. Self-care is an acknowledgement that one is not defined by their ideas, which avoids unhealthy merging with ideas or projects.

Sixth, Fives must live from authentic self with agency. From an authentic place of identity, Type Fives relax their energetic withholding and realize that there is more in the tank. They can live with a grounded sense of competency and sustainability that encourages them to offer more than ideas to their world, but also action. Fives can connect their ideas to the needs of their environment in profound ways.

Seventh, Fives must intentionally continue to do all of the above. The patterns of holding back and holding in are habitual for Type Fives. Fives must pay attention to their responses to fear of depletion and intentionally practice their inherent sustainability and competency. When they do, Fives integrate their ego and flourish.

Why am I here?–Purpose for Type Five

From an authentic place of identity, the Type Five can redirect their gifts of research, analysis, and deep thought toward a purpose that transcends their own defenses. Their energies can shift from an adapted state of preservation and retention to an authentic state of empowering others with wisdom. Rather than merging with their ideas, they fully emerge in their world to help others live their lives with wisdom and intellect. Here the Type Five can employ their intelligence toward flourishing.

When Fives live from the *Imago Dei* within, they find the energy to live with purpose. In seasons of discernment, Fives can ask *Why am I here?* to remind them of their self-giving competency and sustainability.

Where am I going?–Direction for Type Five

Exploring the depths of anything comes easily for Fives. Their challenge lies in fathoming the depths of the here and now, and not waiting to do so when they are in isolation. Fives struggle to believe they have the energy to consider the depths of the here and now. This requires the Type Five to align their body, their heart, and their mind to the present to set healthy trajectories of direction.

When Fives fathom and engage their Gut Center, they can rediscover their sustainable and competent selves in the world. They can be fully present in a world that doesn't threaten their reserves of energy, a world in which others can energize, not simply deplete. Their knowledge and insight is engaged toward action and problem solving. They can pair intuition and action with their deep study. To fathom, Fives should consent to silence, an intentional quieting of the mind in order to listen.[12] In this way, stillness confronts the withdrawing compulsion to a silent environment in order to let the mind race. Consenting to silence cultivates a listening beneath all the thinking where a Five can hear the Divine Voice of abundance, generativity, and wisdom.

Wisdom – Doing, Feeling, Thinking

In Chapters Three and Four, we explored the Triads and the Stances of the enneagram and how they employ the three centers of intelligence: doing, feeling, and thinking. Fives lead with thinking intelligence in their Head Center, supported by Feeling intelligence in their Heart Center, but distort or misuse doing intelligence in their Gut Center. This leads to an over identification with thinking at the expense of action.

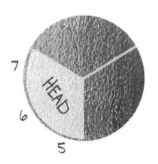 

What am I doing?

Fives' activity is often connected with ideas. Their actions are typically intertwined with their ability to research, study, analyze, etc. The Fives' adaptive state emphasizes attaining and owning knowledge rather than applying and utilizing it.[13] This poses a significant challenge: considering thinking activity as a suitable substitute for more active doing. When Fives invest themselves in something, it's understandably in what is most interesting to them, even if it's at the expense of others. To ask *What am I doing?* helps Fives address their tendency to view action separate from interaction.[14] Fives can be mindful of the temptation to view thinking in isolation as sufficient action.

A healthier approach for Type Fives is to find intentional ways to integrate their thinking and feeling toward application. Asking *What am I doing?* confronts this compartmentalization, and helps Fives consider if their activity is sufficient (or avoidant) for the moment.

Type Fives Engage:

What typically prompts you to act or interact?

_____

What types of settings are challenging for you to engage?

_____

What am I feeling?

The Type Five has a suspicious and cautious relationship with feelings. Therefore, this question is particularly challenging for them in the Way of Discernment. They've developed patterns of automatically and unconsciously detaching from emotions.[15] This preserves the integrity of their objectivity and analysis.

This is why to the outsider, Fives appear outwardly stoic. In reality, they are quite sensitive. Their layers of protection hide a deep inner world that isn't just a rich thought life, but also a rich emotional life. The primary emotional challenge for Fives is this: the fear that their inner sensitivity, when unleashed, will deplete them. Sometimes they will repress their need for relationships, keeping others at a "safe" distance. But, our feelings always need places of expression, particularly relational expression.

Ironically, the Five's efforts to detach and disentangle emotions from thinking can end up backfiring. Fives' over-identification with thoughts and ideas can become possessive.[16] This possessiveness can result in a merging with ideas. As Fives lose themselves in their ideas, they can begin to attach feelings to them: protection, desire, control, craving, etc.

The Way of Discernment poses the question, *What am I feeling?* to help Fives integrate their feelings with their thinking in relationship with others (not simply in isolation). This question helps Type Fives engage their holding back and holding in, and helps them see how their attempts at preservation inhibit their relationship and activity.

What am I thinking?

This is typically the Five's favorite question to answer. Their skills at analysis, study, research, and depth of thought are pronounced. Asking this question of a Five could result in a lengthy and detailed response. Or, it could shut the conversation down, for the Five simply doesn't have the time or energy to go there. For a Five to consider this question within the Way of Discernment is an invitation to integrate their thinking to cultivate holistic wisdom.

When a Five authentically considers *What am I thinking?* they evaluate the health of their withdrawing patters to think. As this is often a response to their fear of depletion and incompetency, this question can open up new ways of thinking beyond dispassionate cognition.

While it may be most comfortable for Fives to get alone and think, The Way of Discernment provides new pathways and venues of thinking. Wise thinking is integrated with feeling and doing, and derives from authentic identity and purpose. Fives can cultivate their thinking skills in relational spaces in ways that activate and animate their lives, not just preserve it.

Practice in Time

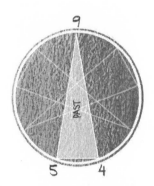

Type Five is a member of the Withdrawn Stance (see Chapter Three) along with Types Four and Nine. The Withdrawn Stance has a preferred past perspective on time, supported by a future perspective, while neglecting the present. The pull on Type Five to withdraw and isolate reveals much about how Fives view time as a precious and finite resource. Fives withdraw to preserve energy and maintain sufficient space to study. This holding back and holding in is a bracing of sorts, a compulsive response to fear of incompetency and depletion. Maintaining what's left, what's been acquired and gathered (notice the past tense in both), is more important than burning through it in the present.

This past orientation is supported by a tendency to bypass the present to scan the future horizon. Intrusions or threats on competency and depletion are everywhere, and Fives are vigilant in their protection of time, energy, and ideas. The future is often ominous for Fives. This results in a push/pull experience in the life of a Five. They often experience a magnetism to retreat or withdraw from their present environment. The past provides its own comfort, so the pull to return to it is strong. And yet Fives also experience an invisible nudge to consider their futures. The fear of depletion and incompetency is likewise strong, pushing Fives out of their havens to see what's ahead. The Five's ability to look back and look ahead is a sophisticated rhythm that protects their thinking.

The Five's greatest struggle is to be fully present. When we understand the powerful fear of depletion and competency, this is understandable. To show up fully is, at some level, an acknowledgement that one has enough energy and competency to contribute. A Five's very presence is a courageous act.

What am I remembering? (Past)

The Type Five's adapted state tends to be fixated on a past perspective. In this egoic pattern, Fives often experience a compulsive retreat to a prior established place to dwell on knowledge and information gained. *What am I remembering?* can conjure positive memories of competency and sufficiency or negative memories of incompetency and depletion. Remembering activates an investigation of lessons taught and events shaped. Regardless, the focus on the past activates the scarcity mindset to hold back, preserve, and maintain. Past experiences and knowledge acquired help assuage the fear that lurks in the present. When Fives ask *What am I remembering?* in the Way of Discernment, they can reflect upon their memories in a manner that informs the present, before a compulsive retreat. They can look anew at their prior life and perhaps see the competency and sustainability that has marked their days.

What am I experiencing? (Present)

Like for the Type Four, the present environment can seem overwhelming. If a Five perceives the present as a threat of depletion, the safest thing to do is to protect. Thus, Fives often feel suspicious of the experiential. Their present world often seems intrusive or neglectful or overwhelming.[17] By considering *What am I experiencing?* in the Way of Discernment, authentic identity, purpose, and direction align with wisdom and practice, allowing Fives to honestly consider their experience in the here and now. Fives can employ their vast resources of study to analyze their present world rather than gathering them and retreating to a safer place.

The Type Five must experience the present not just in their Head Center, but also in their bodies. They must embody the here and now, aligning their physical presence with their thinking and feeling. When they do, Fives can find the energy, the time, and the competency that they fear they lack. When Type Fives worry about depletion, they often fail to recognize their preemptive and proactive role in depletion: depleting themselves from their present environment. The sustainability and competency Fives seek can often by revealed by showing up fully.

Type Fives Engage:

What is your common response to being asked to show up for something new (social event, work project, etc.)?

_____

How do you typically respond to situations that seem emotionally, physically, or mentally draining?

_____

What am I anticipating? (Future)

When Fives anticipate, it is often scarcity-based. Their future-thinking focuses on threats of depletion, intrusions of boundaries, or topics for which they are unprepared. The Five's forecasting tendencies are a form of radar which scans for such threats. Fives are also capable of fantasizing about a future free of the demands that drain. The Way of Discernment invites Fives to consider a future from a grounded, embodied place. This is what sets good trajectories of activity and engagement. *What am I anticipating?* in this way discerns through being informed by the past, activated by the present, all to cast a vision of a hopeful, grounded future.

Discernment

Fives' abundant skills to think, analyze, research, and study can be extremely effective in discernment. Their appreciation of depth, insight, and focus are profoundly helpful. Their capacity to sit with a problem for a sustained period of time gives them a unique ability in decision making. These strengths are weakened by the Five's attempts to assuage their fears of incompetency and depletion. Their scarcity mindset can cause them to withdraw and isolate, cutting off from the wisdom and insight of others. When Fives cater to their fears, they can merge with what is most comfortable to them: their ideas. They lose their sense of authentic self and over-identify with their ideas and their intellect. Fives must be intentional with the following:

- Identity Over Isolation: The Type Five in an adapted state is characterized by a protective isolation to preserve what remains. Fives in their authentic state of identity are marked by sustainability and competency. Make the identity statement for the Type Five a mantra: "I am made in the Divine Image, and in the Divine Image there is not fear of incompetency or depletion. My competency and viability are inner renewable resources to be shared with others."

- Wise Body: Through intentionally practicing doing intelligence, Fives listen to their intuition and actively engage their world, even before they know as much as they want. Engaging in Wise Body helps Fives "get out of their heads" and into embodied living, integrating thinking and feeling with action. In the Way of Discernment, Fives intelligence centers are aligned in healthy rhythms that allow the Five's gifts to flourish in their world.

- Sacred Presence: Fives must practice Sacred Presence (Chapter Three) in order to more wisely discern their lives. This requires showing up fully, bringing the head, the heart, and the gut to the here and now. To show up fully is courageous—a healthy confession that you have the energy and competency for the moment. It's a lived belief that you have plenty to offer, and others have plenty to offer you.

Exercises for the Type Five Within

- <u>Practice need</u>. Pick a topic or issue in which you feel at least mildly incompetent. Instead of engaging in your usual patterns of withdrawal and study, use it as an opportunity to engage others, asking for help. Such confession of need, coupled with asking for help, is good practice for Fives, as it cultivates interdependency, social engagement, and collaboration.

- <u>A generosity of time</u>. Try giving time away, even when it feels wasteful or lavish. If you have a social event, try staying 20-30 minutes longer than you normally would. Pay attention to your thoughts and feelings during this time.

- <u>Sit under a teacher</u>. Fives love learning, but don't always love having teachers. Fives can often find the knowledge they want on their own terms. Practice sitting under the instruction of another person, even if it's just for a short time.

- <u>Join a fitness class</u>. This may seem odd, but physical activity can be really helpful in getting a Type Five out of the head and into the body. Activities such as Yoga, Pilates, or spin classes align thinking with the physicality of the present. It's tough to overthink when you're engaged in strenuous activity.

Questions for the Type Five Within:

- What's mine to know?
- How can I use my knowledge to benefit others?
- What are healthy rhythms of time alone and time with others?

- What am I learning about that I should be acting upon?
- How much information do I really need to act?
- How small is my circle of trust? What do I risk when I widen it to include others?
- What are the things I tend to cling to that are non-negotiable?

Notes

[1]Chestnut, *The Complete Enneagram*, p. 231.

[2]Daniels & Price, *The Essential Enneagram*, p. 37.

[3]Riso & Hudson, *Discover Your Personality Type*, p. 127.

[4]Here's an explanation of the Law of Diminishing Returns: https://www.learning-theories.com/law-diminishing-returns.html.

[5]A. H. Almaas, *Facets of Unity: The Enneagram of Holy Ideas* (Berkeley: Diamond Books, 1998), p. 102.

[6]Schaffer, *Roaming Free Inside the Cage*, p. 84.

[7]Chestnut, *The Complete Enneagram*, p. 235.

[8]Naranjo, *Ennea-type Structures*, p. 81.

[9]Chestnut, *The Complete Enneagram*.

[10]Schafer, *Roaming Free Inside the Cage*, p. 82.

[11]Chestnut, *The Complete Enneagram*, p. 235.

[12]Heuertz, *The Sacred Enneagram*.

[13]Schafer, *Roaming Free Inside the Cage,* p. 84.

[14]Naranjo, *Ennea-type Structures*, p. 88.

[15]Chestnut, *The Complete Enneagram,* p. 240.

[16]Hurley & Donson, *Discover Your Soul Potential*, p. 107.

[17]Chestnut, *The Complete Enneagram*, p. 227.

CHAPTER 12

Type Six: "The Loyalist"

"Courage, dear heart."
—Aslan the Lion, *The Voyage of the Dawn Treader*

Sixes want loyalty but settle for safety.

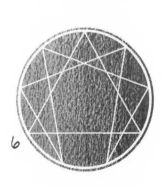

Type Sixes are often labeled as "loyalists." Unlike many other types, this nickname truly does capture what Sixes are truly after. Sixes, at their core, want loyalty. They want to be loyal and supported, and they want the world to be marked by fidelity to one another. But when confronted with a world that isn't always loyal, it feels threatening. They can see need for security everywhere, and they see it most prominently within themselves. This leads Type Sixes to doubt their intuition and

feel anxious about life, and that stress manifests as a particular type of fear: being in an unfaithful environment. Because of their need to cope, this fear of infidelity takes on a more subtle and acceptable version: ensuring one's surroundings are safe and secure. In order to keep the need for loyalty in check, Type Sixes settle for the safety they can acquire in their world. This pursuit of safety can cause Sixes to threat-forecast wherever they go, which can further isolate themselves from others and feed their fear of disloyalty.

The Way of Discernment for the Type Six is to reflectively engage their dominant emotion, fear, in order to work through their compulsion to secure. The fear that Sixes carry is their most significant barrier to discernment. When Sixes return to a place of inner authority, loyalty, and security, then the discernment triads of vocation, wisdom, and practice can align to make good decisions.

When making decisions, Type Sixes perceive their options in the Head Center, and a lack of trust in others and themselves compels them to respond by securing themselves and whatever is near them. Sixes spend significant energy responding to their doubts and skepticism. They hope that the small wins of safety and reliability they can enact will keep the fear at bay. The Type Six believes that if that which is in front of them can be secured, they'll be okay. This unfortunately fails them, because risk abounds in our lives and very little is certain. The fear can grow in strength and power over time, causing the Six to simply avoid risk-taking as a preemptive security measure. Or, some Sixes will blindly charge at their fears without much thought.[1]

Sixes engage their fear by coming alongside others. They share this Dependent Stance posture along with Ones and Twos. Since Sixes value loyalty, support, and guidance so highly, they quickly gravitate toward others, and engage them in one of two ways. The first response is to stick with those they trust the most, at nearly any cost. The second is to be suspicious and cautious with those they don't, and vigilantly be "on guard" in their presence. They can embody the adage "keep your friends close and your enemies closer." By securing their world with others, Sixes hope that they will find the loyalty and authority they've been searching for. When healthy and wise, this can be true. When unhealthy, it leads to perpetual disappointment and a ramping up of fear.

Sixes are highly intuitive people and have a strong sense of the way life ought to be. This is why they are so practical. They can exhibit a sensible confidence in how things should be, and are able to provide tangible solutions to get there. They have a high value in the concrete and the guaranteed. In times of conflict, fear stokes the Six's reactivity, resulting in an emotional response that can sometimes be negative, pessimistic, suspicious, and perhaps blaming.

Sixes are often stereotyped as the worry-warts and the pessimists of the enneagram. This is an unfortunate typecasting. Their perceived pessimism can be more accurately understood as a commitment to finding positive outcomes to the perils of life. Ginger Lapid-Bogda describes this well when she characterizes Sixes as wanting "to enable the best to manifest and the worst from occurring..."[2] Sixes rely upon their intuitive sense of danger to find what they believe to be the safest and most trustworthy way forward for all. Not everyone cares about the support and guidance of others. Sixes truly do. Behind their securing tendencies and threat-forecasting is a quest for a loving, trusting, and loyal world.

Strength – Intuitive Team Players

In seasons of discernment, Sixes have much more to offer than most give them credit for. Type Sixes' sensitivities toward loyalty, support, and guidance compel them to be some of the most trustworthy, dutiful, and responsible types of the enneagram. Sixes are naturally loyal and their team and group orientation makes them great friends and colleagues to have around.

Sixes are consummately good friends and coworkers for their ability to collaborate and cooperate. When healthy, the

Type Six's agenda is the common good, and shared goals drive them to succeed. Because of their strong sense of loyalty, Sixes embody a steadfast presence. This cannot be overstated, for Sixes are often derided for their worry and indecision. This overlooks the fortitude, or "staying power," that Sixes bring to environments. This steadfastness is a powerful resource for discernment.

Because of their heightened thinking, Sixes should rely on their critical thinking skills in decision-making, trusting their own abilities. They have a naturally questioning mind[3] that, when coupled with their intuition, is full of wisdom. This affords Sixes the capacity "for seeing through false pretenses and detecting ulterior motives and hidden agendas."[4] Generally speaking, Sixes are excellent observers. They can pick up on subtle cues and nuances that others miss.

Also, Sixes have a strong wit, and their mental sharpness allows them to easily take the role of the "devil's advocate." In times of important decision-making, taking the opposing view tests the strength and validity of a choice, also testing its veracity.

This all allows Sixes to be the ultimate prepared team players. Type Sixes exhibit a calm and effectiveness in times of crisis or chaos that is surprising to other types. It initially seems counterintuitive to their observable fear and worry. But to a Six, there are very few surprises, for they are well-practiced in preparing for any scenario, far more than any other type. This points to what Sixes offer as a gift to us when healthy: an intuitive courage in the face of risk, uncertainty, and the unknown. When courageous, they embody a wise and inspiring discernment.

Type Sixes Engage:

Can you think of a significant event in which your preparation paid off?

When has your pursuit of the common good for the sake of the team or group helped you discern your path?

Challenge – Problem-Seeking

Type Sixes also experience some challenging patterns that inhibit their discernment. Discernment implies change, which is often threatening to Sixes. One of my teachers, Lynda Roberts (a Type Six) describes Sixes as having "Pre-Traumatic Stress Disorder." This is evidenced by a compulsive shift from the Six's innate *problem solving* abilities to *problem seeking* patterns as a way to feel safe.[5] In this way, an unhealthy Six can become overly-identified with their problems, including the ones of their own making.

This problem-seeking approach can enhance the Six's uncertainty, worry, and caution toward important decisions, the legitimate problems in their lives in need of solutions. They can become distracted by a vigilance for the wrong things. Sixes assume that the world is suspicious, which causes them to experience their own tragic irony: They can be the least trusting type, and yet are the most trustworthy. The lack of trust fosters a persistent doubt in others, in how things will work out, and inevitably a doubt in oneself. This is why those who know Sixes observe their ambivalence, a dissonance of distrust and trust. According to Beatrice Chestnut, this ambivalent dissonance reflects "the ongoing inner conflict a Six experiences between pleasing others and rebelling against them, admiring others and trying to invalidate them."[6] The result can be like sandpaper which, overused, can eventually stop smoothing and actually wear something down.

It's then easy to see how the Six's fear and lack of trust can lead to procrastination, despite their commitment to loyalty. If they wear others down by their problem-seeking and ambivalence, they can isolate themselves from others. Then their ability to practically solve problems can be ceded to the fear of being alone and having to do it (whatever it is) themselves. This can be paralyzing to discernment, for the combination of inner-doubt and external threat(s) is wicked. The Six's ultimate fear is taken to its furthest end: a forced isolation in which there is no possibility of loyalty, support, or guidance.

This is why Sixes are sometimes afraid to act on their own behalf. The instability of an uncertain present or future can lead the Six to constrict themselves, heart and/or body, to cling to safety. The action needed to make a decision and follow through is replaced by thinking: "Thinking replaces doing because attention shifts from the impulse to act on a good idea to an intense questioning of that idea from the point of view of those who might disagree."[7] Inner authority is diminished to a perceived external critique.

The heightened thinking about decisions triggers the Six's primary defense: projection. Projection, according to therapist and enneagram teacher Carolyn Bartlett, is "attributing to other people or objects their own unacceptable thoughts, feelings, motives, or desires. When this defense is active, Sixes see their internal issues as belonging to external forces. Such projection can be negative or positive. Regardless, others are perceived as larger and more powerful."[8] The Six's projection is a way of getting rid of the fear, doubt, and mistrust that overwhelms their inner world. Sixes can also engage in another defense, what Beatrice Chestnut calls "splitting:" an arbitrary categorization of others as "good" or "bad."[9] This simplified "information" is a way for the Six to reduce their fear, for they know who is trustworthy and who isn't.

The results of projection and splitting are damaging to discernment. Intimacy with others can be a challenge, as it's threatening to let people get too close. Paranoia can creep in. Sixes can succumb to linking disparate issues and unrelated encounters as one overarching threat.[10] In an unhealthy state, Sixes will over-control, over-protect and experience a paralysis from making a decision.

It's easy for the Six to play the devil's advocate. It's much more challenging for them to keep the devil's advocate in its proper place. A Six can quickly cede control to the worst-case scenario posed by their own devil's advocate, thus enacting a sort of self-fulfilling prophecy that tells the Six that they shouldn't risk, decide, or act. The lack of risk, decision, and activity can convince the Six that nothing good is for them. Even the prospect of success can seem threatening to them.

When Sixes shift from problem solving to problem seeking, their inner authority is ceded. In times of discernment, Sixes must trust themselves and trust those who are safe and helpful. This requires them to acknowledge their fear and see that the defenses of projection and splitting are not discerning, for wisdom comes from trusting their intuition instead of doubting it.

Type Sixes Engage:

Think of a time in your life when your suspicion prevented you from experiencing something good. What was the result?

_____

Where do you see evidence of projection or splitting in your life?

_____

Vocation – Identity, Purpose, Direction

The Six's compliance to fear can lead to viewing vocation with a suspicious and skeptical eye. Sixes often experience doubt and confusion that questions the legitimacy of the gift of vocation. The Divine Voice of Love is worthy of trust and is calling the Six to rediscover inner authority, trust, and loyalty. This engages The Six's doubt and ambivalence, and is an invitation to find a deeper security and guidance within. By committing to the practice of vocation, Sixes can, step-by-step, learn to trust this inner authority. What Sixes often fail to realize is that their actions of protection often result in distancing themselves from the Divine Call.

The Way of Discernment for Type Sixes begins with trusting and listening to the Divine Voice and not only their devil's advocate. When they acknowledge their authority, intuition, and trustworthiness, their practice of vocation emerges from an inner compass. Healthy vocation "work" for Sixes includes an understanding that change isn't always a threat. There the Six will learn to cast a good and hopeful vision for their future and discover a sense of purpose that guides and directs.

Type Sixes Engage:

When in your life did you feel confident in your direction? How did that feel?

Who am I?—Identity for Type Six

The Way of Discernment Identity Statement for Type Six is:

> *"I am made in the Divine Image, and in the Divine Image there is no fear of being alone.*
> *Support and guidance is within, not simply in what I can secure."*

To live from this authentic identity invites the Type Six to stop shrinking out of fear that they don't have what it takes to be supported and safe. Instead, they must learn to step into their world with courage and faith, free of the defenses of projection and splitting. This comes from a Divine Image that is inherently loyal, trustworthy, and supportive. Here, fear is transformed into courage, and the Six's intuition and loyalty fosters flourishing. When discerning, Sixes must engage *Who am I?* This is the very question that helps Sixes learn to trust themselves and their intuition.

The Way of Discernment for Type Sixes is a reclamation of an identity marked by faith, hope, and love. When Sixes embody these three, they can engage their world with a deeper purpose and clearer direction.

First, Sixes must become more aware of their Sixness. The Six's cycles of projection and splitting can digress into an unhealthy self-fulfilling prophecy that convinces the Six that things won't work out...so they don't. Those who lead with Type Six must notice the ways in which they constrict themselves out of fear and prioritize safety and security at the expense of their own joy and success. Their compliance to fear renders their inner authority as yet another voice to doubt.

Second, Sixes must acknowledge the Divine Voice that calls them beloved. The Six's egoic patterns often compel them to reply, "Yes, but..." to those who have good and beautiful things to say to them. And yet, the still small voice of love whispers an important message of affirmation for the Type Six. Listening helps the Six to stop scanning for an external authority to provide the support and guidance that is within. This inner authority, rooted in the *Imago Dei*, provides the Six a firm foundation: stability, safety, and security. Listening to the Divine Voice within disrupts the Six' tendency to reaching outward to fortify, when the trust and security they seek is within.

Third, Sixes must relinquish the adapted self. This is the true test of the Six's faith and trust: Are they willing to let go of their patterns of monitoring and securing to let their courage flourish? Only when they relinquish their unhealthy attempts to control their environment can Sixes relax their attention on the external in order to turn their focus within.

Fourth, Sixes must live from authentic self with humility. By disrupting their compulsions to project and secure, Sixes can humbly acknowledge what is going on within. Here the Six realizes that healthy humility is not the same thing as having a low view of oneself. Recognizing their power and authority should not threaten healthy humility. Humility from this authentic place believes that the Six is strong and courageous enough to engage doubt and work through it, not bow before it.

Fifth, Sixes must befriend themselves. Self-care for Sixes requires a different framework than safety, for care comes in many forms. Sixes, when they trust themselves, can relax their securing tendencies to care for their other needs. Here, the Six cannot only protect themselves but embrace themselves. Befriending includes tending to other wants and desires that open up their hearts and bodies in courageous and caring ways. Fun, joy, delight, wonder, rest, and renewal find their place.

Sixth, Sixes must live from authentic self with agency. From authentic identity, a Six's energy isn't spent on security and suspicion. Agency can also help the Six work through some common authority issues, in which they can be simultaneously compliant and suspicious. Energy and agency can instead be directed in the service of their intuition and inner authority. The attempts to secure others and themselves can give way to a deeper authority congruent with the Six's purpose and direction.

Seventh, Sixes must intentionally continue to do all of the above. Type Sixes have deep-seated patterns of projection, constriction, and fear-based responses. They must be intentional, and yet loving, to themselves as they seek to live from authentic identity. From a place of inner authority, intuition, support, and loyalty, Sixes can integrate their ego into their authentic self and flourish.

Why am I here?—Purpose for Type Six

From inner authority and a trust in oneself, a Six's purpose clarifies. When a Six trusts themselves, they can begin to trust others with greater discernment on more neutral ground. The result is a grounded and courageous faith that allows Sixes to engage in their world with their full selves, rather than tending to "see themselves small and others as big."[11]

When Sixes recognize their *Imago Dei* and live accordingly, their intuitive listening and observation can be stewarded toward the flourishing of the common good. This is the pursuit of a communal safety and security. In times of discernment, Sixes can ask *Why am I here?* and discover a purpose that isn't merely mitigated by fear, but faith. From faith, fear may still be present, but doesn't rule the day. Faith acknowledges fear and takes the next step with courage. This embodies a loyalty to oneself, a fidelity to the Six's identity and purpose that allows the Six to trust their motivations rather than doubt them.

Where am I going?—Direction for Type Six

To fathom the direction of Sixes requires a depth of presence that relies upon their listening and observation skills, but employ them differently. Sixes are accustomed to finely tuning their listening and observation to address fear. This scanning for any threats leaves little time and energy for depth. This is the difference between simply noticing what's around verses deep exploration.

When Sixes fathom the depths of where they are and where they are going, they encounter their Head Center in a profoundly different way: wise reflection that honestly assesses what surrounds them, congruent with the heart and the body. This integration of the Head Center with heart and body allows fathoming to occur.

It's recommended that Sixes practice engaging in silence, to quell the mind and its bombardment of danger signs and warning signals.[12] This allows Sixes to listen to their hearts and bodies to let them know that they are okay. In this way, fathoming is less about thinking and more about congruence of the Six's entire being. It's a relaxation of the mind's activity to engage in a deeper knowing. From this depth, the Six's way forward becomes more clear.

Wisdom – Doing, Feeling, Thinking

In Chapters Three and Four, we took an in depth look at the Triads and Stances of the enneagram and how they engage the three centers of intelligence: thinking, doing, and feeling. Sixes lead with thinking intelligence in their Head Center, but their thinking tends to be distorted and misused, leading to an over-reliance on feeling and doing intelligence.

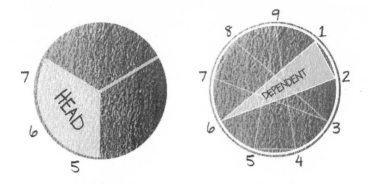

What am I doing?

Sixes can vacillate between engaging in frenetic activity and being stuck, frozen, and immovable. Their activity can often be described as over-complicated action, full of fits and starts. This is because their activity is often dictated by their thinking. And when their thinking is marked with fear, doubt, and uncertainty, the activity of the Six can be frenetically timid.

Another way to consider this is what Eli Jaxon-Bear calls the Six's "mental body."[13] Without some intelligence center work, Sixes can view the body simply as an extension of the mind, and its purpose is simply to avoid fear or threat. Doing intelligence is diminished for the sake of the mind's need for safety.

Here we can make an important distinction between movement and action. Sixes can engage in a lot of movement and yet struggle to act in a meaningful way. Again, Jaxon-Bear describes this well: "The issue for Sixes is movement into action; there are usually a thousand head trips between the idea and acting it out."[14] This is why other types can wonder why Sixes struggle with acting on a decision. The procrastination isn't pretending the need to act isn't there. It's thinking the action through from every possible angle while keeping the body busy.

The Way of Discernment for Sixes is an opportunity to quiet the mind and allow them to get out of their heads and more fully into their bodies. *What am I doing?* is an invitation to let the body speak for itself. For the body knows what the mind doesn't. Accessing and trusting doing intelligence activates the Six's intuition. Here the healthy, discerning Six can find the head space to listen to their body and tend to its needs. They can courageously engage in active, practical, and responsible problem solving. This requires grounding the body in order to align what's going on in the head with the gut.

What am I feeling?

The Type Six's initial response to this question is often marked by feelings associated with safety (or lack thereof) and trust (or skepticism). Such initial responses reveal the extent to which the Six's mind can tell the heart to be closed and protected. Thus, Sixes often present themselves as timid, unsure, and small. Or, interestingly, some Sixes (commonly referred to as "counter-phobic Sixes") can present themselves as the extreme opposite: unnecessarily aggressive, overly confident, and forcefully large.[15] In either instance, fear is the common emotion.

Sixes can more honestly name and recognize feelings of anxiety than most types. This is why we often characterize the Six as being the most anxious type, which isn't always the case. While Sixes can be more visibly anxious, perhaps they are just more honest about it than other types. Beyond this emotional range, Sixes often experience their feelings in relation to others. Their Dependent Stance in the world provides ample feelings in the relational field. When relationships are healthy, the Six's connectivity, loyalty, and support provide ample feelings.

The Six's path on The Way of Discernment includes an exploration of *What am I feeling?* that is less directed by the mind. Rather than thinking through their feelings, Sixes must truly experience them. This invites them to enter a richer and deeper emotional world, and engage their feelings with a sense of authority and authenticity.

What am I thinking?

As I've already indicated, this is the Six's most challenging question with regards to discernment. Some interpret the Six's thinking as silly, wasteful, or foolish. I don't think this is truly the case. Sixes are deeply thoughtful and intelligent, but too much of their cognition is devoted to their fear. This limits their thinking intelligence to survival-oriented pursuits, even when their survival isn't at risk. This results in Sixes being the type most disconnected from their thought life.

Sixes, due to their struggles with trust and doubt, interpret their world with a cognitive bias toward suspicion. Suspicion demands significant cognitive energy, requiring additional information, further questioning, and more corroboration. This is especially true of the Six's scanning for threats, which leads to worst-case scenarios dominating their head space.

Often when Sixes find their way through the many stages of suspicious thinking about something, they doubt their ability to make a firm judgment or decision about it. This, for the Six, can be a cruel experience: to go through so much thinking work and then feel the need to ask others to help them make the decision.

The Way of Discernment for Type Sixes provides an invitation to a different relationship with their cognition. This requires initially disentangling thinking from feeling and doing. In their adapted state, these are jumbled, and in the confusion the Six's mind calls the shots. When loosened from one another, Sixes can more wisely and productively use their thinking intelligence with faith and courage. Thinking in the present doesn't wear the Six out, for it is aligned and integrated with feeling and doing. This allows the Six to not be so overwhelmed by their present, preserving energy to engage their future.

Type Sixes Engage:

How often do you feel exhausted by all that's going on in your head?

What are the majority of your thoughts focused on?

Practice in Time

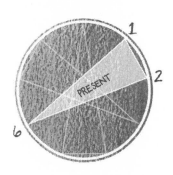

The Six's residence in the Dependent Stance (Chapter Three) along with Ones and Twos results in a common "stacking" of time perspectives. Sixes are present focused. They support this present orientation with the past, while too often neglecting the future. This is evidenced by the Sixes' focus on their present world in three primary ways. First, Sixes perpetually scan their present environment for threat or risk. Second, they assess their present company for their trustworthiness and loyalty. Third, they busy themselves in the present securing anything that feels unsafe or insecure. This present focus is often a rapid-fire series of responses to the Six's mind, which works strenuously to address fear.

This present orientation is supported by a past perspective. Sixes in their adapted state have a way of carrying past fear and doubt into their present situations. Prior instances of insecurity, scenarios that went awry, and memories of feeling alone shape the way Sixes engage their present world. As children, Sixes often remember vividly how they would threat-forecast and plan while trying to fall asleep. This is often paired with the Six's lifelong role of being the one concerned about the group, about safety, or being the devil's advocate. The past provides ample reminders of what demands the Six's attention in the here and now.

What Sixes struggle with the most is the future. With all that needs to be watched, secured, and evaluated in the present, it's very difficult for Sixes to let it be and enjoy a clear outlook for the future. Like Ones and Twos, they have a prevailing sense that so much requires their attention right now, therefore they don't have sufficient time to plan too far ahead. Granted, Sixes anticipate often, but it's a narrow anticipation to what can be done in the present to prevent something bad from happening. An unknown future can breed doubt. Many Sixes prefer to focus on what they can control or affect immediately.

Please know that this doesn't mean that the Six should forsake the present and those close to them. But critical time-work for the Sixes includes opening themselves up and experiencing a greater vantage of their life. This allows them to steward their discerning skills for their futures. When this occurs, Sixes become more courageous and faithful in their present and can find more peace with it.

What am I remembering? (Past)

As explained above, Type Sixes are prone to bring prior doubt, fear, and uncertainty into their present world. Sixes can even have memories, whether they be painful or nostalgic, of being the loyal one in their family or the (only?) one who tended to safety and security. Many remember playing the role of the devil's advocate, letting their practical reasoning guide and shape their family's decisions. When in their present environment, many Sixes recall deficit-based messages that can fuel their expectation that things will not work out.

By engaging The Way of Discernment, Sixes can reflect upon their past with greater clarity. Through healthy reflection, *What am I remembering?* is an invitation for Sixes to allow past events of belonging, loyalty, and trust to also guide their present engagement. Sixes can employ their intuition toward their stewardship of memory, considering its validity for the present and welcoming a full range of past experience. Does the past only stoke our fear, doubt, and mistrust? Or can it help us cultivate faith and courage in the here and now?

What am I experiencing? (Present)

Sixes, like their fellow Ones and Twos, often experience a present that is overwhelming. They suffer from a tyranny of the urgent that often doesn't allow Sixes to relax or think about anything else until the urgent is attended to. When particularly stressed or unhealthy, the shift from problem solving to problem seeking results in hyper-vigilant Sixes responding to danger, threats, or insecurity that don't warrant their attention or energy in the present. In this way, Sixes can feel "suspended in the now,"[16] keenly aware of all they think they should attend to, but uncertain how to handle it all. This fuels the Six's doubt and uncertainty, and leads to Sixes often feeling fatigued by their present condition. Guards take shifts in their around-the-clock security work. Sixes don't feel they have the luxury to take time off and often struggle to let others take the burden from them, for they believe they must be their own security detail.

For Sixes to follow the Way of Discernment, they must develop a different frame for their present engagement. By considering *What am I experiencing?* they can invite their hearts and bodies to speak for themselves. This is an opportunity for Sixes to listen to their bodies and not simply tell them what to do. This is an occasion for Sixes to sense and experience their emotions in ways that aren't so mitigated by the mind, free of thinking through them and doubting them. This creates a hospitable environment for the Six to engage their inner authority, and learn to trust themselves.

What am I anticipating? (Future)

As outlined above, this is the most challenging time perspective for the Type Six. The Six's anticipation is perpetual and palpable, a constant expectation that things will go sideways unless they are addressed now. The threat-forecasting in worst-case scenarios alerts the Six's Head Center to batten down the hatches as quickly as possible. When not listening to their own intuition or guided by their inner authority, the Six's doubt and timidity can cause them to be fearful of the future consequences of their own actions.[17]

When Sixes journey The Way of Discernment and engage in Sacred Vision, they can relax their fixation on security as an attempt to preemptively control the future. They can look up and out at a future that includes trust, togetherness, guidance, and positive outcomes. They can eventually envision a future that isn't so split into categories of good and bad. By asking *What am I anticipating?* Sixes can name their anticipation and let their intuition and inner authority deem it appropriate or valid. They can envision an active role for themselves, in which their skills and gifts are used for flourishing.

Type Sixes Engage:

When you tend to consider future scenarios, how would you describe them? Positive? Negative? Any other descriptors?

How do you initially respond to engaging in thinking about a future that is safe and trustworthy?

Discernment

Six's natural skills to be a prepared, loyal, and supportive member of the team are so valuable in discernment. Their intuitive approach to problem solving, their abilities to see through pretense, and their skills of observation and questioning are profoundly helpful. Sixes must learn when to let down their guard and trust in their own abilities to discern. This is their greatest challenge: Their fear, doubt, and uncertainty can fuel a problem-seeking approach that distracts them from the real problems of discernment. They must learn to engage their fear less compulsively. This means welcoming their doubts, trusting in their intuition to engage them, for doubt is a common human experience. When Sixes rediscover their inner authority and access their intuition, attention becomes more than keeping watch and scanning for threat. It becomes an embodied posture of searching for places in which they can courageously step in with their gifts and skills to embody their loyalty, trust, and support. Then the loyalty they want is not secured and pinned down, but instead released in flourishing expression. They can live the seemingly unmanageable truth of Julian of Norwich, who writes, "All shall be well, and all manner of things shall be well."[18] Sixes should be mindful of the following when engaging decision-making:

- Identity Over Insecurity. The journey to authentic self for Sixes can be rife with doubt and uncertainty. Relaxing the securing tendencies can feel vulnerable. The Six's compulsions to constrict, scan, and problem-seek lead the mind to work on overdrive in attempting to assuage fear. Make the identity statement for the Type Six a mantra: "I am made in the Divine Image, and in the Divine Image there is no fear of being alone. Support and guidance is within, not simply in what I can secure."

- Wise Mind. The Head Center holds a dominant and complex role for Sixes. Wise Mind for the Type Six means allowing the heart and body to have an equal voice. Correcting the mind's unhelpful power trips over heart and body allow them to have a healthier conversation. This allows the body's intuition and the heart's emotional landscape to be accessed and included in the cultivation of wisdom. Wise Mind helps Sixes align and integrate their active thinking with doing and feeling in a way that empowers themselves, building trust and courage. In this way, Wise Mind is *less, but better* thinking, making room for the heart and body to have a say.

- Sacred Vision. Sacred Vision (Chapter Three) for the Six is crucial in finding freedom from the bombardment of present threats. With intention and attention, Sixes can rise above the problems they sometimes seek and set their focus more distantly in the future. When they do, they access the courage that's been there all along.

This is the courage that "has to do with what it takes to pay attention to our inner reality."[19] This is the courage that emboldens them to take the next right step with faith and hope.

Exercises for the Type Six Within

- Breathing in Silence, For Sixes, engaging in silence must practically help them quiet their minds and the numerous signals, forecasts, scenarios, etc. One helpful practice is called "four-sided breathing," and consists of engaging in a rhythm of breathe-pause-exhale-pause. Count four seconds for each step, and continue the cycle multiple times until your mind feels more at ease. The combination of counting and breathing quiets the mind in helpful ways.

- Visualization. Studies have proven the effectiveness of intentional visualization work to improve motivation and effectiveness. Such practices even create new neural pathways in the brain. For Sixes, visualizing realistic positive outcomes can be profoundly helpful in disrupting their tendencies in anticipating worst-case scenarios. Experiment with one form of visualization called "picture and describe."[20] Spend time picturing and describing a future goal you hope to achieve to a trusted friend or on paper in written form. Use all of your senses to describe this picture of you achieving your goal. Add more and more detail until it feels real, until you feel like you are experiencing it. This can help soften the Six's skepticism to a hopeful and realistic optimism about their future.

- Brain Dump. With so much going on in the mind, a helpful and disarming technique for Sixes is to practice a five-minute "brain dump" to help them feel less overwhelmed. Take a sheet of paper and write down everything that's going on in your brain. Once you've got it down, try to identify which items are *problem-seeking* and which require legitimate *problem-solving*.

- <u>Power Pose</u>. This will sound silly initially, but hear me out. Intentionally standing in a posture that you believe to be powerful has been scientifically proven to increase one's feeling of being empowered.[21] And when we are empowered, we are more courageous, engaged, and confident. Power posing counters the timidity and constriction many Sixes experience. For Sixes, this is an intentional practice in the body talking to the mind (and not the other way around). Before entering a stressful meeting or situation, if you're in a place where you can power pose without being too self-conscious, try it out. See what effect it has on your presence and engagement.

Questions for the Type Six Within

- What is mine to secure?
- Am I trusting in myself or giving others too much power and authority over my decisions?
- Is my skepticism the best use of my intelligence?
- How can I see beyond the present dangers to the future?
- How much of my time and energy is devoted to thinking about that which is unlikely to occur?
- Do my actions convey what I know to be true?

Notes

[1]This would be an example of what many call the "counter-phobic Six." In some circles, this is the countertype Six, the subtype that is unlike the others. In other circles, this is the Sexual (Sx) Six, which is a Type Six with a dominant sexual instinct. The instinctual drives are beyond the scope of this book, but here we must acknowledge that some Sixes' fears compel them to lash out or respond with force or aggression. This often confuses non-Six types, for it can appear as confidence and power. For the Six, such assertion is often a reaction to fear.

[2]Lapid-Bogda, *The Art of Typing*, p. 18.

[3]Daniels & Price, *The Essential Enneagram*, p. 42.

[4]Chestnut, *The Complete Enneagram*, p. 185.

[5]Naranjo, *Ennea-type Structures*, p. 102.

[6]Chestnut, *The Complete Enneagram*, p. 199.

[7]Palmer, *The Enneagram*, p. 237.

[8]Bartlett, *The Enneagram Field Guide*, p. 94.

[9]Chestnut, *The Complete Enneagram*, p. 191.

[10]Hurley and Donson talking about this linking in their book, *Discover Your Soul Potential*, p. 121.

[11]Bartlett, *The Enneagram Field Guide*, p. 101.

[12]Heuertz, *The Sacred Enneagram*.

[13]Jaxon-Bear, *Fixation to Freedom*, p. 175.

[14]Ibid, p. 176.

[15]In many enneagram contexts, this is known as the counter-phobic Six, characterized by fear-based aggression.

[16]Hurley & Donson, *Discover Your Soul Potential*, p. 129.

[17]Naranjo, *Ennea-type Structures*, p. 101.

[18]Dan Graves, "Article 31," *Christian History Institute*. Accessed Jan 12, 2020. Retrieved from https://christianhistoryinstitute.org/incontext/article/julian.

[19]Maitri, *The Enneagram of Passions and Virtues*, p. 168.

[20]Read more about som helpful visualization techniques here: https://www.psychologytoday.com/us/blog/living-forward/201806/3-effective-visualization-techniques-change-your-life.

[21]Amy Cuddy has conducted extensive research on power posing, summarized here: https://www.forbes.com/sites/kimelsesser/2018/04/03/power-posing-is-back-amy-cuddy-successfully-refutes-criticism/#1b16092e3b8e.

CHAPTER 13

Type Seven: "The Enthusiast"

"Be content with what you have;
rejoice in the way things are.
When you realize there is nothing lacking,
the whole world belongs to you."
—Lao Tzu

Sevens want contentment but settle for excitement.

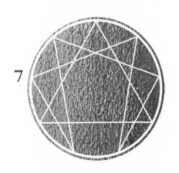
7

Type Sevens are often labeled as "enthusiasts." While this describes some common expressions of Sevens, it doesn't capture what Sevens are truly after. Sevens, at their core, want contentment. They want to be content, and they want the world to be marked by contentment. But when confronted with a world that isn't always satisfactory, it feels threatening. They can see need for satisfaction and contentment everywhere, and they see it most prominently within themselves. This leads Type Sevens to feel anxious about life, and that stress manifests as a particular type of fear: being in a painful or deprived environment. Because of their need to cope, this fear of pain or deprivation takes on a more subtle and acceptable version: planning1 for the next adventure or immersing themselves in another story. In order to keep the need for contentment in check, Type Sevens settle for the excitement they can manifest in their world. This pursuit of excitement can cause Sevens to hyper-plan wherever they go, which can cause Sevens to overlook the goodness of the ordinary and mundane.

The Way of Discernment for the Type Seven is to relinquish the planning for excitement as a defense against their dominant emotion: fear. The fear of being restrained or trapped is the Seven's most significant barrier. When Sevens intentionally return to an authentic place of inherent contentment and wholeness, vocation, wisdom, and practice align to make good decisions. In decision making, Sevens perceive the possibilities in their Head Center, which quickly initiates activity toward the option that will bring the most excitement and satisfaction, free of pain. In this manner, Sevens think and do in response to two metrics: avoiding pain and increasing satisfaction. In so doing, they bypass the Heart Center to maintain the patterns of pain avoidance and pleasure-seeking.

This is why Sevens tend to be charmingly assertive in groups. Their idealism is contagious. They have a knack for dreaming up plans and easily convincing others to join with their charm and fun, energetic demeanor. They pose a large but welcomed presence in any environment, in hopes that their optimism and enthusiasm will lead to a positive future. When conflict arises, Sevens have a tendency to reframe the situation in as positive a light as possible, sailing through any choppy waters to calmer seas. Upon reflection, they consider past conflict with a rose-colored memory.[2]

Strength – Embracing the Unknown

The enthusiasm of the Type Seven seems to have magical qualities. Their charming and disarming nature can generate much that is good. Sevens' abundant positivity can be infectious in seasons of discernment. They are curious, imaginative, spontaneous (to others), and creative. Times of discernment often require generating and testing ideas, which Sevens do quite naturally.

Sevens have a special ability to diffuse tension through humor. Levity can be a helpful release valve to think and see more clearly. Their good-natured approach to difficult situations can be grounding. Often important decisions are not as life-or-death as we make them out to be. Sevens can approach such forks in the road of life with a lightheartedness that prevents paralysis.

Type Sevens naturally want to try out new ideas. In times of transition, many types are hesitant to dip their toes in the water. Not Sevens. They're eager to dive in headfirst. That which is new is not scary to Sevens. They often welcome the unfolding nature of life. William Schafer describes the Seven experience this way: "Sevens are particularly alive to this structure of life's unfolding, awareness of which can be likened to beholding a waterfall."[3] They embrace it, approaching the unknown with arms open wide.

Sevens move through life with an infectious buoyancy, which compels them to embrace risk. The fear of the unknown is less than the fear of staying in the present. Seasons of discernment can be exhilarating, as it puts the Sevens' fixation on what's next in overdrive. The dreaming, scheming, planning, testing, and recruiting skills of Type Seven are all enhanced when making important decisions. When discerning, Sevens are more than happy to employ them.

Type Sevens Engage:

What are a few things that you are enthusiastic about right now?

Describe a recent event in which you coaxed others who were hesitant?

Challenge – Ever the Tourist, Rarely the Resident

Sevens' optimism can be valuable, but also comes with some caution. Their commitment to a glass-half-full approach can be an overcompensation and can cloud their judgment. Sevens are prone to leave situations too soon, unwilling to commit to seeing something through to completion. They can be perpetually restless, struggling to be fully present. This is largely due to the fear of being restrained and stuck. Sevens' fears center on being trapped and experiencing life in lack. They can abandon projects or groups too soon, failing to see the fruits of their labor.

Sevens adamantly keep their options open. They struggle to say no. They also struggle to see their commitments through. In each situation, freedom reigns supreme. Keeping all options on the table results in shallow, easily breakable commitments. Left unchecked, Sevens can risk being tourists in their lives, failing to settle down and sink roots in any one place. They become vagabonds, and life is defined more by transition than stability.

We all live life differently while on vacation. Our expectations and behavior are more indulgent and excessive. Sevens can struggle with this mindset as their default setting. They can get away with a charming rebelliousness that allows them to indulge in the excess of life. Those around Sevens enjoy the perpetual party and are happy to encourage a Type Seven to keep it going.

When this occurs, discernment is thwarted in a number of ways. Sevens' abilities to manifest what they want can shortcut receiving the gift. Think of it as putting an item on your birthday wish list and then buying it for yourself before your party. Forgoing discipline and overindulging in life stuffs down the fears of lack and deprivation and fails to cultivate the habit of listening well. To be a tourist in one's life is to be in the midst of others, but risks focusing simply on what to get out of an experience before moving on to the next adventure.

Here we find a tragic irony. Sevens tend to be fully committed to not being fully committed. They are charmingly forceful in keeping their options open. Over time, this rigid openness becomes the very thing they are working against. Sevens must be aware of the temptation to settle for excitement when they truly need wisdom and authenticity. Sevens must realize that decisions must be made, not hedged. In the investment of right and good commitments lies transformation.

Type Sevens Engage:

How would those close to you describe your ability to follow through?

Can you think of a time in which you left something too soon?

Vocation – Identity, Purpose, Direction

Type Sevens struggle with viewing vocation as an exciting possibility rather than a gift to receive and a practice to cultivate. A gift comes to us. Our only activity is to open ourselves to receive it. Sevens are prone to go after the exciting. It's an assertive rather than receptive posture. A practice is something forged over time, with repetition. Exciting possibilities are fresh and new. Similar to Threes and Eights, identity, purpose, and direction are often described using active verbs with an eye to the future. The Way of Discernment for Type Sevens requires an understanding of the fear they hold and then a distinguishing between planning and calling. There is certainly an important connection between the two, but it is dangerous to consider them the same thing. Healthy vocation "work" for Sevens includes cultivating a grounded sense of identity, a sense of purpose that integrates the importance of the mundane and slowing down to let the past speak. This cultivates wisdom and maturity in vocation.

Type Seven Engage:

If you were to stop and wait for your future to come to you, how would that feel?

Who am I?—Identity for Type Seven

The Way of Discernment Identity Statement for Type Seven is:

"I am made in the Divine Image, and in the Divine Image there is no fear of lack.
My contentment is in who I am, not simply what I can plan or experience."

The work required of Type Sevens to live from authentic identity is often uncomfortable. The journey from adapted self to authentic self (Chapter Two) provides insight for Sevens to stop searching for contentment and sufficiency and instead live from an Image that is inherently content and sufficient. In seasons of discernment, Sevens must begin by asking the question *Who am I?* To do so helps Sevens search for provision within.

First, Sevens must become more aware of their Sevenness. Acknowledging the power that fear plays in the life of Sevens helps them see the ways in which they externalize their fear of being trapped or deprived, and how they seek excitement and fulfillment elsewhere. Sevens: Notice when you begin to feel restless in various situations throughout the week. Observe the ways in which you are ready to move on more quickly than others. Consider how you plan to keep options open. These are all indicators of your Sevenness.

Second, Sevens must acknowledge the Divine Voice that calls them beloved. Most Sevens I know came to a point where they realized: "I have more to bring to my world than levity and fun."

Listening to others tell them how fun they are eventually loses its power. Consider the Divine Voice speaking into your being. This is the Voice that grounds you in the here and now, so that compulsive planning gives way to listening. Engaging the Divine Image within helps Sevens find contentment and fulfillment in identity, not simply adventure.

Third, Sevens must relinquish the adapted self. When Type Sevens relinquish their egocentricity, they learn to trust in the abundance of the present, rooted in the authentic self. Their fun and pleasant disposition emerges from a place of wholeness. Contentment and fulfillment begins within, not in what can be found or conjured in our world.

Fourth, Sevens must live from authentic self with humility. Sevens often ask the question *What could go wrong?* when in planning and recruiting mode. Their unspoken but clear answer to others is, "Nothing. It'll be fine." Their winsome ability to coax, unfettered from humility, can be manipulative. The journey to authentic self requires humility to honor others, even their concerns, and be honest with themselves on limits and capacities.

Fifth, Sevens must befriend themselves. Deep inner work can be particularly challenging for Sevens. They're savvy at keeping a step (or two) ahead of pain and discomfort. When they stop their excitement-seeking tendencies, they may struggle to know how to love themselves. Self-care is rest, not another adventure to experience. It's a loving embrace of oneself in the present, free of excitement.

Sixth, Sevens must live from authentic self with agency. Sevens relish a sense of freedom that keeps options open. From authentic identity, their abilities to woo and diffuse tension can help others experience freedom from their own compulsions and limitations. Their ability to get others to join them in the adventures of life help them move from tourists to pilgrims in their worlds.

Seventh, Sevens must intentionally continue to do all of the above. The tendency to want to chase after the adventure will persist in Type Sevens. It takes lifelong, intentional work to make sure that what we experience is from a place of contentment and fulfillment. When this occurs, wonder and awe permeate our world.

Why am I here?

Rooted in a place of authentic self, a Seven's purpose comes into focus. The freedom that Sevens work so hard to maintain in their world gives way to the true freedom that comes from making decisions from a place of inherent contentment and fulfillment. Purpose is refined, and hope and possibilities are assessed from a purer place. This is *shalom*. The Seven's adapted self seeks to pursue what brings excitement and satisfaction. The Seven's authentic self seeks to cultivate flourishing with others, that they may find contentment and fulfillment.

When a Seven lives from their identity in the *Imago Dei*, they are motivated for others to do the same. This is profound discernment: For a Seven to see beneath and through the excitement and satisfaction to remind them of their self-giving, not self-serving, identity. By asking *Why am I here?* Sevens can get beneath and through a surface-level enthusiasm and excitement for that which is more sustainable: flourishing.

Where am I going?

The Way of Discernment for Type Sevens asks this question from the perspective of depth, not simply forward movement. Sevens often have a spring in their step. Their buoyant positivity almost always lightens the mood of any room. This "lightness" has another effect, allowing the Seven to quickly move on to what's next.

The Sevens' fixation on the next excitement impedes their ability to discern with depth. Depth requires a more focused attention on the here and now. Depth requires letting the heart catch up with the head and the body. When Sevens discern with depth, they sink roots that allow them to engage a more complete range of emotions. While this can feel like the walls are closing in, it's important work in discernment. Sevens struggle to believe that one can possibly have too much of a good thing. By dialing down their wanderlust, Sevens can learn to be more content with what is. When Sevens practice resting in stillness they can intentionally silence the mind.[4] Here we plunge the depths beneath the bursts of enthusiasm: a sober wisdom.

Wisdom – Doing, Feeling, Thinking

Chapters Three and Four introduced the Triads and the Stances of the enneagram and how they each use (or misuse) the three centers of intelligence: thinking, doing, and feeling. Sevens lead with thinking in the head center, supported by doing intelligence. They struggle to align their feeling intelligence with their thinking and doing.

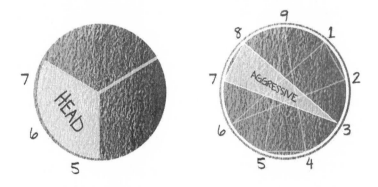

What am I doing?

Sevens are most often engaged in a multitude of activities. They are frequently multitasking, reminiscent of a juggler eager to add objects to the juggling rotation. They tend to thrive on variety, not wanting to spend too much time on one activity. To pose this question to a Seven often results in some version of this response: "Right now, I'm doing x and y. I'm about to do z."

A healthier approach for Type Sevens is to be slower to move on to the next task, project, or event. The famous German industrial designer Dieter Rams was known for championing

"*Weniger, aber besser,*" which translates "less, but better."[5] If Sevens can answer the question of doing intelligence with this phrase, they're on the right track. It's important for Sevens to align their activity with the authentic self, which is inherently content and fulfilled. This shifts the metric for evaluating activity from excitement and satisfaction to authenticity.

What am I feeling?

Sevens have an imbalanced relationship to their feelings. They are quickly able to recognize positive emotions: happy, excited, surprised, etc. Identifying negative or darker emotions is much more difficult. Sevens' overreliance on thinking and doing keeps the darkness away, as Sevens are always chasing light. Their charming assertiveness often results in positive encounters and environments. But often Sevens' ability to get a party kickstarted is a defense against fear, sadness, anger, loneliness, etc.

Without feeling intelligence (or EQ, emotional intelligence), Sevens are prone to some common mistakes. Sevens can lift the mood of the room, often shortcutting empathy, lament, and other means of bonding with one another through pain and suffering. Quick escapes to find the next source of pleasure or adventure can avoid problems that need to be engaged. The Seven's fear of being trapped or stuck is a powerful motivator, and energizes their activity in the world. But it can also thwart the growth and development that comes with working through suffering. A Type Seven friend of mine, Jeremy, walked in patience and love for years with his wife while she battled a terminal disease. Upon reflection, he said the experience was like being "stuck in a Seven's nightmare. You can't escape the pain." But it also forced him, through time and intention, to confront his pain and suffering. His ability to employ his feeling intelligence is much more natural as a result.

Wisdom in discernment requires that a Seven realize that a rich social life is not the same thing as a rich emotional life. Continually living to keep the prospect of pain and confinement away is its own prison, where the Seven is in a cage of expectation. Sevens must develop practices to engage their feelings, both positive and negative. This puts the ego in its proper place, and lets the authentic self flourish.

Type Sevens Engage:

When were you last exhausted from activity? How did you respond?

_____

What do you do when you feel sad? How do you engage, or avoid the sadness?

_____

What am I thinking?

Given the Type Seven's location in the Head Center, they are always thinking. Type Sevens are founts of ideas, consistently creating what Hurley and Donson refer to as "plans, projects, and possibilities."[6] Sevens are quick and clever thinkers, but tend to struggle with sustained thought. Their thought life mirrors their activity: quickly moving from one thing to the next, avoiding getting stuck as much as possible. They "love to skate on new ideas."[7]

For a Seven to honestly consider *What am I thinking?* requires a disentangling of thinking from doing. Here the practice of silence is helpful. This reflective silence disrupts the Type Seven's plan-act-plan-act cycle to cultivate wisdom. The restraint of thinking without action helps Type Sevens consider their thought life and observe ways in which it focuses on what's next.

Type Seven's Way of Discernment requires wisdom that more deeply and authentically engages doing and thinking, and properly integrates feelings as intelligence. Wise rhythms of doing, feeling, and thinking foster holistic discernment, drawn from deep wells of contentment and fulfillment.

Practice in Time

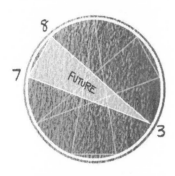

As we learned in Chapter Three, Type Sevens are in the Aggressive Stance (with Threes and Eights) and have a preferred future perspective on time, supported by the present, while neglecting the past. Sevens are future-focused, always ready for when the present begins to feel suffocating, boring, or awkward. They always have a plan for what comes next, though their quick shifts in activity often seem spontaneous to others.

This future fixation is supported by a present perspective on time that allows them to enjoy the thrill of the moment. As long as the present is free of pain or difficulty, Sevens stick around. As long as their enthusiasm lasts, they appear fully engaged in whatever they are doing. They thrive off of the adventure, the thrill, and the enjoyment. But as soon as it's gone, Sevens have also moved on.

What Sevens struggle to integrate in their practice is the past. This is understandable. If Sevens live from a fearful place of being trapped our deprived, the prospect of returning to such places is daunting. Pain, lack, and insufficiency all mark the past. It's easier to look ahead. Turning a Seven's attention to the past encourages them to slow down and let their feelings catch up to them. To discern well, Sevens must practice reflecting on the past to keep them more grounded in the present, and prevent them from compulsively chasing a future of excitement for the wrong reasons. Practices that require silencing the brain and body are critical to Sevens' healthy engagement with the past. This means Sevens must no longer avoid the prospect of pain, but engage it to see what it may teach.

What am I remembering? (Past)

In times of discernment, this is the most challenging time question to answer. It requires practicing Sacred Delay to look to the past as teacher. Our past is part of the equation and includes seasons of pain and joy. By accessing our memory, we engage our fear, rather than run from it. When Sevens turn to face their fears, the shadows don't seem so ominous. The fear of being trapped and restrained is alleviated by recognizing the freedom and agency you always have.

Type Sevens Engage:

When is the last time you've allowed yourself to be nostalgic?

_____

What do you risk when you take time to look to the past?

_____

What am I experiencing? (Present)

For Sevens in their adapted state, "the present is made tolerable by the future."[8] Such a future orientation inhibits their ability to be fully present. For Sevens, it's important to ask the question, *What am I experiencing?* a few times to get beneath the outer layers. An initial response often is enthusiasm or excitement. What else is being experienced? In the body? In the heart? In the head? This helps deepen awareness in the present, shifting from the constant "mental mapping" of the future to the surprise of the moment.[9] Pondering this question also provides Sevens with a chance to assess their consumption: is it excessive?

What am I anticipating? (Future)

This question gets at the heart of the Sevens' time compulsion: the future. Ask a Seven what they're anticipating, they'll likely enthusiastically offer their plan, and invite you to join them. Hurley and Donson describe it this way: "For Sevens, keeping a positive attitude and dreaming new dreams seems as vital to life as breathing."[10] The Seven's way of living is a preoccupation with "What's next?" But taking time to consider anticipation helps Sevens be more aware of their future fixation. Sevens, acknowledge your anticipations.

When Type Sevens arrive at decisions from authentic identity, grounded purpose, and a direction of depth, they can learn from the past (Sacred Delay), live in sustained presence (Sacred Presence), and consider a healthy future (Sacred Vision). The frantic planning for excitement gives way to wisdom for the journey.

Discernment

Discernment requires making plans and having the ability to hope. These are natural skills for Sevens. A Seven's charming energy can be helpful when discerning, but often a Seven's planning can get ahead of the natural unfolding of life. Challenge comes when Sevens must slow down, be still, and listen to the heart in order to make good and right decisions. Keeping all options open is antithetical to discernment. One has to say "yes" to something, which means saying "no" to other things. It's important for Sevens to be intentional with the following when it comes to important decisions:

- Identity Over Adventure. The journey to authentic self for Sevens is fraught with fear. The prospect of pain and lack is prominent. Living from inherent contentment and sufficiency is essential for Type Sevens. This requires an exploration of being that isn't so enmeshed with frenetic activity. Make the identity statement for Type Seven a mantra: "I am made in the Divine Image, and in the Divine Image there is no fear of lack. My contentment is in who I am, not simply what I can plan or experience." This will cultivate a constancy that quiets the mind, awakens the heart, and sustains the body.

- <u>Wise Heart</u>. Let the heart catch up to the mind and body. Face the fear of the complexities within: the positive and the negative, the light and the dark. Instead of running from feelings to pursue the exciting, listen to the heart. In seasons of discernment, feeling intelligence is critical to cultivating wisdom. In transition, it's tempting to revert to planning and action. It is here that Schafer advises Sevens to "tolerate the tension of these transitional states."[11]

- <u>Sacred Delay</u>. By intentionally and habitually pausing to look back, Sevens learn to trust in their inherent freedom. The restraint of stillness provides a good boundary. Such a boundary can feel confining, but there is a wise freedom within chosen limits. Here the Seven can truly let the past help them in the present, and inform their future plans. Friends I know who are Sevens have found journaling and spiritual direction to be particularly helpful in cultivating Sacred Delay.

Exercises for the Type Seven Within:

- <u>Be still and listen</u>. If a Seven simply tries to be still, they'll go insane. Consider practicing *Lectio Divina*, a contemplative spiritual reading practice, which slowly and repeatedly reads a sacred text in order to see what emerges.[12] As one reads and rereads, there are four "movements": read, meditate, pray, and contemplate. With each pass at the text, an inner focus strengthens, and new insights emerge.

- <u>Plant something</u>. This may seem silly, but Sevens can struggle with patience. They are accustomed to searching for, and finding, quick hits of excitement and gratification. By planting a garden, or a houseplant from seed, patience and commitment is fostered. Such small opportunities to develop grit and determination are important for Sevens.

- <u>Liturgy of the ordinary</u>. Borrowing from Tish Harrison Warren's central theme of her book by the same title, practice reflecting upon the awe and wonder in the midst of the ordinary and mundane aspects of the day.[13] This tempers the compulsion to go find the exciting.

- <u>Time audit</u>. A small way to practice Sacred Delay is by keeping a time audit. Choose an amount of time, at least 24 hours and up to one week, and track how you spend your time. At the end of your time audit, take some time to look back and reflect upon the life you've been living. What do you notice? What do you observe?

Questions for Discussion on the Type Seven Within:

- What is mine to experience?
- Sincerely: What could go wrong?
- Is it time for a change or am I simply bored?
- What do I have to offer when my enthusiasm wanes?
- How can my feelings help me better discern?
- What commitments am I most afraid to make?

Notes

[1] A word on the "planning" of the Type Seven is needed, as it is often misunderstood by other types. Everyone plans, but the difference with Sevens is that they often plan in the middle of something that they've already planned. Think of planning the next vacation while presently on vacation.

[2] Thanks to my friend and Type Seven, Jeremy Sims, for this term.

[3] Schafer, *Roaming Free Inside the Cage*, p. 109.

[4] Heuertz, *Sacred Enneagram*, p. 124.

[5] The "less, but better" philosophy is a central theme in Greg McKeown's fantastic book, *Essentialism: The Disciplined Pursuit of Less* (New York: Currency, 2014).

[6] Hurley & Donson, *Discover Your Soul Potential*, p. 135.

[7] Jaxon-Bear, *Fixation to Freedom*, p. 198.

[8] Ibid.

[9] Schafer, *Roaming Free Inside the Cage*, p. 112.

[10] Hurley & Donson, *Discover Your Soul Potential*, p. 135.

[11] Schafer, *Roaming Free Inside the Cage*, p. 112.

[12] You can find a helpful introduction to Lectio Divina here: https://bustedhalo.com/ministry-resources/lectio-divina-beginners-guide.

[13] Seriously, Tish Harrison Warren's *Liturgy of the Ordinary: Sacred Practices in Everyday Life* (Downer's Grove: IVP Books, 2016) is fantastic.

CONCLUSION
Living the Way of Discernment

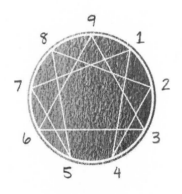

In the Introduction, I wrote about the power of a map. Granted, it's an odd illustration, for we hardly use maps anymore. Technology has rendered physical maps somewhat obsolete. But I've always found maps miraculous: a simple piece of paper can guide your steps in the world. They're practical and yet beautiful. Simple and yet intricate.

I proposed the Enneagram of Discernment to you as a "triadic map of applied identity." This particular map that you've held in your hands includes three such triads: Vocation, Wisdom, and Practice. I encouraged you to hold the map and learn to make sense of it.

For any map to be useful, you have to figure out where you are and plot your journey from there. Our dominant enneagram type is the trailhead to a deeper journey of discernment.

Type is simply the starting point. If we're willing to walk, we encounter the beautiful and brutal journey known as The Way of Discernment. Walking The Way helps us navigate the countless decisions that comprise a life. It's a pilgrimage of sorts, a sacred journey to discover who we are, why we are here, and where we are heading. There's a Latin phrase that captures this well: *solvitor ambulando*. Translated it means, "it is solved by walking." This is the profound truth of the enneagram and discernment. We discern by walking, beginning at the trailhead, and taking each next right step.

Here I must confess something to you. In my map-holding imagery, I intentionally withheld something from you out of fear of piling on too much, too soon. I must share it now, although you've probably discovered it yourself already. Holding the map of your inner life and making sense of it requires you to become a **cartographer**. Cartography is the art and practice of drawing maps. This Way of Discernment requires each of us to draw the maps we hold, for they initially seem incomplete to us. We've found the trailhead, and we have guidance through the triads of Vocation, Wisdom, and Practice. But as we discover, learn, stretch, suffer, and grow, we engage in a cartography that connects the disparate experiences of our lives into a more coherent path. We connect the dots. We get the lay of the land. We can see the topography.

The enneagram helps us in this cartography work, raising our awareness of our adapted, ego-driven state, so that we can rediscover our authentic selves. When we depart from the trailhead, we learn what discernment truly means:

> *Discernment is the gift and practice of living our lives*
> *from a deep sense of vocation, with wisdom,*
> *in the fullness of time.*

Barriers to Invitations

Any honest journey to self-discovery engages our inner world in profound ways. In Chapter One, we explored our most significant barriers to discernment. These are the dominant emotions of the enneagram: anger, shame, and fear. By reading this book, I hope you discovered that The Way of Discernment transforms our most significant barriers into invitations. From authentic identity, purpose, and direction, our barriers invite us to engage our dominant emotion in loving and courageous ways.

Discernment is a way of seeing *beneath* and *through*. The Way of Discernment helps us see beneath and through our type's dominant barriers. Instead of running into them, and limping away bruised and confused, discernment helps us see what they may be inviting us into. They become holy biddings to listen, sense, consider, tend, and engage.

Anger, the dominant barrier of the Gut Triad (Types Eight, Nine, and One), becomes an invitation to flourishing action. Each type must discern its transformation of anger to action.

- The Type Eights need for protection is empowered in flourishing action that protects the most vulnerable in the world.
- The Type Nines need for peace is empowered in flourishing action that makes peace in the world.
- The Type Ones need for goodness is empowered in flourishing action to cultivate goodness in the world.

Shame, the dominant barrier of the Heart Triad (Types Two, Three, and Four), becomes an invitation to flourishing humility.

- The Type Twos need for unconditional love is empowered in flourishing humility to freely love others.
- The Type Threes need for value and worth is empowered in flourishing humility to cultivate the value and worth of others in their world.
- The Type Fours need for belonging and significance is empowered in flourishing humility to foster the belonging and significance of others.

Fear, the dominant barrier of the Head Triad (Types Five, Six, and Seven), becomes an invitation to flourishing courage.

- The Type Fives need for competency is empowered in flourishing courage to steward their knowledge for the sake of the common good.

- The Type Sixes need for loyalty is empowered in flourishing courage to intuitively trust themselves and bring others together.

- The Type Sevens need for contentment is empowered in flourishing courage to be content with what is, and what is within them.

With action, humility, and courage, we respond to the invitation of our dominant emotion. This doesn't mean future decisions will be easy. On the contrary, they may be more difficult. Integrity and authenticity has a more difficult time in today's world. It's often easier to approach decisions from our adapted, unaware self. Autopilot takes much less thought, emotion, and physicality than doing things manually.

When we engage life's decisions, big and small, The Way of Discernment provides the questions we need to ponder our steps forward with wisdom. When you face a decision and are unsure what to do, journey through the nine questions. For some, this can occur internally. For others, writing it out can be helpful. And for some, talking it through with a friend is best. Regardless, with a deeper understanding of your dominant enneagram type, considering these nine questions will engage vocation, wisdom, and the fullness of time.

The Vocation Triad

- *Who am I?*—Affirm your authentic identity. How does your identity as one made in the *Imago Dei* inform this decision?

- *Why am I here?*—Align your pursuits with your deeper purpose of flourishing (*shalom*). What options before you make way for flourishing? What options don't?

- *Where am I going?*—Fathom the depths of where you are, so you can more wisely discern where you are going. How can you fathom where you are so you can more clearly see the road ahead?

The Wisdom Triad

- *What am I doing?*—Sense what your body is telling you. Engage your instincts and intuition to assess your activity. Is my activity (or lack thereof) wise considering the options before me?
- *What am I feeling?*—Enter into the richness of your emotional world. Allow your feelings to teach you. What do your emotions have to say about the decision?
- *What am I thinking?*—Reflect upon your cognition. Consider how your thinking is helping or hindering your decision-making? How can you engage your brain to productively think your way through this decision?

The Practice Triad

- *What am I remembering?*—The past is a powerful teacher. We must be careful not to ignore it or wallow in it. How can memory help me engage this decision with wisdom? What should I be reflecting upon?
- *What am I experiencing?*—Our present engagement in the world is fraught with distraction and mixed messages. What are my gut, my heart, and my head experiencing in this decision-making process?
- *What am I anticipating?*—While the future is unknown, our ability to fixate on what could be, or fail to give ourselves permission to dream can radically impact our ability to discern. What do my anticipations tell me about the future I'm stepping into?

If we all journeyed through these nine questions, even briefly, consider the impact it would have on the quality of our lives, our relationships, our work, and our communities. Remember, we don't need more information. We really don't need any more knowledge. What we desperately need is wisdom to discern our individual and collective lives.

Go Back and Get It

The West African concept of "Sankofa" gives a concept for this type of discernment, capturing the essence of the journey. Sankofa is a mythical bird with its body forward and head turned backward. Roughly translated, "Go back and get it," the bird is a reminder that we must remember to fetch what is at risk of being left behind.

- SAN [Return]
- KO [Go]
- FA [Look, fetch]

Any work involving the enneagram and discernment is Sankofa work. We must go back and fetch what's at risk of being left behind: our identity, our purpose, our direction.

- SAN: We must return to our authentic identity as one made in the *Imago Dei*.

- KO: We must move forward with flourishing purpose, fathoming our direction.

- FA: We must engage our present in the fullness of *kairos* time, with head, heart, and gut aligned to cultivate wisdom.

This is the discerning life: *Sankofa* over and over again. As our dominant type doesn't change, our need to walk The Way of Discernment is lifelong. We will always have to go back and fetch what we risk leaving behind. We must give ourselves permission to take out our maps and consult them. The Jewish sacred text

Avot D'Rabbi Natan offers us an encouragement for this lifelong task: "Don't be afraid of work that has no end."[1]

Endless work can seem overwhelming. But it can also be evergreen. And that's a good thing. It's probably best that we perpetually and humbly receive the gift of discernment while consistently committing to its practice, over and over again. The ego will always want to shove its way to the fore and call the shots. The default patterns prowl. The dominant emotions lurk. This endless evergreen work is a lifelong practice of aligning and integrating our ego into our authentic self.

The Way of Discernment is no express lane. While it can provide momentary help in times of decision, it's a longsuffering journey. So, when the next decision comes, journey through The Way of Discernment. Hear the call to go back and get it, and discern your life with flourishing abundance. And do it over and over again, because it's worth it this way. You're worth it.

A Final Blessing

May your life be marked with the gift and practice of discernment.

May you see your dominant enneagram type as the trailhead to your inner landscape, and may you have the courage to take one step after another as a pilgrim journeying back to your authentic self.

May this pilgrimage include receiving the gift of vocation, the divine call to identity in the Imago Dei. *May it include invitations to practice your calling with flourishing purpose, fathoming the depths of the path that lies ahead.*

May you walk the path with loving wisdom through rhythms of Wise Mind, Wise Heart, and Wise Body.

May you discern your life in the fullness of kairos *time through the integration of Sacred Delay, Sacred Presence, and Sacred Vision.*

May it be so for you, and for us.

Notes

[1]Avot D'Rabbi Natan, https://www.sefaria.org/Avot_D'Rabbi_Natan?lang=bi.

ACKNOWLEDGMENTS

Writing an enneagram book truly takes a village, and I'm thankful to all the villagers who pitched in on this project to get me to the finish line.

My Family

Bekah—Your loving encouragement and challenge gave me healthy pauses (Sacred Delay) and sufficient hope. Thanks for putting up with a spouse consumed with the writing process. Plus, your copy-editing skills made the drafts less offensive to the English language. All my love.

My children—Ben, Isa, Sam, Stella, and Will, you make me want to be a better person in all the right ways. Thanks for your patience and forgiveness for all the times I had to shut myself in the office and write.

My Teachers

Suzanne Stabile—When I cracked open the door to peek into what a deeper study of the enneagram looked like, I came to you. You kicked that door wide open for me, and I'm grateful. Thanks for your wisdom, your Texan hospitality, and your love for the enneagram and your students.

Nan Henson—When I was searching for a place to deepen my studies, I never imagined Atlanta would be my enneagram home. What you are doing in the ATL, which reaches around the world, is simply beautiful. Thanks for your hospitable wisdom, caring disposition, and sweet brilliance.

Lynda Roberts—Your quiet strength and profound insight helped me engage parts of the enneagram in unexpected ways. I deeply appreciate the way you hold space for your students to be their true selves. Thanks for taking a chance with your certification program. May every cohort be packed with engaging students.

My Publisher

Dr. Keith Martel and the team at Falls City Press: Your belief in this project gave these words a home. When many "traditional" publishers were unwilling to take a chance on this "nontraditional" approach to the enneagram, you made room. May Falls City Press flourish in today's tumultuous terrain of publishing.

My Illustrator

Rachel Aupperle: Thanks for your brilliant and thoughtful work visually depicting so many of these concepts.

My Advisory Readers

It takes a pretty special group of friends to willingly sacrifice their time and energy to read my drafts and lovingly, yet firmly help me improve them.

My advisory readers group—Seth Abram, Seth Creekmore, Dr. Julia Hurlow, and K. J. Ramsey thanks for the many, many, many hours you spent wrestling with my words. I am truly blessed to call you friends, and this book is infinitely better because of your wisdom.

My type-chapter readers—It's a daunting and nerve-wracking thing to write about other personality types. Thanks for your grace, mercy, and wisdom in helping me better understand you and your fellow types. Seth Abram, Dr. Jeff & Rachel Aupperle, Kate Austin, Jordan Bolte, Hope & Jesse Brown, Seth Creekmore, Bill Cummings, Shelby Delay, Rachel Demarse, Whitney Drake, Hannah Goebel, Sara James, Dr. Julia Hurlow, Dr. Jerome Lubbe, the incomparable Bekah Moser, Chin Ai Oh, Amy Peterson, K. J. Ramsey, Jeremy Sims, Jake Smith, Kevin Smith, Amber Stanley, Kim Stave, Troy Tiberi, and Peter Yeung, I honor you.

My Fellow Enneanerds

Seth Abram, Seth Creekmore, and Kevin Smith—Thanks for your steadfast engagement and presence, even though we're all hundreds of miles apart. (Thank goodness for Marco Polo!) I'm grateful to learn so much from each of you.

Dr. Jerome Lubbe—Thanks for the late-night whiteboard sessions at your office. You helped refine my concepts in important ways.

Drew

The Nine Questions of The Way of Discernment

Dr. Drew Moser

When facing a decision, and you're struggling to know what to do, consider the following…

The Vocation Triad

- Who am I? (Identity)
- Why am I here? (Purpose)
- Where am I going? (Direction)

The Wisdom Triad

- What am I doing? (Gut Center)
- What am I feeling? (Heart Center)
- What am I thinking? (Head Center)

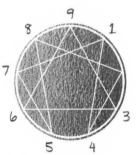

The Practice Triad

- What am I remembering? (Past)
- What am I experiencing? (Present)
- What am I anticipating? (Future)

Five Axioms of Discernment

Dr. Drew Moser

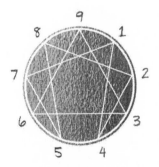

Discernment is one of those elusive ideas that's hard to describe, but we know it when we see it. The Latin root of the verb "to discern" means "to discriminate." In spirituality, discernment refers to the ability to sort out what is of God and what is not. Obviously, this is easier said than done. For *The Enneagram of Discernment*, the following five axioms of discernment help us better listen and see with depth and clarity:

Axiom 1: Discernment is a gift and a practice. Much of the spiritual life is the art of letting go so we can open ourselves: our minds, our hearts, and our bodies, to receive gifts from God. Discernment is one of those gifts. Often our ability to listen and see the depth and reality of what is, and respond faithfully, is a spiritual gift from God. Discernment is also a habit to be cultivated through intentional practice. Through our practice, we become more receptive to the divine gift. Much like an important conversation with a loved one, we receive such a conversation as a gift, and yet we also intentionally develop the habit of listening to our loved one well.

Axiom 2: Discernment requires self-knowledge, humility, and courage. In order to receive the gift and cultivate the habit of discernment, certain dispositions must be present. First, we must know who we are. Self-knowledge brings an honest assessment of our capacities and limits from a place of integrity. Second, we must receive the gift with humility, and allow humility to fuel our practice. Third, from a place of integrity and humility, we must embody courage to respond to the gift.

Axiom 3: Discernment is a process. Despite cartoonish notions of light bulb moments that instantaneously provide insight, discernment is much more of a process. It is the process of listening and living well, aligning interior movements with exterior action. It's a process of living from a place of internal freedom from making decisions based on selfish, ulterior, or unhealthy motives. Discernment cultivates awareness of God and the work of God in our present world in the contexts of solitude and community.

Axiom 4: Discernment is complex. Simple decisions don't require discernment. Mere choice or judgment will do. But discernment engages bigger questions than what to eat for lunch. Discernment is for deeper questions. Such complexity honors the depth of what matters most, and often leads us to explore other unforeseen questions. Discernment raises questions that beget other good questions. It is manifold and generative. Discernment acknowledges mystery, and is willing to explore it.

Axiom 5: Discernment is holistic. The process of discernment permeates our entire being: head, heart, and body. When we cultivate the ability to discern with wisdom, we learn to pay attention to our whole selves. This is how we see, as Nouwen would put it, "through appearances to the interconnectedness of all things." This is where true vision lies. Cultivating discernment draws from the intelligence available to us from our cognition, our emotional center, and our body awareness.[1] This holism also has a relational dimension. Not only do we discern from our entire being. We also discern from our interconnectedness with God, others, and creation.

Notes

[1] The Ignation concept of consolations and desolations is helpful here.

Enneagram Settling Statements

Dr. Drew Moser

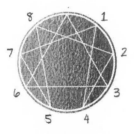

We too often settle for less than what we truly want.

The enneagram helps us become aware of the ways in which we project our core desires. When we project, we distort, and our core desires become cheap imitations of the real thing. It's a main pathway away from our Authentic Self to the Adapted Self, where the ego takes the reins.

We reason: "It's safer this way. It helps us get through our day."

But if we're honest, it's no way to live a life. If we simply settle, we'll always long for deeper things that our settling will never satisfy. Here are the Nine Settling Statements of the Enneagram.

Type 1—Ones want goodness but settle for order.

Type 2—Twos want unconditional love but settler for niceness.

Type 3—Threes want worth but settle for image.

Type 4—Fours want belonging but settle for longing.

Type 5—Fives want competency but settle for knowledge.

Type 6—Sixes want loyalty but settle for safety.

Type 7—Sevens want contentment but settle for excitement.

Type 8—Eights want protection but settle for control.

Type 9—Nines want peace but settle for calm.

Nine Tips for Enneagram Typing

Dr. Drew Moser

1. *Patience*—Be patient with yourself. Forcing yourself into a "type" doesn't work. This takes time.

2. *Read*—Pick up the time-tested enneagram books. Consider which description resonates the most, hurts the most, or feels the most unfair (or some combination of these three).

3. *Ask*—Ask those who know you well AND will steward such important conversations with love and grace.

4. *Listen*—Listen to all of the enneagram songs from *Sleeping at Last*. Pay attention to the song that makes you cry. If they

all make you cry, pay attention to the one that makes you UGLY CRY.

5. ***Listen Again***—Listen to all of the Enneagram podcasts from *Sleeping at Last*. Each episode dives deeply into an Enneagram song and includes profound descriptions of each type by Chris Heuertz.

6. ***Listen Yet Again***—Sit at the feet of a trusted Enneagram teacher in a live workshop. This is an oral tradition and learning from a master teacher can be incredibly helpful.

7. ***Focus***—Focus your attention on the small and big motivations that drive your behavior. They'll provide clarity.

8. ***Reflect***—Find pockets of time in your day to reflect on what's happening in your mind, your heart, and your body. What patterns emerge?

9. ***Relax***—Some take years to discover their dominant type. If you think everyone around you has everything figured out, you're wrong. They don't. We're all fumbling forward.

The Nine Identity Statements of the Enneagram

Dr. Drew Moser

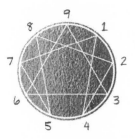

Type 1: "I am made in the Divine Image, and in the Divine Image there is no condemnation. My goodness is in who I am, not simply what I improve."

Type 2: "I am made in the Divine Image, and in the Divine Image there is no shame of being unlovable. I am loved and appreciated for who I am, not simply what I do for others."

Type 3: "I am made in the Divine Image, and in the Divine Image there is no shame of being worthless. My worth and value are in who I am, not simply what I do."

Type 4: "I am made in the Divine Image, and in the Divine Image there is no shame of being unknown or excluded. My belonging and significance is in who I am, not simply what I uniquely express."

Type 5: "I am made in the Divine Image, and in the Divine Image there is no fear of incompetency or depletion. My competency and viability are inner renewable resources to be shared with others."

Type 6: "I am made in the Divine Image, and in the Divine Image there is no fear of being alone. Support and guidance is within, not simply in what I can secure."

Type 7: "I am made in the Divine Image, and in the Divine Image there is no fear of lack. My contentment is in who I am, not simply what I can plan or experience."

Type 8: "I am made in the Divine Image, and in the Divine Image, anger is refined.
My protection is in who I am, not simply what I control."

Type 9: "I am made in the Divine Image, and in the Divine Image, anger is resolved.
My peace and wholeness is in who I am, not simply in what I keep calm."

Nine Stages of Enneagram Learning

Dr. Drew Moser

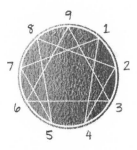

The Way of Disorientation

- Stage 1-CONFUSION | "What is any-gram? Never heard of it."
    - While easy to understand this stage, it's important to remember that we all start our journeys here. All of us experienced a moment in which we first heard about the enneagram. Remembering this point is an important perspective as we follow the path.

- Stage 2-SKEPTICISM | "This enneagram thing is garbage. I don't know why everyone is so obsessed with it."
  - You may scoff at the naysayers, but it's important to honor this step. It's a natural response to encounter something new and strange to us with skepticism.

- Stage 3-RESIGNATION | "Fine. I'll look into it. It's all anyone is talking about so I might as well give it a go."
  - At this stage, it's critically important to honor the wisdom of the enneagram AND the person who is willing to explore it. We must tend to both with care.

The Way of Discovery

- Stage 4-WONDER | "Holy crap! This thing reads my mail!"
  - This is the stage where we begin to be truly honest in acknowledging our dominant type. Once we see how our dominant type explains so much of what motivates us, we sit in wonder.

- Stage 5-SIMPLISM | "I read a few books and listened to some podcasts. It's so helpful to have everyone I know figured out."
  - At this stage, we begin to turn our working knowledge of the Enneagram toward others. It becomes a lens through which we make sense of the world. Unfortunately, it's a simple lens that, left unchecked can lead to stereotyping and weaponizing the enneagram.

- Stage 6-EVANGELISM | "The enneagram is everything and I have to tell everyone about it."
  - Almost coinciding with Stage 5 is an evangelistic fervor of Stage 6. The Enneagram becomes

the THING we talk about in social settings. At this stage books and podcasts are PASSION-ATELY recommended.

The Way of Descent

- Stage 7-COMPLEXITY | "The more I learn about the enneagram, the more I realize how little I know."
  - o If we're honest, once we think we've reached the limits on this framework, new questions emerge. This stages requires a 'learned humility' that recognizes there's always more we can know.

- Stage 8-SUFFERING | "The deeper I get into this thing, the tougher it gets confronting my own stuff. Real inner work is hard."
  - o If the enneagram is simply a way to label yourself and others, then there's no change. Those who stick with the work that the enneagram can provide find a painful, but worthwhile path of acknowledging and naming the darker parts of ourselves. This stage of the journey is the type of suffering that refines us.

- Stage 9-GROWTH | "The enneagram doesn't do the work of growth for me. It helps me realize my blind spots, where I need to let go of things, and where I need to change habits and practices. The rest is up to me."
  - o At this stage, we recognize that the enneagram isn't everything. It's incredibly helpful, but only to the extent that we are willing to engage what we learn with attention and intention. The enneagram gives language and light to many parts of who we are, but it's up to us to cultivate the habits and practices for lasting growth.

Recommended Enneagram Resources

Books (An Initial List)

- *Discovering Your Personality Type: The Essential Introduction to the Enneagram*, by Don Richard Riso and Russ Hudson

- *Discover Your Soul Potential: Using the Enneagram to Awaken Spiritual Vitality,* by Kathy Hurley and Theodorre Donson

- *The Complete Enneagram: 27 Paths to Greater Self-Knowledge*, by Beatrice Chestnut

- *The Essential Enneagram: The Definitive Personality Test and Self-Discovery Guide*, by David Daniels and Virginia Price

- *The Road Back to You: An Enneagram Journey to Self-Discovery*, by Ian Morgan Cron and Suzanne Stabile

- *Roaming Free Inside the Cage: A Daoist Approach to the Enneagram and Spiritual Transformation*, by William M. Schafer

- *Spiritual Rhythms for the Enneagram: A Handbook for Harmony and Transformation*, by Adel and Doug Calhoun, Clare and Scott Loughrige
- *Whole Identity: A Brain-Based Enneagram Model for (W)holistic Human Thriving*, by Jerome Lubbe

Websites

- International Enneagram Association – https://www.internationalenneagram.org/
- The Enneagram Institute – https://www.enneagraminstitute.com/
- The Narrative Enneagram – https://www.enneagramworldwide.com/
- Integrated Enneagram – https://www.integratedenneagram.com
- Enneagram Indiana – https://www.enneagramindiana.com

Podcasts

- Fathoms | An Enneagram Podcast, featuring Seth Abram, Seth Creekmore, & Drew Moser
- The Real Enneagram Podcast by Dr. Joseph Howell
- The Enneagram Journey Podcast with Suzanne Stabile
- Do it for the Gram: An Enneagram Podcast by Milton Stewart
- Typology with Ian Morgan Cron

Other Books by Dr. Drew Moser:

Scholarship Reconsidered [Expanded Edition]

Ready or Not: Leaning into Life in Our Twenties

Campus Life: In Search of Community

Follow Drew's Work:

www.drewmoser.com
www.enneagramindiana.com

Fathoms | An Enneagram Podcast

Twitter: @drewmoser
Facebook: www.facebook.com/drewmoserauthor
Instagram: @drewmoser // @enneagrammers

Booking Inquiries: drewmoser@gmail.com

Made in the USA
Middletown, DE
03 March 2021